NEW GUIDE
FOR
TOASTMASTERS
AND
SPEAKERS

NEW GUIDE
FOR
TOASTMASTERS
AND
SPEAKERS

by

Herbert V. Prochnow

PRENTICE-HALL, INC.   ENGLEWOOD CLIFFS, N. J.

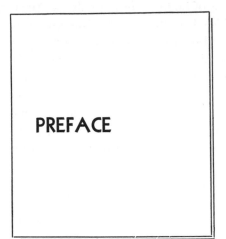

PREFACE

CLARENCE BUDINGTON KELLAND ONCE SAID, "The obvious duty of a toastmaster is to be so infernally dull that the succeeding speakers will appear brilliant by contrast." Someone else has said that any toastmaster will be a success if he can be dull in a new way. These are interesting quips, but they are not true. A dull toastmaster does nothing to enhance the speaker he introduces. He may even speak so long and in so tiresome a manner that he wears out the audience and handicaps the speaker.

A great deal of material has been brought together in this book to help the chairman or the toastmaster of a meeting to discharge his responsibilities efficiently and effectively. There are literally thousands of luncheons, dinners, convention sessions, forums, discussion groups, clinics, conferences and other types of meetings held every week at which someone has the responsibility of presiding. The ability with which the chairman or toastmaster arranges the event, provides the speakers, and handles the meeting itself will be a major factor in determining whether those in attendance waste their time or profit from the experience.

A mathematical genius or an electronic brain would be required to determine the fantastic number of hours spent not only by Americans, but also by Canadians, British, French, Scandinavians, Germans, Japanese, Brazilians and peoples all over the world in meetings. The Rotarians, Lions, Kiwanis, Optimists, Toastmasters and Toastmistresses clubs alone are responsible for thousands of meetings every week over the entire world. Then, if you add the conventions of business, industry and the professions, the time spent in meetings increases to millions of hours a year. Any steps which can be taken by those in charge of these events to make them more worthwhile can do immeasurable good.

This book contains some fundamental rules for organizing and conducting meetings. It also contains thousands of helpful items for assisting the chairman or toastmaster. Among these items are a number of actual introductions used on different occasions, responses to introductions, humorous stories and verse, unusual illustrations and excerpts from speeches, epigrams, quotations from literature and from many other sources, and interesting stories of well-known statesmen. These materials will be invaluable in helping the chairman to prepare introductions that arouse the interest of an audience and win its attention. They will also save valuable time for the chairman.

Some of the material has been arranged alphabetically by subject in the book and all of it has been classified in the index.

If this reference book helps to provide more efficiently organized and conducted meetings and better introductions, it will have served its purpose in a field where there is vast opportunity for improvement.

H.V.P.

TABLE OF CONTENTS

NEW GUIDE

FOR

TOASTMASTERS

AND

SPEAKERS

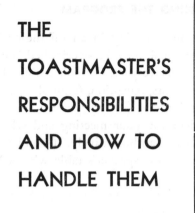

THE TOASTMASTER'S RESPONSIBILITIES AND HOW TO HANDLE THEM

To CONSERVE THE TIME of the reader, and yet to cover the subject comprehensively, there are presented here in outline form the various responsibilities of the toastmaster. It is hoped that the use of an outline will help to point up more sharply the toastmaster's several responsibilities.

Later in the book there are presented hundreds of items useful to toastmasters. These items include examples of introductions used by successful speakers; responses to introductions; humorous, serious, and inspirational anecdotes; light verse; interesting excerpts and stories from speeches; humorous epigrams; quips, and witty comments; literary quotations; selected quotations from modern sources; and unusual, attention-winning stories about well-known national and world figures. These hundreds of items will help the toastmaster on countless occasions in discharging his responsibilities.

Now we shall outline specifically the many responsibilities which are yours as toastmaster. It is important that you keep these fundamentals clearly in mind. You have no right to blame anyone else if your meeting does not go well. You are the toastmaster or chairman.

1

You are in charge. You are responsible for making the meeting a success. If the meeting goes well, you are entitled to the credit.

TEN RULES FOR PLANNING THE PROGRAM

1. Never arrange or conduct any meeting in an off-the-cuff, careless manner. No detail, however small, must be overlooked. The arrangements must be perfected in every respect. Committees should be appointed to handle table arrangements, reception, fellowship, and all matters that require special attention.

2. Choose an appropriate subject for your meeting and select speakers who can speak interestingly and authoritatively. If you have a luncheon or dinner, select guests for the speaker's table who will be a compliment to the speaker.

3. Determine exactly how much time the meeting will take and set up a precise schedule for every part of the meeting.

4. Make certain that the meeting room is suitable.

5. Carefully check the qualifications of the speaker and satisfy yourself regarding his ability before you present him to an audience. You have no right to inflict on any audience a program that is not good, or a speaker about whose qualifications you are not fully informed.

6. Have a clear understanding with each speaker regarding his subject, the date and the location of the meeting room, the exact place you will meet him, the nature of his audience, and the time he is to be allowed for his address.

7. Provide proper publicity for the meeting so that all who may attend are fully informed and in order that the press may have adequate information.

8. Obtain information from each speaker which will help you to introduce him properly.

9. If you have several speakers, it is best, as a general rule, to have your strongest speaker last.

10. If you have several speakers, you must make certain that your program is not too long and that no one speaker has too long a speech. It is better to err on the side of falling short of the time, rather than running over.

TEN RULES FOR CONDUCTING THE MEETING

1. Have your guests at the speaker's table meet before the luncheon or dinner and become acquainted with each other and with the speaker.

2. Start the meeting on time, and keep it *strictly* on schedule. That is your responsibility. Do not clutter up a program with all kinds of announcements and extra items that rob the principal speaker of his time and bore the audience. Permit an audience to stand up and stretch in the middle of a long afternoon or evening program.

3. Be certain the audience knows who you are.

4. Before the meeting begins, check to see that the room is in proper order, the ventilation good, and a lectern available for the speaker. You may also need a microphone.

5. If you have a luncheon or dinner, have place-cards at the speaker's table and see that each person at the table knows where he is to sit.

6. Your own list of guests should have brief information about each guest for your use in introducing him. Have each guest's name in the order of introduction.

7. Introduce the guests at the speaker's table loudly and plainly so that the audience hears each person's name. Give a brief item of information about each guest as you introduce him. Be certain you have the correct pronunciation for each name.

8. Give the speaker a strong introduction. Commend his achievements and let your audience know it is a privilege to hear the speaker. However, do not become so extravagant in praise and so flowery in language that your audience will expect the speaker to be a combination of Socrates, Patrick Henry, and Churchill. No speaker can overcome such an introduction. Remember, also, that your job is to make the introduction, and his job is to make the speech. Make your introduction brief. Give the speaker his full time.

9. If the meeting permits—and most meetings do—add a light touch, a bit of humor, to your comments.

10. After the speech, always express appreciation to the speaker on behalf of the audience and thank the speaker personally. If your speaker is appearing on your program without payment of a fee, it is a good idea, if your treasury has some funds, to show your appreciation by giving him a modest gift.

2

INTERESTING
INTRODUCTIONS
FOR MANY
OCCASIONS

James E. Day, *past President of the Executives' Club of Chicago, and President of the Midwest Stock Exchange introduces* **Robert H. Jackson,** *Associate Justice of the Supreme Court of the United States.*

I THINK I SHOULD TELL YOU that when we had the reception for those at our speaker's table, I walked in and said, "Hello, Judge," and nine people shook hands with me.

I see we have a great many lawyers here today, which is fine. A lawyer is a man who takes 50 per cent of the money that you just got through proving you didn't steal. Or maybe it's 75 per cent.

Our microphone has welcomed, over the years, many famous men. It has been my great, good fortune to introduce a number of them.

In preparing an introduction for our speaker, I could find no justifiable reason for taking any time to give you his background, for the very self-evident fact that his career has been amply spotlighted by the numerous history-making events in which he has participated. To present even briefly his brilliant career in law and international

4

affairs would be repetitious to every man in this room. Therefore, I'm going to tell you about my grandmother.

Now, my grandmother was a very intelligent, warm-hearted and patient person. My mother was a semi-invalid and so the onerous task of raising your president fell to grandmother's lot.

One thing I remember very vividly about her on those innumerable occasions when she would insist that I study my lessons was the expression that she used at the end of all her arguments. It was, "Jimmy, I want you to make a name for yourself." Through the earlier years, this expression continued to run through my head like a popular song will sometimes do. After we lost her and the years went along, I forgot the refrain. This year, however, it has been brought back to me on the many occasions when I have been privileged to introduce men who have, most certainly, made a name for themselves.

Though one never gives up hope, it seems rather remote now that I will ever attain grandmother's goal; but, knowing her, I am sure she wouldn't be too disappointed, and I think she would be proud of the fact that I have, at least, the opportunity to introduce men who have attained this goal.

I can say quite sincerely to you gentlemen that no one has graced our platform this year that I could introduce with more pride than I do our speaker today, and I wish there were some way I could be sure she could hear me when I say, "Grandmother, here is a man who has made a name for himself."

The Honorable Robert H. Jackson.

༄

John J. McDonough, *past President of the Executives' Club of Chicago, and Vice-President of the Harris Trust and Savings Bank of Chicago, introduces* **Lester B. Pearson,** *Canadian statesman.*

IN THESE TURBULENT TIMES of international bitterness and political strife, it is indeed comforting and heart-warming to pause, and consider for a moment, the ideal of international amity and understanding, which is exemplified by the friendly relations between Canada and the United States.

American businessmen are fully aware, I'm sure, of Canada's amazing internal economic expansion since World War II. They know too that Canada is our best customer. It is more important, however, in my judgment, for all of our citizens to remember constantly that Canada is also our best friend among the great independent nations of the world.

The extremely close integration and implementation of our respective national efforts in both war and peace have no parallel in world history, and certainly it is our earnest desire in America to do all in our power to strengthen this unique relationship.

Today, gentlemen, we are greatly privileged to have with us as our guest of honor a distinguished Canadian statesman who understands thoroughly the relations between our nations.

In order to prepare himself properly for his extraordinary career in diplomacy Mr. Pearson, (or "Mike" as he is affectionately known to his many American friends) made a very wise choice of his university.

I am delighted to point out, gentlemen, that he is an Oxford man, and like most of the Canadians I knew at Oxford "Mike" Pearson was both a brilliant student and a star athlete.

After receiving his B.A. degree from Oxford, our honored guest returned to Toronto University for a brief fling at teaching and coaching. He tells me he is the only international diplomat who has a pass to both American and National League baseball parks in New York.

In 1928, however, he quit the cloisters for a career in the Department of External Affairs.

Recognition and high honors came quickly and in steady succession to Mr. Pearson and there soon followed important assignments in London, Ottawa, and Washington where, you will recall, he served two years as Canadian Ambassador to the United States, and where, incidentally, he made more good friends for Canada than any of his predecessors.

In 1948, he was called to the Cabinet at Ottawa as Secretary of State for External Affairs and four years later he served with great distinction as President of the United Nations Assembly, of which, of course, he continues to be a member.

Gentlemen, I feel greatly honored and pleased to present to you

Canada's most famous and most colorful diplomat and our good neighbor, the honorable Lester B. Pearson, Canadian Secretary of State for External Affairs.

⁓

John J. McDonough, *past President of the Executives' Club of Chicago, and Vice-President of the Harris Trust and Savings Bank of Chicago, introduces* **Allan Shivers,** *Governor of Texas.*

I AM VERY HAPPY indeed to extend a most cordial welcome to the thirty-sixth Governor of the fabulous State of Texas.

Texas, as you know, is the state which has more oil, more natural and conversational gas, more cattle and more Cadillacs than any state in the Union.

Speaking of the great size and importance of the State of Texas, I am reminded of the story about the tiny midget in the side show of a traveling circus who was asked by a friend one day why he continued through the years to submit himself to the hardships and indignities of side show life.

"I stay here," said the midget, "because I love this life. I don't have to stay, you know, because I have a nice outside income."

"Outside income?" his friend said, "What kind of an income do you have?"

"Confidentially," said the midget, looking furtively around, "I receive a big check every month from the treasurer of the State of Texas for never telling anyone I was born in Texas!"

It is interesting to point out that the careers of so many of the distinguished young leaders in our national political life seem to follow a remarkably similar pattern. As in other instances, we all know our honored guest today chose the legal profession as a training ground for his political career and success came quickly to Allan Shivers once he decided to enter politics.

At the age of twenty-six, he was the youngest state senator Texas ever had. After being re-elected to the Senate and after winning five battle stars and a Bronze Star in World War II, he moved on quickly to new heights of political accomplishment.

In 1946, he was elected Lieutenant Governor and has been acclaimed as the most effective and influential Lieutenant Governor in the State's history. Certainly, devotees of Texas have not been surprised that he has continued to do a brilliant job as Governor.

I should like also to add a word of personal admiration for our honored guest, not only for the forthright stand he has taken on some very highly controversial issues, but also for the courageous decision he made to support his fellow Texan candidate, Dwight D. Eisenhower.

Gentlemen, it is a great personal pleasure to present the very able and distinguished Governor of the great State of Texas, the Honorable Allan Shivers.

✦

Homer J. Livingston, *President, The First National Bank of Chicago, introduces* **Clarence B. Randall,** *Chairman of the Inland Steel Company.*

THE CHAIRMAN of the panel on "Our Foreign Economic Policy" is, I am certain, known to all of you by reputation and to many of you personally. He is Chairman of the Board of the Inland Steel Company, which is a very important and demanding responsibility. But Mr. Randall is also a man of large and generous interests in many fields, and his mind ranges freely over wide horizons.

On one occasion, you will recall, when an issue of constitutional government was at stake in the United States, he was the eloquent spokesman for the entire steel industry, and in many respects for all of us.

Time does not permit me to tell you of his high standing as an ornithologist, or of his distinguished authorship of thoughtful and scholarly books on the American economy, and specifically on private enterprise.

Some months ago the President of the United States wisely selected Mr. Randall to become Chairman of a "Commission on Foreign Economic Policy," and many of you are familiar with the recent report of that Commission. It seemed quite imperative that we include in this conference a discussion of this important subject. I am afraid that the sagacity for which we should like to be known as bankers and businessmen seems to take a vacation when it faces some of the difficult and challenging problems of our foreign economic policy.

We are fortunate in having a chairman and a panel today all of whom are experts on the subject. I am pleased now to present the chairman of the panel, Mr. Clarence B. Randall.

❧

Herbert V. Prochnow, *Vice-President, The First National Bank of Chicago, introduces* **Clarence B. Randall,** *Chairman of the Inland Steel Company, at a dinner of the Bankers' Club of Chicago.*

SOMEONE ONCE SAID that most of us will listen to people who are smarter than we are—the trouble is we can't find any. But this audience of seven hundred thirty-eight persons—by far the largest in the Club's history—clearly indicates that we have found persons tonight to whom we should like to listen. Certainly, no audience has ever had a more distinguished panel to discuss the business outlook.

The moderator of this panel is known not only to every one here but to men and women over the United States. One evening last April when the American people had an uneasy sense of impending disaster to a great industry, he placed all of us in his debt, for he made a frank and fearless statement over television and radio on the principles of constitutional government. In the front row of that great audience was a well-known citizen from Independence, Missouri, who had been having a little difficulty with those principles. Our moderator helped to resolve that difficulty, and to clarify the issues for the American people.

On some other occasion, but not tonight, I might have said that the moderator is the author of *A Creed for Free Enterprise,* which competent reviewers state is one of the most significant books published in recent years.

On some other occasion, I might also have said that this book is available for $2.75 per copy at all leading bookstores and should be in the library of every bank and business executive, but I shall not mention that tonight.

As Chairman of the Inland Steel Company and a participant in a generous range of civic, community, educational, and business activities, Mr. Randall contributes to many facets of American life. He brings to these activities, convictions with courage, vision with a sense of reality, and wisdom with eloquence. It is a privilege to present the moderator, Mr. Clarence B. Randall.

༞

Clifford S. Young, *President of the Federal Reserve Bank of Chicago, introduces* **William McChesney Martin,** *Chairman of the Board of Governors of the Federal Reserve System, to the Bankers' Club of Chicago.*

I SHALL NOT encroach upon your time or our speaker's this evening to review his career and then embark upon the customary eulogy. He and you are entitled to this forebearance on my part. A lesser person than Bill Martin might require an introductory build-up. He doesn't.

I will, however, cite just one paragraph from an article about him that appeared in *Business Week* shortly after he took the oath of office as Chairman of the Board of Governors of the Federal Reserve System. Under a sub-title, "The Pragmatic Mind," this article said:

"At 44, Martin is the second-youngest man ever to sit at the head of the table in the Federal Reserve System's handsome board room. (Marriner Eccles has the edge by two months.) He looks even younger than his years. Buoyant cheerfulness, obvious good health, a friendly manner, a good mind, immense modesty combine to make him one of the most attractive top men in Washington. He has a good record—Martin has made good in every big chance he's had."

That is a meager, thumb-nail sketch but it is inaccurate in only one minor detail. He grew up in the atmosphere of a Federal Reserve Bank and, on graduating from college, took a job in the Bank Examination Department of the Federal Reserve Bank of St. Louis in 1928. He was fired not long afterward. Let me hasten to add that this was not due to incompetence. His father, then governor of the Bank, is a most punctilious man. He could not countenance any progress for his son in that institution lest it fall under the ban of nepotism. Accordingly, the young man was advised to seek employment elsewhere. The Bank's loss has meant a great gain for the rest of the community, especially the financial world on which his pragmatic mind—in the best sense of pragmatism—has left a deep and admirable imprint as he progressed along the road from university via private business to president of the New York Stock Exchange in 1938 and then, after an interlude in the army from 1941 to the end of World War II (he was drafted as a private, honorably discharged as a colonel), he served as Chairman of the Board and President of the Export-Import Bank, as Assistant Secretary of the Treasury, as United States Executive Director of the International Bank for Reconstruction and Development, and as a member of the National Advisory Council on International Monetary and Financial matters. He has attended all meetings of the Board of Governors of the International Monetary Fund and the International Bank for Reconstruction and Development, and he has represented the United States at various international conferences. The banking fraternity can well be thankful that the President of the United States selected William McChesney Martin, Jr., to be the Chairman of the Board of Governors of the Federal Reserve System.

But I am lapsing into biography when I should be lapsing into silence.

It is a pleasure and an honor to have him here.

⌣

Rufin W. Boyd, *Assistant Principal, Lincoln High School, Manitowoc, Wisconsin, introduces his former pastor.*

As YOU KNOW, our speaker served a parish in Billings, Montana, up until five years ago. When I was there, I stayed at the home of one of his former parishioners. The conversation got around to ministers, and I asked about Pastor Johnson. One day I said to this lady, "How was Pastor Johnson with the youth of the congregation?"

"Oh, he was wonderful. We really didn't know what youth work was until he came to us."

"Was Pastor Johnson a good speaker?"

"Oh, yes, his sermons were just wonderful, in fact, until Pastor Johnson came to Billings we really didn't know what *sin was!*"

⌣

James E. Day, *President of the Midwest Stock Exchange, introduces* **Lee Wulff,** *who presented fishing and hunting films.*

I THINK that it was very nice of the Program Committee to arrange this particular meeting, as I have just returned from a fishing trip. It was very thoughtful.

Our speaker today needs no introduction; therefore, I would like to take a couple of minutes and tell you about my fishing trip. I may never have an opportunity like this again.

To start out with, Mrs. Day went along on this trip and I have been teaching her to fish. Now, if any of you gentlemen have an idea about teaching your wife how to fish, you might think about it again.

You will find that in teaching your wife to fish, you get into strange territory. All sportsmen like to get into strange territory and new places; however, most of the new places that I got into were called "gift" shops.

I will say one thing for Mrs. Day—she isn't extravagant about anything except money. We had a wonderful time together and we caught some fish.

I remember one day it was blowing and I suggested that we go to the lee side and do a little casting off the pier. We were having fun and getting a few fish. Finally, here came a little barracuda about this long. Well, I threw a plug out, he took a look at it and turned up his nose. I then put on a bucktail, he took another look and again ignored the bait. I finally turned to Mrs. Day and said, "What do you suppose is wrong with that stupid fish?" She replied, "Maybe he doesn't know that you are president of the Executives' Club." You just can't win!

Now, in introducing Mr. Wulff I know that you are all aware that he is probably the top sportsman in the country. We have had him with us before and those of you that have been here know that you are in for a treat.

We are very happy to have him today and I would like to present him by quoting an old proverb, as follows: "Allah does not deduct from the time of man those hours spent in fishing."

I'm sure, Mr. Wulff, that this also applies to you.
Gentlemen, Mr. Lee Wulff.

~

| **John J. McDonough,** *President of the Executives' Club of Chicago,*
introduces **Joseph M. Dodge,** *Director of the Bureau of the*
Budget of the United States.

IT IS A GREAT PLEASURE today to welcome to the Executives' Club of
Chicago the best qualified and the most distinguished Director of the
Bureau of the Budget in our country's history. We all recognize our
honored guest to be a man of unquestioned integrity and exceptional
competence and ability. We further know him to be an outstanding
member of a very select and dedicated group of men of similar character and capability who are restoring the faith and confidence of
the people of the United States in our Federal Government.

One of the more partisan members of Congress recently said, "Joe
Dodge is one of those extraordinary citizens who proved that they
were able and loyal long before they received their Eisenhower
appointments, and who, incidentally, made their money before they
got to Washington."

For reasons that I am sure are obvious to you, I take special
pleasure in reminding you that Mr. Dodge was one of the country's
leading bankers before entering his long and rewarding career in
government service. Particularly noteworthy in his banking career
was his promotion, at the tender age of 43, to the presidency of
The Detroit Bank, and not many years thereafter, his election to the
presidency of the American Bankers' Association.

Mr. Dodge long ago established himself as a bitter foe of inflation,
and as a militant believer in balanced budgets. He first demonstrated
this rare ability to put those strong convictions into practice in Germany, where, in association with Generals Eisenhower and Clay, he
won his initial battle against inflation. In a later assignment in Japan,
in 1948 and '49, as financial adviser to General MacArthur, with the
rank of minister, he won another great victory over economic decay
and disorder by insisting on a balanced budget for Japan.

In recent months, gentlemen, Mr. Dodge has been making the

most heroic fight of his life for his sound principles, and today we eagerly await his report on the progress he is making in helping to balance one of the biggest budgets in our history.

Gentlemen, it is a great personal pleasure to present to you a banker and a great public servant, who will speak to us on the subject, "Our Budget and Fiscal Problems."

꜒

John Nuveen, *Director of the Executives' Club of Chicago, introduces* **Dr. Walter H. Judd,** *Congressman from Minnesota.*

I HAD THE PRIVILEGE of hearing Dr. Judd in 1938 in one of the first talks he made in Chicago after he had returned from China. I had never heard anybody who spoke with such energy and conviction. His rapid-fire delivery didn't seem to be able to keep up with his anxiety to get across the message that was in his heart.

I do not think he was the subject of a couple of men who, upon leaving a meeting at which they had heard a very eloquent speech, were discussing the speaker. One said to the other, "How could any one man learn to speak so fast?" The other fellow said, "That's easy. His father was a tobacco auctioneer and his mother was a woman."

In the June 18, 1945, issue of *Time* magazine, the editors did something which I don't think they have done before or since. They devoted four pages to the speech of one congressman in the House. They introduced that comment with these words: "Of all Americans occupying elective office, the man who knows most about the Far East is almost certainly Congressman Walter H. Judd."

We have a man here today to tell us something about the Far East. He didn't go there to learn any diplomatic tricks; he went there to help the people.

Around the world today, where we are looking for help to solve the problems in most countries, we will find that the men who can be the most helpful, who have the most good will back of them, are those who have gone their way with a similar purpose, and perhaps if we can recognize it when our total foreign policy becomes of that nature, rather than one of cleverness or political intrigue, we will have better success in what we are trying to do.

I think you all read yesterday's "Chuckle" in the *Daily News* and I only repeat it for Dr. Judd's benefit. It was to the effect that all people can be divided into three classes, those who watch things happen, those who make things happen, and those who don't know anything is happening.

Dr. Judd is one who is making things happen. We are thankful for him, and we are happy to have him here.

_____

James E. Day, *President, Midwest Stock Exchange, introduces* **Gardner Cowles,** *publisher.*

AT ELEVEN O'CLOCK today we received word that the Twentieth Century—on which Mr. Cowles was coming here so there wouldn't be any slip-ups on his date—was five hours late. It looked like a long introduction. But Mr. Cowles left the train at Cleveland and chartered a plane to be here with you.

These things come in pairs. I thought it would be a very nice idea to have Mr. Cowles introduced today by our director, Mr. Otis Kline of United Air Lines. Mr. Cowles is a director of United. Well, everything was fine, and we hadn't a worry in the world, but Mr. Kline shows up today with no voice. So you're stuck with me.

In that short space of time I haven't had much opportunity to find any additional things about Mr. Cowles, other than the information contained in the folder we sent you. I did quiz him here on a few things, and found out that he is a golfer. I'd like to tell him a story that I heard recently about a golf game, and I'd like to have you listen in on it. This is a true story told to me by a friend of mine of the First California Company by the name of Jack Egan.

He said that a year ago he was entertaining the new president of the American Stock Exchange who wanted to play the famous Pebble Beach Course.

Jack said, "Well, I didn't know what kind of game Mr. McCormick of American played, so I had one golfer who could shoot around par and another who shot around my game—around 105— and we started out.

"I think I should tell you that at all these 'name' golf courses they have what we call tramp caddies who come in from all over and follow the circuit around. Some of them are perfectly magnificent golfers; they can make shots the pros can't make."

Jack said that on this particular day he had a short little fellow for a caddy, who didn't have much to say.

Well, Jack said they teed off for the 13th, and the other fellows were right down the middle, while Jack was over behind a big sand dune, 190 yards from the green. Jack walked over with his caddy and looked at his ball, in the rough, with this big sand dune there, and 190 yards to the green. He turned to the caddy and said, "What in the world would you do with that?"

The caddy looked at him and said, "If it was me, I'd belt it on the green."

Jack said, "I know, but what will I do with it?"

The caddy said, "If it was me, I'd still belt it on the green."

Jack said, "I don't believe you could do it."

The caddy said, "All right, I'll show you." He reached over and yanked a 2 iron out of the bag. Jack looked over the situation, and could just see the top of McCormick's head, so he said to the caddy, "Wait a minute. Let me take a club, you count three, and I'll lift my club with you and swing, and they'll think it's me." The caddy said, "Okay, Doc."

Jack yanked a club out of the bag. The caddy looked the shot over, got down and swung. It was a magnificent shot—the ball zoomed right up there on the green, four feet from the cup.

Jack said McCormick and this other chap went berserk. They dropped their clubs and came running over to him behind the sand dune. McCormick said, "My Gosh, I never saw a shot like that in my life. That's impossible! What did you hit it with?"

Jack handed his club to him, and he said, "Man—a *6 iron?*"

Gentlemen, your guest speaker is President of the Des Moines Register and Tribune, the Cowles Broadcasting Company and Cowles Magazines, chief of which, as you all know, is the very popular *Look* magazine. He is Chairman of the Board of the *Minneapolis Star* and *Tribune*, and the Massachusetts Broadcasting Company. He is also a director of Bankers Life, the Iowa-Des Moines National Bank & Trust Company, and United Airlines. He is a trustee of Drake University and Iowa Wesleyan College.

It is my very real pleasure to present a man who, in order to be with us, jumped from train to plane—a man to be admired for his integrity, audacity, and most certainly his—solvency.

Gentlemen, Mr. Cowles.

❧

William G. Stratton, *Governor of the State of Illinois, introduces* **Herbert Brownell, Jr.,** *Attorney General of the United States to the Executives' Club in Chicago.*

THIS IS ONE OF THOSE occasions that most of us look forward to and dream about but rarely ever have consummated. This happens to be the first time that, as your Governor, I have had the privilege of introducing a distinguished member of the President's Cabinet, and so you can understand that in addition to the elation and, shall I say, the good will present in the audience, that your Governor, too, feels proud today to be able to introduce and to act in this capacity with our distinguished guest speaker.

The gentleman I am about to introduce has already, in a few short months, established a new and, shall I say, a refreshing pattern in the conduct of the office of Attorney General of the United States.

I hope that people will not too soon forget, at least, the fact that when this gentleman took office, the Department had achieved a reputation that was far from good, the people had little confidence in its operation, and there was great difficulty in carrying on this important branch of the government dedicated to law enforcement and dedicated to helping the Administration in carrying out its duty. But since this gentleman has taken over, I am proud to say here today—and I'm sure you share the feeling with me—that now we have an example of an Attorney General—not only in the conduct of that office (and it is a great and a far-reaching office), but in the example he has set for all of the other departments of the national government—that is contributing a great deal to the progress and success that is being achieved by the President and his entire Cabinet.

So, today, I am proud to present to you not just another Attorney General, great as that office may be, but the leader, the man who has done so much to build and to help solve these tremendous problems facing the country—the man who is the closest adviser to the President of the United States—our distinguished guest, the Attorney General of the United States, Herbert Brownell, Jr.

◆

Joseph R. Knight, *a director of the Executives' Club of Chicago, introduces* **H. E. Humphreys, Jr.,** *Chairman of the U. S. Rubber Company.*

I FIND MYSELF TRYING to fill rather big shoes today in the absence of our President, Jim Day, who is on a fishing vacation in Florida. I think Jim must wear about size 12 Triple E shoes, while I wear only 1½ D. The Triple E is for triple excellence for him as the President of our Club and his weekly introduction of our guest speakers. I know that you miss him.

Our speaker today heads one of the "Big Four" companies in the rubber industry, and we are greatly pleased to have him with us. He has expressed himself forcefully on national issues and public affairs.

Hundreds of years ago the Indians of Central and South America discovered a strange tree in their hot, wet jungles. They named the tree "caoutchouc" meaning "weeping wood" because of a milky liquid which exuded from the cut bark like big, white tears. When Columbus made his second voyage to the New World, he reported the Indians were playing with balls "made of the gum of a tree." Cortez watched the Aztecs use a bouncing ball to play games something like our soccer and basketball today. The Valley of the Amazon seemed then to be the favorite home of the rubber tree.

Early European scientists experimented with rubber, and in 1823 a Scottish manufacturer by the name of Macintosh made the first raincoat, and a new word was coined when that raincoat was called a "macintosh."

In 1833 America's first rubber plant was started in Massachusetts. In 1839, vulcanized rubber was born, which was really the beginning of the rubber industry as we know it today.

I think we should not be unmindful of the rubber crisis of World War II, which was finally overcome by the industry's magnificent job in the production of synthetic rubber.

Earliest work on synthetic rubber occurred in U. S. Rubber laboratories more than twenty-five years ago.

Our speaker today is Chairman and President of the U. S. Rubber Company, which, as I mentioned before, is one of the "Big Four" companies in the industry.

I could build a Horatio Alger story in presenting our speaker, and I should like to say to our young men here today that we have an outstanding example here of a man who, coming from a very humble beginning, found that there was plenty of room at the top of the ladder.

He was born in Philadelphia, the son of a city policeman, and obtained his higher education in the night classes—seven years, incidentally—at the Wharton School of Finance of the University of Pennsylvania. He now holds an honorary degree of Doctor of Laws from that University.

In 1938 he was elected a Vice-President and Director of U. S. Rubber Company; President and Vice-Chairman of the Executive Committee in 1949; Chairman of the Board in September, 1951.

One way to learn something about anyone is to ask a friend or business associate. I did both. A business associate said of him, "There are two kinds of people in the world—those who want to be somebody, and those who want to get something done. Harry made his choice early. He would get things done." A friend appraised him in a very few words when he said, "Harry is a good American." I think you will agree with me that no greater tribute can be paid any man.

Gentlemen, it is a pleasure to give you the Chairman and President of the United States Rubber Company—Mr. Harry E. Humphreys, Jr.

❧

James E. Day, *President, Midwest Stock Exchange, introduces* **John L. Lewis,** *American labor leader.*

FOR AN INDETERMINABLE number of years we have worked long and patiently to sign up our speaker of today. It is then with pardonable pride that I have the privilege to introduce him.

Now, it is a matter of record that the Empire State Building sways over three feet in a strong wind. In the lifetime of our speaker, in the most violent winds of controversy, there has never been a perceptible movement. To withstand such winds that at times have reached almost hurricane force would require a sound and solid base.

After interviewing both friend and foe, you soon discover the qualities that give our speaker his unwavering stability. His friends point admirably to his fortitude and integrity; his enemies invariably, but grudgingly, admit that there never was a question about his courage and honesty.

Yes, our speaker has his share of enemies, but he has more than an ample quota of real friends. A number of them are the heads of our largest coal companies, with whom he has had many a rough battle.

I happen to come from a coal-mining town downstate. As a boy, I knew many men who worked in the deep mines, never seeing the sun. I can tell you that these men hold "John L.," as they call him, in high regard and with deep affection.

One of my interviews was with the chairman of the board of one of our outstanding coal companies headquartered here in Chicago. In reminiscing on Mr. Lewis, he said, "You know, John would have made a great general. Whenever he went into battle for his union, he always had several plans of attack. He could switch from one to another, as the circumstances warranted. I guess that's one of the reasons he generally won. I could almost say 'Ouch' right now when I think of some of the hard bargains he struck with me."

Gentlemen, the Executives' Club of Chicago is proud to present American Labor's five-star general, Mr. John L. Lewis.

❧

M. Glen Miller, *Owner, M. Glen Miller, Advertising, introduces* **Jesse M. Donaldson,** *Postmaster General of the United States.*

NOT SINCE BENJAMIN FRANKLIN held the job from 1775 to 1776 has the United States had a Postmaster General who knew anything about the job when he took office. By that I don't mean to deny the obvious fact that a certain few did pick up some odds and ends of information while occupying this high cabinet position. I suppose it would have seemed as remarkable for a post office official to look to his chief for advice about running his part of the postal system as it would now for the President to call in Jesse Donaldson for lunch to snag a bit of advice on political strategy. Traditionally, the post office has provided a cabinet position for a political head—never for a postal administrator.

That is why it was a perfectly normal thing for Jesse Donaldson to be non-plussed when the President of the United States casually rang him on the phone one day and asked him to be Postmaster General.

Said the modest and unassuming career man, "Mr. President ... you've knocked me off my chair."

But you can bet Mr. Donaldson, with the cheers of post office workers right down to the lowliest porter ringing in his ears, climbed right back in a hurry. For here was one of the world's biggest businesses to be run.

I suspect Mr. Donaldson slid into his new job without very strenuous adjustment from his post as First Assistant Postmaster General.

He knows more about the Post Office Department than any man alive or dead! And why shouldn't he. Before he was out of school he began in vacations for $11 a week to help the Postmaster of Hanson, Illinois, near where he was born on a farm. And who was the Postmaster at Hanson? His own father. Later on he quit a school teacher's job to become a city letter carrier at Shelbyville, Illinois.

And what do you suppose he does for a hobby ... he collects stamps.

Gentlemen—a member of the Cabinet of the President of the United States, the Postmaster General, the Honorable Jesse M. Donaldson.

♰

John J. McDonough, *Vice-President, Harris Trust and Savings Bank, Chicago, introduces* **Dr. Will Durant,** *author and philosopher.*

IT IS PRESUMPTUOUS of me to try in the usual way to introduce Dr. Will Durant to you, or vice versa, not only because he is a very old friend of the members of the Executives' Club, but also because of his fabulous "History of Philosophy" and his other monumental books that have made him so well known to millions of Americans. However, I do wish to say to Dr. Durant how happy we are that he has flown two thousand miles from California only to be with us on this very auspicious occasion, and we all look forward with the greatest of pleasure to enjoying his prodigious learning, his brilliant wit, and his great personal charm.

Dr. Will Durant, who will speak to us on the subject, "The Destiny of Civilization."

⁓

M. Glen Miller, *Owner, M. Glen Miller, Advertising, introduces* **Dr. Robert E. Wilson,** *Chairman, Standard Oil Company of Indiana. (Many petroleum company executives were present.)*

BY ALL ODDS this ought to be the smoothest and most powerful meeting of the year. Never before have we had such an array of talent dedicated to the elimination of friction and the increase of explosive impact. Never have we had on hand at one time so many oleaginous specimens fairly bristling with octanes.

Our speaker today is not only an outstanding executive administrator in the oil industry, but a trained scientist with more than ninety patents to his credit. He sits at the controls of a great corporation, with oil can in hand, and squirts oil into the far recesses of a vast and far flung industrial empire—third largest oil company in the country—and he also sees to it that the very oil in the can is the product of the most advanced and precise scientific research.

It is unusual in big businesses that directing heads are selected from the ranks of research men, let alone professors, who notoriously are poor administrators. But Standard's selection of Dr. Wilson bespeaks not only a vast confidence in the man but a recognition of the great importance of the laboratory in the future of the business.

Bob Wilson early gave promise of an important future. His mother had bought a crib from a Mrs. Midgley, and little Bobby squirmed and gurgled and slept in the self-same crib that had sheltered little Thomas Midgley, later to become the wizard of chemistry, who discovered the value of tetraethyl lead in gasoline. These two men had more to do with making ethyl gas available to all of us than anyone else. Yet, they were both famous and close friends before they discovered the strange sharing of a baby crib.

By the time he was twenty-five, little Robert had become a Major in the Chemical Warfare Service in the First World War. Success and honors and promotion followed in rapid succession. His contributions to the oil industry were phenomenal and his executive talent soon became too obvious to ignore.

He has received honorary degrees from five institutions. He has won the coveted Perkin Medal, the highest recognition attainable in applied chemistry in the United States. The vestibule of his life is littered with directorates and trusteeships in universities, banks, museums, associations, and institutes.

His great mind delves deep into scientific mysteries. He can tell us precisely what happens to every precious particle of energy in gasoline; he even knows the exact amount of wasted energy in the sun's rays, and he can measure to the infinitesimal the energy dissipated in giving a vice-president the hotfoot.

To you men whose lives would be utterly blighted without lubricants and gasoline, I am happy to present one of the men who makes them—Dr. Robert Erastus Wilson, Chairman of Standard Oil Company of Indiana.

~∂⌐

John E. Stipp, *President of the Federal Home Loan Bank of Chicago, introduces* **Ralph D. Paine, Jr.,** *Publisher of Fortune.*

As our guest speaker today, it is our good fortune to have *Fortune's* good fortune—its publisher, Mr. Ralph D. Paine, Jr. Mr. Paine will speak on "Changing American Markets," and for the sake of those of us who are interested in the current economic situation of this country, let us hope that he does not live up to his office reputation as a "strong, silent man."

In this connection, let me quote from a recent article in *Fortune* concerning him.

"During his 22 years in Time, Inc., Del Paine has been a practitioner of heroic silence. His reputation as an originator of many ideas and speaker of few words gives rise to staff ribs like this one: 'A story conference with Paine isn't a conference at all. You talk for yourself and for Paine. First you present your idea, then you express what you think his reaction is likely to be, then you try to judge from the sound he emits whether you have said what he would have said if he were speaking.' "

After graduation from Yale in 1929, Mr. Paine spent two years in

Wall Street as a securities analyst before joining Time, Inc., as a writer. He was appointed business editor of the magazine in 1933, and he held that post until 1938, when he was named editorial assistant to the then president of *Time*, Mr. Henry Luce.

While he was vacationing in Europe in 1939, Mr. Paine was asked to remain abroad and to direct the London and Paris bureaus of *Time*. He became the managing director of *March of Time, Ltd.*, of London, and had charge of European operations for all Time, Inc. publications. When the Germans moved into Paris, Mr. Paine returned to the United States as head of the Washington bureau of *Time*. In 1941, he joined *Fortune*, and later that year was appointed managing editor, which position he held until he became Publisher of *Fortune* in February of 1953. His one escape from the editorial desk during his career at *Fortune* came in 1945, when he went to the Pacific as a war correspondent to cover the Okinawa operation with the navy.

I am very pleased and happy now to present Mr. Paine to you.

꧁

John J. McDonough, *Vice-President, Harris Trust and Savings Bank, Chicago, introduces* **Fulton Lewis, Jr.,** *radio and TV commentator.*

IN EXTENDING a most cordial welcome today to Mr. Fulton Lewis, Jr., I want, first of all, to point out that we, in the Executives' Club, are particularly enthusiastic about guest speakers whose first name is Fulton.

Even though the Fulton who is with us today wears no bishop's purple, he has many similar forensic and semantic capabilities, and nearly as great an audience as his namesake who opened our Club year.

Amazing versatility is another similar characteristic and I should guess that few of you realize that our guest of honor today, in addition to his distinction as a radio commentator, is also a well-known boat builder, carpenter and cabinet maker, stamp collector, dirt farmer, composer, choirmaster, and since the departure of the Democratic administration, is the most celebrated amateur pianist in Washington.

For all his tremendous popularity, Mr. Fulton Lewis, Jr. is not a commentator who always tries to evoke a uniform or neutral response from his vast audience. His listeners do agree, however, that his newscasting technique is thoroughly poised, incisive, and fluent, and that he has a genius for exerting a very powerful influence at timely moments when his less courageous rivals prefer to preserve their silence.

I have in mind, for example, the relentless and dramatic attack some years ago on O.P.A. by Mr. Lewis, which, according to one top O.P.A. official, contributed more than any other single effort to the abolition of price control.

There have been many compliments paid Mr. Lewis by many distinguished citizens, but one is especially noteworthy. This was the high tribute paid to him by ex-President Hoover back in the dark days when the Republicans were out of power. Mr. Hoover wrote, "In these days when our precious liberties are being menaced by the machinations of treacherous and faithless men who masquerade as 'liberals' and 'champions of the people,' Fulton Lewis' lucid, fearless and exhaustive examinations of the vital issues of our time are of profound importance to all good Americans."

Gentlemen, it is a real pleasure to present the popular and resourceful purveyor of the "Top of the News from Washington" Mr. Fulton Lewis, Jr.

⌐↝

M. Glen Miller, *Owner, M. Glen Miller, Advertising, introduces* **Charles F. Brannan,** *Secretary of Agriculture.*

I SHOULD LIKE to give you a statistic. There are 27,000,000 people living on farms in the United States. By a strange alchemy of democracy, this represents just 27,000,000 votes.

Now, I would be among the last to suspect that our speaker today has the least interest in such a squalid, mundane thing as 27,000,000 votes. Rather, I believe Mr. Brannan recognizes that this vast number of people represents a magnificent market for goods, so long as a high level of farm income is maintained.

His intent is to establish a procedure by which farm purchasing power may be sustained, and yet which allows the public to benefit by fluctuations in prices. This seeming anomaly is overcome by direct subsidy payments to the farmer by the government.

I am quite sure there is no one in the room who is not conscious of the fact that when government spends money, it is taxpayers' money, and I suppose that there is no one present today who is not a farmer, a Republican, or a taxpayer.

I hope Mr. Brannan will be patient with our inability to understand how it is possible to subsidize one impressive factor of our population without doing similar subsidizing for other organized groups. I hope he will also make clear to us how we are to have such bureaucratic control without completely socializing farming operations.

Mr. Brannan has come up the hard way. He was a farmer himself and he is completely surcharged with this idea to keep farmers prosperous. He has achieved a point of high eminence for a man of his youthfulness.

I am proud now to present the Honorable Charles F. Brannan, Secretary of Agriculture in the Cabinet of the President of the United States.

⌖

John J. McDonough, *as President of the Executives' Club of Chicago, introduces* **Edward T. McCormick,** *President of the American Stock Exchange.*

TODAY IT IS A GREAT pleasure to introduce a young man who defied Horace Greeley and came East instead of going West to find his fame and fortune. Our guest of honor was born in Tucson, Arizona, and—the Arizona Chamber of Commerce notwithstanding—the record shows that he got out of there as soon as possible, after obtaining all his basic education in that state.

Incidentally, Mr. McCormick took a B.A. degree at the University of Arizona, and picked up a beautiful gold Phi Beta Kappa key which, as you can all see, he is modestly concealing today by not wearing a vest.

Mr. McCormick's academic pedigree is very impressive. In addition to that B.A. he has an M. Sc., C.P.A., Ph. D., and on top of all that, he is a Democrat.

Fully intending to devote himself to a cloistered life in some ivory tower as a professor of economics, Mr. McCormick somehow suffered a metamorphosis in 1934, when he suddenly decided to enter the government service as a securities analyst of the Securities and Exchange Commission. After 18 years of very outstanding and rewarding association with the SEC—which, incidentally, included much lecturing and much writing, and a lot of golf—our guest of honor rose to be a Commissioner of the SEC in 1949.

So well did he perform his duties as Commissioner that the titans of Wall Street finance persuaded him to exchange Washington for New York, and to embrace a career in private industry rather than in public service.

Under his able and resourceful leadership, the American Stock Exchange—the second largest in the country—has grown and prospered until today it handles approximately 800 domestic and foreign issues, has approximately 500 members who operate 1700 offices in 400 cities in the United States.

With his exceptional educational background and his splendid record of public service, his ready smile and great personal charm, Mr. McCormick, I am fully confident, will enjoy a long and distinguished career.

In view of what has been happening in the stock markets recently, we are all vitally interested in his message today, and I am delighted to present Mr. Edward T. McCormick, President of the American Stock Exchange, who will speak to us on the subject, "The Need for National Optimism."

⤳

John J. McDonough, *Vice-President, Harris Trust and Savings Bank, Chicago, introduces* **Lester L. Colbert,** *President, Chrysler Corporation.*

GENTLEMEN, this is Texas Week in Chicago!

Yesterday, the very charming Miss Sue White from Big Springs, Texas, received a sensational new all-time record price for her Grand Champion steer at the Live Stock Show.

Today we pay our respects here at the Executives' Club to the most famous son of Oakwood, Texas—600 people. And next Friday, the Governor of Texas will be here to tell us how Texans frequently win such high honors and accomplish so much so easily.

Incidentally, I am delighted also to announce that last week at the Dallas State Fair, Governor Shivers designated our guest of honor today as The Texan of the Year! I think we ought to give him a hand for that.

Seriously, we are happy indeed to welcome back to this community an old friend, not only of so many men in this room, but in all Chicago, who will never forget "Tex" Colbert's superb achievements here as a wartime executive.

Many years before Mr. Colbert set his amazing production record at the Dodge Plant, he was busy preparing himself for a successful career in industry.

Like many discerning Texans, Mr. Colbert added a Harvard Law Degree to the B.A. he received from the University of Texas and, gentlemen, that combination proved unbeatable.

After a short but enlightening tour of duty with a prominent New York law firm, our honored guest was brought to Detroit as House Counsel by the late, great Walter P. Chrysler.

There quickly followed for Mr. Colbert some extremely valuable experience in labor relations, production, and administration, and this, coupled with his exceptional native sales ability, moved him rapidly along the high road of success.

We have recalled, of course, the fact that World War II diverted him for a time to Chicago where he did such a magnificent job in running the largest aircraft plant in the world.

In 1945, however, he returned to Detroit and in less than five years he was elected President of Chrysler Corporation.

How very fortunate for Chrysler Corporation in these highly competitive years ahead that they have as their President not only a seasoned lawyer, a labor relations expert, a production genius, but also, and perhaps, most important, a superb salesman.

I don't think we could find anyone in the country better qualified to speak on the subject of "Competition."

Gentlemen, it is a great personal pleasure to present to you the genial and dynamic President of the Chrysler Corporation, Mr. Lester L. Colbert.

෴

| **John E. Stipp,** *President, Federal Home Loan Bank of Chicago, introduces* **Nathan M. Pusey,** *President, Harvard University.*

HARVARD UNIVERSITY has had twenty-three consecutive presidents born and raised in New England. It has had twenty-two presidents who were Bostonians. From that, you might say that a kind of tradition had developed.

But last year the oldest university in the United States broke this tradition and picked its 24th president—a man who was born and raised in Council Bluffs, Iowa, and who was President of Appleton, Wisconsin's Lawrence College at the time of his election to the presidency of Harvard.

The president of Brown University, Henry Wriston, when he was president of Lawrence, noted that he had on his faculty "the most brilliant young teacher I have ever known." This brilliant young teacher, who had worked his way across country to California and back, teaching, was Nathan Marsh Pusey, our guest speaker today.

President Pusey, of the Harvard Class of '28, Magna Cum Laude, has studied in Europe, and has a master's and doctorate degree from Harvard, specializing in ancient history and Athenian civilization. Incidentally, he wrote his doctorate paper in the Greek language. From all of this you will readily see that he is an outstanding scholar. He has taught at Lawrence, Riverdale Country School, Scripps College at Claremont, California, and Wesleyan University.

He did a remarkable job as president of Lawrence, in the fields of both school studies and the endowment fund, which almost doubled under his leadership.

An Appleton reporter, upon the occasion of Dr. Pusey's receiving the news of his new appointment as president of Harvard, wrote that when the students serenaded him that night, he told them, "I don't want you to think that we're going to a better college. That's not true. It's bigger, but not essentially better."

Well, it certainly was bigger, with 10,000 students compared to 800; with an endowment of $210 millions compared to $2.5 millions.

A national magazine quoted President Pusey's philosophy of higher education in these words: "Christopher Fry said recently that 'affairs are now soul-size.' The American colleges must recognize this fact, and remember again that the true business of liberal education is greatness. It is our task not to produce 'safe' men, in whom our safety can never, in any case, lie, but to keep alive in young people the courage to dare to seek the truth, to be free, to establish in them a compelling desire to live greatly and magnanimously, and to give them the knowledge and awareness, the faith and the trained facility, to get on with the job. Especially the faith, for as someone has said, the whole world now looks to us for a creed to believe and a song to sing. The whole world—and our young people first of all."

Gentlemen, to discuss the question, "What's Going on at Harvard," I present President Pusey.

⤳

John J. McDonough, *as President of the Executives' Club of Chicago, introduces* **Gene Flack,** *Sales Counsel and Advertising Director, Sunshine Biscuits, Inc.*

IT IS A GREAT PLEASURE to welcome back to the Executives' Club our favorite sales expert who also specializes in making business executives feel better about life.

While I realize that there are many fine salesmen in this audience, I am particularly happy about the idea of exposing Gene Flack to our good friends in the club who are lawyers, doctors, politicians, philosophers and other equally cloistered members and guests who have never had to meet a sales quota!

I know that they will enjoy, equally with us working men, Gene's rare genius as an inspirational speaker and as a raconteur!

Like some other great salesmen I know, Gene Flack chose to graduate from Northwestern University, instead of Yale or Princeton, and I am delighted to tell you that not long ago N.U. bestowed upon our guest of honor a special award for meritorious service to his Alma Mater.

While it is a well known fact that Gene Flack has sold many trainloads of Sunshine Biscuits, I want you to know also that he took time out of his colorful and successful career to serve his country in two world wars. In the first, he was a fighting soldier; in the second he was a vocal but an extremely effective "Citizen Soldier" in the ranks of the U.S.O., the C.E.D., the Red Cross, and the U. S. Treasury.

The one and only Gene Flack.

⤳

| **John E. Stipp,** *President of the Federal Home Loan Bank of Chicago, introduces* **Edmund S. Muskie,** *Governor-elect of Maine.*

ACCORDING TO the modern press, as well as historians, there are two explosions in connection with the state of Maine that have "rocked the nation." One of these explosions had to do with the U. S. S. Maine, and resulted in that famed call to the colors, "Remember the Maine!" The second happened recently, and according to *Newsweek*, was a "shock" and "surprised the nation." Furthermore, and still quoting *Newsweek*, the surprising thing about the September elections in Maine was "the force of the explosion." This was all tied to another adage—"As Maine Goes, So Goes the Nation."

Overnight, the first Democratic Candidate for Governor to carry rock-ribbed Republican Maine in twenty years became a national figure—a cause of studious comment by both of the political parties.

Vice-President Nixon, who took part in the Maine campaign, said the vote there should serve warning to Republicans to "run scared." The Democrats hailed the victory as the handwriting on the wall. Everyone's first reaction was "What happened?"

Today we have the man who can answer that question "what happened?" Today we have as our guest, forty-year-old lawyer, Edmund Sixtus Muskie, the man who carried Maine for the Democrats.

Governor-elect Muskie is the son of a Polish immigrant. His father fled as a youth of fifteen from czarist military conscription in Poland. He settled in Maine, and became a confirmed outdoorsman.

The son became an enthusiastic fisherman, a good skier, and a competent track man. At Bates College he was president of his class, a Phi Beta Kappa, and was voted the most respected senior, the most likely to succeed, and the best scholar.

Time Magazine reports that when the Governor-elect was in college, he was something of a political oddity. When the President of

Bates College was introduced to Mr. Muskie, he remarked, "Oh, so *you're* the Democrat."

He practised law at Cornell, and served four years in the United States Navy as an engineering officer on a destroyer escort. After the war he returned to his law practice, tried unsuccessfully to become elected Mayor of Waterville, won a seat in the state legislature, and later became Director of the Office of Price Stabilization in Maine. Governor-elect Muskie describes himself as "neither a New Deal nor a Fair Deal Democrat, but rather, a Maine Democrat."

Republican apologists in Maine are said to be excusing the results of the election there on the grounds that the state, which is renown for its bountiful fishing and the sportsmanlike character of its fishermen, simply could not reject a man with the name that our guest bears.

Gentlemen, Governor-elect Muskie.

⌒

John E. Stipp, *President, Federal Home Loan Bank of Chicago, introduces* **Warren Lee Pierson** *of Trans-World Airlines.*

MANY, MANY TIMES we hear a person described by that time-honored and well-worn phrase, "He is a man of the world." And yet, it is seldom, indeed, that we have the opportunity to see a person to whom that phrase is appropriate in a literal sense. But today we have the pleasure of seeing—and listening to—a man to whom that description does apply, both figuratively and literally.

World War I found him a student at the University of California. He left the University in his senior year to join the French Ambulance Corps overseas and later served the United States as an artillery officer. Following the war, and in rapid succession, he became a lawyer, president of an international holding company, the American Cable & Radio Corporation, chairman of the Board of Trans-World Airlines and president of the International Air Transport Association. All of this gave him the background for his subsequent "man of the world" activities.

He became general counsel and later president of the Export-Import Bank, financial adviser to the United States delegation at the

Bretton Woods Monetary Conference, a member of the Inter-American Financial and Economic Advisory Committee, and advisor to the Inter-American Conference of Problems of War and Peace at Mexico City. As a special United States ambassador, he represented this nation on the Tripartite Commission on German debts and is now chairman of the United States Council of the International Chamber of Commerce.

I suppose in the interest of accuracy, we really should refer to him as a "Businessman of the World." With all of his international activity, it would be small wonder, indeed, if our guest is becoming impatient at the seemingly slow progress that is being made in the field of interplanetary space travel.

It is a real pleasure to present to you a man who has indeed won the right to represent the world at the first monetary and business Conference of the United Planets—Mr. Warren Lee Pierson.

✒

Melvin Brorby, *President of the Chicago Council on Foreign Relations, introduces* **Chester Bowles,** *former United States Ambassador in India.*

I FEEL VERY MUCH SET UP these days, having so much to do with ambassadors and such distinguished guests. Only last Friday, you remember, we had the President of Turkey and many of his ambassadors with us.

I think you will be interested in a comment made to me during that luncheon by Mme. Bayar, the President's very charming wife. She was the only lady at the speaker's table, and across the room the balcony was crowded with ladies, including my wife. When I introduced my wife to Mme. Bayar with gestures across the room, she said, "Well, you know in Turkey we have abandoned the harem system—it looks as if you have taken it up!"

I am especially pleased to have the privilege of introducing our guest of honor today for two reasons:

One: He represents what I think is one of the most important trends or symbols of our American life today. He is one of those men who turned from a very successful career in business to public service. Having first proved that our so-called free enterprise way of life is a sound one, he showed his willingness to dedicate himself to the public interest. We are completely safe when Americans are willing to do that.

Two: I have a personal interest in India because I spent a year there many years ago, living with the Indian people, studying their way of life. In those days, of course, public officials were not apt to mingle with the people. I can remember one high British official who said he missed being Governor of a Province because he went to the Indian wedding of Indian friends.

During the time that Mr. Bowles was Ambassador in India, I had many letters from friends of mine there saying how much they liked his basic attitude of cooperation and understanding. He very evidently went more than half way to meet the Indian people, and they liked it immensely.

In the year and a half he was Ambassador, he drove 60,000 miles inside the country in a battered car, only using his official limousine and flag on state occasions. Both he and his wife learned to speak the language and sent their children to Indian schools. I am sure that this attitude of friendliness to a people for whom friendliness is very important, made a great contribution to the cause of our relationship, not only with India but with the entire East.

Last May, after he finished his book, both he and Mrs. Bowles decided to set aside one year going through the United States, sharing their experiences in India, so people here could have a clear idea of what is going on in India today.

I said that he was successful in business. That is an understatement. He was one of the founders of Benton & Bowles, which became one of the most successful advertising agencies in America.

In 1941, he entered government service, was head of OPA in 1943, Director of Economic Stabilization in 1946 and also Delegate to the UNESCO Conference in Paris. In 1949, he became Governor of Connecticut. Then in October, 1951, he became our Ambassador to India.

From that high post he had a chance to see much farther than India itself and to understand the implications of the entire Asian scene to America today and tomorrow. He is fresh from having studied the whole Asian problem, and we are very fortunate to have him here today to speak to us on the "Asian Revolution."

Following the Council custom, there will be a brief period of question and answer following his talk.

It is a privilege to present to you the Honorable Chester Bowles.

~∽~

| **M. Glen Miller,** *Owner, M. Glen Miller, Advertising, introduces* **Henry J. Taylor,** *radio commentator.*

AT THE MENTION OF A NAME like Truman or Eisenhower, there is no question about whom one is speaking. When you say Farley or DeMille or Kaltenborn, an individual person pops into mind. But what happens when you say Taylor? Not a thing! What about Hank Taylor? Still blank. But the moment I say Henry J. Taylor, a very definite character comes instantly to life, and what a character!

Your Program Committee has been besieged for years to get this guy, Henry J. Taylor—more than for any other man who ever stood on our platform. Well, today he is here. As you can see, he is too mature to be called Young Taylor, yet—good as the name sounds to some of you—it doesn't seem appropriate to call him Old Taylor. At any rate, we are grateful to him for bringing his authoritative, compelling, dramatic voice to our own private microphone.

Most of us think of Henry J. Taylor as a radio commentator. That is only a superficial identification, for fundamentally he is an economist. Some years ago Mr. Taylor "retired." He wanted to devote full time to the study of world affairs, to his radio work, and to writing. What a retirement that turned out to be, for only last year he traveled 35,000 miles in a three-month, around-the-world trip to find out first hand exactly what was happening in this old, beaten-up world of ours. He has talked with political leaders everywhere, but closest to his heart have been the many, many intimate conversations he had with shopkeepers, farmers, soldiers, clerks, laborers and others on the levels where the real attitude of the nation is expressed.

Mr. Taylor commutes all over the world, as simply as you fellows commute from Barrington and Highland Park and Olympia Fields and Streeterville. He has been in almost all the troubled spots of the world during the past decade. I wouldn't want to say he started them, but he was there.

Mr. Taylor was born in Chicago, just after the turn of the century, and it's good to have him back again. No part of this program is an electrical transcription, and the next sound you will hear will be the well-known voice of the noted journalist, economist, author, and radio reporter, Mr. Henry J. Taylor, in person, who will talk to you about "Our Future Around the World."

⤙⤚

James E. Day, *President of the Midwest Stock Exchange, introduces United States Senator* **Alexander Wiley** *at a luncheon of the Executives' Club of Chicago.*

INTRODUCING ANYONE from the State of Wisconsin brings back very pleasant thoughts—memories of a black bass on the business end of a fly rod, or the first leap of a 20-pound muskie who looks about the size of a hard-top convertible.

Here at the Executives' Club we always try to set up pleasant memories for our guest speaker, and I can think of no better way to do that than to pay homage to the Senator's favorite product—Wisconsin cheese.

I took the liberty of seeing to it that you all had a piece of genuine Wisconsin "imported" cheddar with your apple pie. Did you notice its tangy goodness? Its tantalizing bouquet? To say nothing of its mellow lusciousness?

I thought it would be nice to get a few official statements about the Senator's product. First, of course, it was necessary to make a survey. If you're going to make a survey, you don't go to engineers or analysts. You all know you go to the cigarette people. They make more surveys than a government bureau.

Seriously, gentlemen, we are honored to have the Senator from Wisconsin with us—a conservative Republican who has served in the United States Senate since 1939.

In 1937 he was named Chairman of the Judiciary Committee—the only Wisconsin Senator in history to be so honored. He is now Chairman of the Senate Foreign Relations Committee.

Last summer he traveled over 13,000 miles in foreign countries on a tour of inspection, along with the several other members of the Senate Foreign Relations Committee.

In view of current events, it would be difficult to choose a more timely subject than that selected by our speaker today, entitled, "What Is Our Foreign Policy?"

We are pleased to welcome the Senator from Wisconsin, the Honorable Alexander Wiley.

᠆᠊᠌᠍ᔓᔓ᠊

Walter M. Heymann, *Executive Vice-President of The First National Bank of Chicago, introduces* **Fayette H. Elwell,** *then Dean of the School of Commerce of the University of Wisconsin.*

THE ABSENT-MINDED PROFESSOR has been the butt of a great many comments, most of which have been half-truths. For example, someone has said that the absent-minded professor used to be a joke, but now he is a government economist.

All of us here today who have known the speaker will readily certify that he is not absent-minded. In fact, those of us for whom the advancing years have not sufficiently mellowed our recollections of Accounting #181 (as I recall the number of the course) will testify that Fay Elwell was—to put it mildly—never absent-minded.

He was a critical professor, but it was the kind of sound, constructive criticism that made young men and women able accountants and efficient business leaders.

I might say as a banker that when one lends money to a going concern, he needs to know, with reasonable certainty, which way it is going, and Fay Elwell did a great deal to give his students the hard facts which enabled them later to form sound judgments and guide businesses in the right direction.

Time does not permit me to dwell at length upon the significant contribution he has made to the growth of the School of Commerce, and to its widespread recognition among both academic and business institutions.

It is a pleasure to present to this audience of his friends and former students, the dean of the School of Commerce of the University of Wisconsin, Fay Elwell.

᠆᠊᠌᠍ᔓᔓ᠊

Thomas H. Coulter, *President, Executives' Club of Chicago, intro-duces* **W. Alton Jones,** *President, Cities Service Company.*

THE EXECUTIVES' CLUB is honored to be host again to the oil men of Chicago, and to take part in the activities of Oil Progress Week. We are proud of the extensive research and oil refining facilities in Chicago which make it the greatest center of oil technology and oil distribution in the world.

We are also proud of the tremendous contribution the oil industry has made in improving our way of life and strengthening our economy. Oil men have provided the outstanding example of how well the individual initiative, free enterprise system can work in a free society. This applies not only to the big operators, but also to the independent wildcatter who gets by on a shoestring, and to the dealer who starts a service station on a vacant lot. While we usually think of oil companies as "Industrial Goliaths"—and many are—the major operators are smitten regularly by some 34,000 "Little Davids" —who pack a terrific octane-rating when competing for oil properties and consumer preference.

It may surprise you to learn that most of the major oil companies produce much less than half of their crude oil requirements. The rest they have to buy from some little guy who got there first.

As a matter of fact, some big oil companies recently started drilling wells many miles out in the ocean, to try and escape the competition of small operators, who get around so fast on land.

The little wildcatter may be temporarily stymied for lack of the expensive equipment required in deep-sea drilling, but, if taxes don't kill his incentive, I think he'll find a way to fry fish on the ocean floor with the big boys.

And speaking of big boys . . . we have Exhibit "A" with us today. Our guest speaker is not only the president of a major oil company, but also Chairman of the oil industry's top organization—The American Petroleum Institute.

Like most successful oil men, he has spent his entire business career in the petroleum business, and with the same concern—the Cities Service Company.

He joined Cities Service after attending Vanderbilt University, and his record in the company reads exactly like the man who was nominated "most likely to succeed."

He has done almost everything—and done it well. Aside from his own company responsibilities, he has always been willing to assume the additional burden of the executive statesman, who steps outside the confines of his own business life to work in the public interest.

Numbered among his many outstanding achievements are the building of the "Big" and "Little" Inch pipelines during the war, as President of the War Emergency Pipelines, Inc., and Chairman of the Petroleum Administration for War.

For almost every year of service in the oil industry, he has been elected an officer or director of some company. His tally at the moment numbers twenty-eight.

No one is better qualified to represent the oil industry in today's Oil Progress Celebration. He will speak to us on the subject, "Freedom's Price Tag."

Gentlemen, the President of Cities Service Company, Mr. W. Alton Jones.

࿔

Melvin Brorby, *President of the Chicago Council on Foreign Relations, introduces* **Arnold J. Toynbee,** *distinguished professor, author, and historian of Great Britain.*

GOOD AFTERNOON, ladies and gentlemen. I am sure I don't need to tell you that this is a gala occasion. I have decided to omit the usual announcements of coming Council activities. But it would break my official Council heart if I did not extend to all of you who are not already members, an invitation to join the Council on Foreign Relations. Out of this sea of shining faces, I am sure there are at least a few of you who would like to join with us. To anyone who has the slightest impulse in this direction, I urge you to follow it recklessly! You will find application forms in the lobby and young ladies to answer your questions.

It is always a pleasure to introduce the distinguished guests at our Speakers' Table, but especially so today.

If I seem a little wiser-looking to you today, it's of course because of the privilege of sitting next to Professor Toynbee. What a fine and civilizing thing it would be if wisdom and vision were more contagious—but actually, and fortunately to a certain extent, this really is so, as you will experience yourselves within the hour.

The name of Arnold Toynbee has been something to conjure with, among intellectual circles, for a very long time. For he has set a tremendously high mark in the world of scholarship. But how wonderful it is that his magic has spread far beyond the boundaries of erudition!

Why is this? Many reasons, perhaps, but isn't this one of them? ... In a world that has specialized in analysis, the taking of things apart, he has brought a genius for synthesis, the putting of things together. And so, instead of the trees, we see the forest! And rising higher and higher, we see the setting, the forest in the whole world —and life itself as a whole thing. For that rare gift, Dr. Toynbee, we thank you.

Arnold J. Toynbee first became interested in international affairs while he was a student in the British Archaeological School in Athens. He has never turned back from that interest, particularly the world history that lies behind. This has led him to produce 3,150,000 words, now bound into a 10-volume set called *A Study of History*.

In 1921, Dr. Toynbee first set down the plan for the *Study*. The notes he wrote on half a sheet of paper listed about a dozen headings. These headings stand with very little change as the titles of the thirteen parts now published in ten volumes.

The last four volumes, just published, have special interest and impact, because in them he sums up his views of society as a whole and states his strongly felt conclusions on the purpose and meaning of history and the future of Western civilization.

We are fortunate indeed to have him here today on a subject of vital interest to every one of us, "World Peace and World History." Dr. Toynbee.

～

M. Glen Miller, *Owner, M. Glen Miller, Advertising, introduces* **Commander Irving Johnson.**

ONCE UPON A TIME on a miserable day of sleet and wind, I chanced upon an acquaintance whose forbears I knew had been men of the sea. Wanting to impress him with my knowledge of sailing, I said, "How'd you like to be standing out on the ol' fo'castle on a day like this?" His lip curled and he sneered, "You poor dope, the 'fo'castle' is where the crew sleeps, as anybody knows!"

I vowed then, that I'd never again encroach on a professional's territory. But here I am in the midst of grave temptation to talk about stuns'ls, spankers, shrouds, flying jib, and martingale stays.

Commander Johnson and his family are no strangers to sailing, for the pictures we are to see are of their fourth trip around the world on windjammers. The majority of the crew, however, was absolutely green, and at the first showdown with bad weather some turned even greener.

Commander Johnson is a man of great charm and a wonderful raconteur—that means story-teller. You'll get acquainted with him and Mrs. Johnson and his amazing son, Arthur, as well as the whole crew as we get under weigh. So let's douse the mains'l and heave to, and take the skipper aboard. Gentlemen: Commander Irving Johnson, and his magnificent natural color film.

෴

John J. McDonough, *Vice-President, Harris Trust and Savings Bank, introduces United States Senator* **William F. Knowland.**

IT IS A GREAT PLEASURE to extend a most cordial welcome to the senator from California.

He will speak to us today on an extremely timely and vital subject, upon which he is one of America's best-informed authorities, a subject which daily grows more confusing and more controversial as crisis after crisis explodes in strategic areas throughout the Far East.

And now a personal word about our honored guest. His record is extraordinary in many ways. Like England's immortal William Pitt, he has always been precocious politically and his unusual promise, which became so apparent in his early youth, has indeed flowered into a brilliant career of dedicated service to his country.

Speaking of his youth, it is significant to recall that the Hon. William Fife Knowland at the age of twelve fought like a tiger for a Harding-Coolidge victory; at twenty-five, he was California's youngest assemblyman; at thirty-seven, he was the then youngest member of the United States Senate. Today, he is the youngest Republican majority leader in the history of the Senate.

In addition to all these striking political successes, our guest of honor found the time not only to complete his education at the University of California, and to marry at the age of eighteen, but also to enjoy (in association with his illustrious father) the power and prestige of the newspaper publishing business into which he entered immediately after his Bachelor of Arts diploma was safely tucked away.

Another very noteworthy distinction in Senator Knowland's eventful career was his splendid war record. After being drafted, he earned a commission the hard way at Fort Benning, and he eventually wound up in Europe in 1945 with the rank of major.

One bright day in August of that year, the then Major Knowland was startled and happily surprised to read in the *Stars and Stripes* that Governor Warren had appointed him to the U. S. Senate to succeed the late Hiram Johnson.

Thus began Senator Knowland's remarkable career in Washington which is leading him so impressively to the highest pinnacles of attainment.

Gentlemen, it is with very special personal pleasure that I present to you one of America's most distinguished statesmen and the new "Mr. Republican," the Hon. William F. Knowland.

❧

Excerpts from an introduction of **John Foster Dulles** by **M. Glen Miller,** *then President, Executives' Club of Chicago.*

MINISTERS' SONS, I suppose, grow up under a handicap. There must be some of you who are ministers' sons, and you probably keep the fact well preserved and out of sight, unless perhaps you want some stranger to cash a check.

If ministers' sons turn out to be ministers, nobody asks questions. But when they grow up to be lawyers, especially in Wall Street, they must continue to pack a handicap as big as a dromedary's hump.

John Foster Dulles is the son of a Presbyterian minister. But Mr. Dulles is at least one minister's son who turned out well and who continues to practice and preach the precepts which must have constituted the basis of his early training.

He is a driving force in the Federal Council of the Churches of Christ in America, for which he served as Chairman of the Commission on a Just and Durable Peace. He says, "I want to make my life count for something for peace in the world." Despite, or perhaps because of, his open acknowledgment of the principles of the Prince of Peace, Mr. Dulles has achieved the position of senior partner of what is perhaps the richest and most powerful law firm in downtown New York—Sullivan and Cromwell...

His biography states he is a tall, stoop-shouldered man, with a forbidding manner and a rocky Puritan profile. There are even some who say he is a "cold sort of fish." And so we dish him up to you on a Friday, although I warn you he's hot today, and even the Presbyterians will find that he is sincere, warm, amiable, and honest as well as a clear, penetrating, logical thinker.

༄

Thomas H. Coulter, *President, Executives' Club of Chicago, introduces* **Dr. Will Durant,** *author and philosopher.*

ON THIS, THE OCCASION of the first Ladies' Day of our 40th Anniversary Year, it is most gratifying to be able to welcome so many lovely members of the distaff side, among the wives, secretaries, and special guests present.

You ladies should know that you create a problem in this Club. Every year, we have a wrangle over how many times you should be invited to our meetings. Some of our more avid members—particularly among the younger men—think you should be here every week.

There is a hard core of conservative reactionaries among the older members, however, who still believe that woman's place is in the home, and will only bring their wives when they know they won't understand what our speaker is saying and will need someone to explain it to them after the meeting.

Others in this same group who want to be oracles, just won't bring their wives for fear they will be discovered to be the parrots they really are—repeating what our speakers say here on Friday noon.

I know that whenever I attempt to be profound on the problems of the day, my wife always asks, "My, who have you heard at The Executives' Club lately?"

The main reason you are invited to hear Dr. Will Durant today is that none of our members would dare plagiarize any of his profundities for the obvious reason you will discover when he starts speaking.

When Vice-President Barkley addressed our opening meeting this year, he was tremendously gratified by the large audience that turned out to hear him, inasmuch as it marked his fourth appearance before our Club, and he observed that maybe he had carried his pitcher to the well once too often.

No such concern confronts our guest today, however, for he is about to address this forum for the ninth time.

While Mr. Barkley mainly attracts Democrats, Will Durant has universal appeal, and he, too, is very popular with the ladies as evidenced by the attendance here today.

Back in 1915, as a young man, he decided to dedicate his life's work to writing a comprehensive story of civilization. For the next ten years, he almost starved while doing the research necessary for the preparation of his first major work, *The Story of Philosophy*, which has sold over two million copies and been translated into twelve languages.

The success of his first great book enabled him to become a capitalistic scholar, and to devote all of his time to his long-cherished objective.

Subsequently, three more books appeared: *Our Oriental Heritage*, *The Life of Greece*, and *Caesar and Cleopatra*,—all of which won worldwide acclaim. Next week, his latest work, *The Age of Faith*, will be released. Presently, he is working on *The Renaissance and the Reformation*, which will be published in 1955, and *The Age of Reason*, which is scheduled for 1960.

Ladies and gentlemen, it is an unusual privilege to present the world's greatest living philosopher and historian, Dr. Will Durant.

John J. McDonough, *Vice-President of the Harris Trust and Savings Bank, introduces* **Clarence E. Manion,** *attorney, and formerly Dean of the Law School of Notre Dame University.*

CERTAINLY, one of the most widely debated and controversial issues of our time is the Bricker Amendment.

Today we are extremely fortunate to have with us as our honored guest one of the best-informed, most eloquent and courageous protagonists of the Bricker side of this furious national argument.

Underlying Dean Manion's strong convictions in this matter is a brilliant record of scholarship and specialized experience which is rarely found in an ex-public servant.

For the past twenty-five years Dean Manion has been one of America's most noted professors of constitutional law at Notre Dame, while at the same time continuing in the private practice of law as a member of the firm of Doran and Manion.

"Pat" Manion, as he is affectionately known by all Notre Dame men everywhere, will remain immortal at his alma mater not only because of his superb record as dean of the Notre Dame Law School but also because he was the founder and builder of the now internationally-famous Natural Law Institute.

As you also well know, gentlemen, our guest of honor is likewise a distinguished lecturer and author. His current best seller, *The Key to Peace,* is a thrilling message of hope and inspiration which has won the highest acclaim of discriminating men of all religious creeds and political faiths.

In addition to all his high personal and professional honors and achievements, Dean Manion has one further rare distinction. For many years he has shared the spotlight with Frank Leahy as one of Notre Dame's great family men. At the last count there were five little Manions!

Gentlemen, it is a great personal pleasure to present to you the scholarly and outspoken ex-Chairman of the Commission on Inter-Governmental Relations who will tell us his side of the story, Dr. Manion.

John J. McDonough, *Vice-President of the Harris Trust and Savings Bank, Chicago, introduces* **Heinz L. Krekeler,** *Ambassador of the Federal Republic of Germany to the United States, to the Executives' Club of Chicago.*

GENTLEMEN, TODAY the foreign ministers of the free nations of the Western world are departing from Berlin with increased feelings of disgust and disillusionment because of the utter and tragic failure of the Soviets to cooperate in any reasonable plan to unify Germany and to sign an Austrian peace treaty. I know you will all agree that the visit of our honored guest today could not be more perfectly timed, nor could his subject be more appropriate to this occasion.

We have a very special welcome to extend to Dr. Krekeler today. We acknowledge, of course, his many distinctions and honors as a skilled diplomat, but I take particular pleasure in pointing out to you that Dr. Krekeler was, first of all, a successful chemist and business executive in Germany before his career in diplomacy began.

In these critical days when so many of our ablest business leaders are concerning themselves with the problems of our national government, it is fitting, indeed, that so great an industrial nation as West Germany be represented in this country by a seasoned businessman who can speak and understand the language of the new administration in Washington.

Dr. Krekeler was born in Westphalia in the North Rhine country. His higher education was completed at the Universities of Munich, Freiburg, Göttingen and, finally, Berlin, where he received his Doctor of Philosophy degree in chemistry in 1930.

For many years Dr. Krekeler was associated with the famous I. G. Farbenindustrie organization, and following the war he became successively, partner, director and chairman of several German business firms.

Gentlemen, it is a privilege indeed to present to you our distinguished guest, who has done so much to restore and strengthen friendly relations between Germany and America: His Excellency, Dr. Heinz L. Krekeler, Ambassador of the Federal Republic of Germany to the United States.

Dr. Krekeler.

M. Glen Miller, *Owner, M. Glen Miller, Advertising, introduces*
Lee Wulff, *lecturer with films.*

THERE WAS ONCE A TIME when all of us hunted and fished every day. That is, speaking of the human race. But that was before someone discovered economics, and taxes, and we can't do it anymore. Life is finer and fuller now and hunting and fishing is out nowadays because we have to stay home and work so we can enjoy the finer and fuller life.

Does anybody think we have given up that savage and brutal life joyously? Just watch the crowd in front of any sporting goods store, or stand and contemplate the shining eyes outside the TWA ticket office on Wabash Avenue, where this week a deft-fingered girl has been tying trout flies all day long.

Today we have with us again a man who refused the heritage of civilization; who thinks a lonely stroll up a white water stream in Newfoundland beats horse trading any day. A man who would rather stalk a deer in bitter Maine weather than put over a fast one in a heated stock exchange.

And what do the rest of us think about this guy? What do you suppose brought a thousand of you busy businessmen out here today?

Lee Wulff is the most envied man in this room despite the business tycoons who are planted at every table. He, too, was misled in his youth and he graduated from Leland Stanford University as a civil engineer. Then he studied art in Europe and came back to practice advertising art and design in New York City.

But the alchemy of his birth in Alaska must have been working all the time, for finally it lured him out into the open spaces and he never went back to work. It's been all fun since then. He gets mail at a place called Shushan, New York. But when the mailman calls he is likely to find Lee Wulff in the high mountains of Montana, lost in the vast interior of the Gaspe, bucking the harness of a tackle chair off Guymas or backing up his ten-year-old-squirrel-shooting son in the back country of New Hampshire.

The world is Lee Wulff's oyster. And he shamelessly steals any part of it with his magnificent camera equipment and his eye for beauty and action in the great outdoors. That is what he has brought us today—deer, pheasant, squirrel and goose-shooting; and on the water, we'll get salmon and trout and we'll have a glorious time harpooning pilot whales. One of the most fascinating sport films you have ever seen.

So let's away on a vicarious trip this afternoon with rod and gun. And the last one in stinks.

∽

M. Glen Miller, *Owner, M. Glen Miller, Advertising, introduces* **Dr. Will Durant,** *author and philosopher.*

TODAY IT IS DISTINCTLY disconcerting to have to introduce a man like Dr. Durant. In the first place this is, I believe, the eighth time he has stood on this platform, which is more times than I have, and you already know more about him than you do about me. Secondly, he gets a lot of money for this, whereas, for me, I have to pay for my own lunch.

Thirdly, Dr. Durant is a philosopher. Now, if I should say something uncomplimentary about Dr. Durant, he would merely smile benignly and forgive me instantly. If I say something patronizing, he will again look like a Cheshire cat but be unmoved because of his vast modesty. For, you see, the very word *philosophy* comes from two Greek words meaning "loving" and "wise," and Dr. Durant is both.

The good doctor represents the very epitome of philosophy. He will rationalize anything. If you go fishing and catch nothing, he says, "Think how good that is for the fish." If you are pinched for speeding on the Outer Drive when you actually were not, Dr. Durant will philosophize, "Think how many times you escaped just retribution when you were making sixty and there were no cops there."

In short, if I may take one side of an argument, Dr. Durant will take the other and logic me right out of the picture.

Just when we're beginning to realize the grandeur of human dignity, Dr. Durant comes along and points out that we are only slightly superior to the amoeba. Well, how can you argue? We all know people we'd gladly trade any day for a healthy amoeba.

The point of importance, ladies and gentlemen, is that we love the way Dr. Durant tells us these things. He always leaves us with a feeling that we have learned a great deal.

If we were to advertise a mere philosopher as our speaker, no one would show up, but we mention the magic word, "Durant," and 800 people beat down the doors. Those of you who have heard this adorable philosopher know what is in store for you. Those of you who have never heard him before will begin to love him before his discourse is finished.

For me it is a great joy to present to you today this man of vast human understanding, this man of wit and erudition, this man with the mind of a grandfather and the heart of a child, this one and only Dr. Will Durant.

⌐᠊

John E. Stipp, *President of the Federal Home Loan Bank of Chicago, introduces* **Dr. Will Durant,** *distinguished philosopher.*

TODAY I FIND MYSELF in a most unusual situation. Normally, you know, it is the function of the president of this Club to introduce the guest speaker. However, today we are in the position where we have never had a guest who has been so thoroughly introduced to an organization as has our guest been introduced to us. This luncheon marks the twelfth occasion on which he has appeared before us, and he has had the full treatment each time.

I am fully aware that your intense interest in this program is exceeded only by your impatience at the time I am consuming in this presentation, in which impatience I fully join you. Consequently, I have decided not to tell you one single thing about our guest. Your presence here today is a far more eloquent tribute to him than any I could possibly frame in words. Your eager enthusiasm to hear him is proof of the fact that you know him well by his works, and whatever I say could not add to the luster of that profound interest with which you already regard him.

I think it is sufficient for me to say that, to him, there is nothing so human as human nature—there is nothing so interesting as human life.

And so, fully realizing the distinguished privilege that is mine, and anticipating the rare pleasure that is to be yours, I present Dr. Will Durant.

3

EXAMPLES OF
RESPONSES TO
INTRODUCTIONS

Robert E. Wilson, *Chairman of the Board, Standard Oil Co. of Indiana, begins an address before the Associated Colleges of Indiana Dinner, Indianapolis.*

IT WOULD BE CUSTOMARY, if not true, to say that I am happy to speak to this group tonight, but it would not be entirely true. While I *am* happy to have a part in encouraging the fine work of the Associated Colleges of Indiana and in urging businessmen to support it, I am rather appalled at having to address an audience comprising 100 educators and nearly 200 businessmen. The latter group I could take in my stride, and I might even tackle the former by themselves if I didn't have a lot of businessmen looking over my shoulder—but the combination is a bit rough!

However, and more seriously, I do think that educators and businessmen can both profit by striving for better mutual understanding and by doing some serious thinking together about the problems and purposes of higher education, and its relation to business and industry.

Walter H. Judd, *Congressional Representative from Minnesota, responds to an introduction.*

I EXPECT WHEN YOU saw on the program that I was to be here today, you felt a little like the man who had an obscure eruption on his skin and went to his doctor to see about it. His doctor looked at it, changed the light and looked at it again, oohed and aahed, finally took some scales off, and looked at them under the microscope. Then he said, "Um, you've had this before?"
The patient said, "Yes."
The doctor said, "Well, you've got it again."
So you have again the same person you have had on several previous occasions when you have been nice enough to invite me to talk to you. And on the same theme—the same theme that I talked about before.

⤶

Donald R. Richberg, *attorney, responds to an introduction at an annual meeting of the Industrial Research Institute.*

PERMIT ME to introduce myself as a battle-scarred veteran of the last fifty years of industrial warfare. I have fought with and against labor organizations, with and against employers, and with and against government. Probably no one will accuse me of any timid pacifism— or even of any excessive partisanship! But let me claim one consistency in this motley record. I have consistently opposed tyranny and oppression. To me, employers, labor leaders, or public officials, who think they have been divinely anointed to rule over their fellow men, are equally absurd and pestiferous.

⤶

Dwight D. Eisenhower, *President of the United States, responds to an introduction by the Prime Minister of Canada, in the House of Commons, Ottawa, Canada.*

MR. PRIME MINISTER, for the very great generosity of the personal sentiments you expressed toward me I am humbly grateful. For the reception that Mrs. Eisenhower and I have experienced here throughout this city we should like to extend to all of your citizens, from all our people, our very deep appreciation, especially for the honor of being received before this body. I assure you, you have given us a distinction we shall never forget.

⤻

James Barrington, *Ambassador of Burma to the United States of America, responds to an introduction at an International Conference on Asian Problems.*

WHEN I WAS FIRST approached to be a sponsor of this Conference and to speak at its opening session, I must say that my immediate reaction was one of doubt. My misgivings arose not from any lack of interest in the conference, because the questions to be discussed here are very close to me both in my official and personal capacity, but from my fear that my other duties would not permit me to give sufficient time and attention to matters pertaining to this conference. However, I was persuaded that some kind of contribution on my part might be useful, and I am glad to have this opportunity to say a few words to you on the theme of this evening, Asian-Western understanding.

Whenever I think of Asian-Western understanding, I never fail to recall the well-known quotation from Kipling:

> East is East, and West is West
> And never the twain shall meet.

Thinking people all over the world have long since discarded this as representing the truth, and in fairness to Kipling I have to say that even he did not make it quite as uncompromising as it sounds. But despite this, there still remains some kind of belief that the differences between Asia and the West are so great in terms of race, religion, culture and general philosophy, that the bridging of the gap, though not impossible, requires some kind of superhuman intervention. I venture to suggest that this is also fallacious.

⤻

Howard Pyle, *Governor of Arizona, begins an address before the Los Angeles Bar Association.*

ON BEING ASKED to meet with you today my first thought was: What in the world could one say to some of Southern California's finest legal minds that would be worth the listening time required to tell it?

Not being a lawyer by profession automatically closed a lot of doors. Being from the other side of the River just as automatically closed at least one other.

Then I remembered the case of a cowboy over in my country who found himself in court for the second time on similar charges. The first time he was acquitted. The second time he was arraigned he found himself before a newly qualified judge who was by no means a stranger. The judge's first question was, "Well, Slim, I see you're in trouble again." "Yes, I guess I am," said Slim. Then, thinking it might be a point in his favor, he reminded the new judge that the last time he was in trouble the judge himself had been his lawyer. The judge's reply was, "Well, where is your lawyer this time?" Slim's reply has something in it worth remembering I think. Said he, "I don't need one, this time! I'm going to tell the truth!" So, for a few minutes, let's examine some truths about a fact that I feel we have taken too lightly too long.

⌒

H. C. Conick, *President, the National Board of Fire Underwriters, begins an address on the occasion of the 88th Annual Meeting, New York City.*

THIS IS AN INSPIRING occasion for me. To all of you here, my friends and associates, this is the 88th Annual Meeting of the National Board of Fire Underwriters. It is far more than that to me. I have been privileged to attend many other meetings of the National Board, but this year I have the supreme honor of serving as your President and delivering this address to your distinguished membership. That distinction can be given only to a few and I am humbly grateful for it.

I have the fondest memories of my work over the years with all of you in the National Board and in this business. Once a man is in our field of insurance, usually he stays for his business lifetime. Perhaps there are many reasons why this is so, but one that always occurs to me is that personal satisfactions in our kind of work are so great that few insurance men ever risk losing them by going into other fields. I don't know where else in business anyone can find more of the feeling that he is doing a worth-while work. Pride in our calling has very real and tangible bases.

᛬᛬

Joseph W. Martin, Jr., *Congressional Representative from Massachusetts, begins an address at the Lions International Convention, New York City.*

I AM PROUD TO COME and speak at this great convention of one of the great forces for building a more peaceful and understanding world. I am also proud of my membership in the Attleboro Club of your organization. Through that membership I am cognizant of the fine part this organization performs in building better communities and supporting and sustaining the more unfortunate.

I hope you will forgive me if I borrow for my speech today our slogan: "Liberty, Intelligence, Our Nation's Safety."

One of the great men of our times, the President of the United States, Dwight D. Eisenhower, has said we live in an "age of peril." I agree with him. I would like to discuss with you the nature of that peril. I would like to hold it up in its true perspective and examine it in the terms of liberty, intelligence, and the safety of all our nations.

Actually, we of this twentieth century are confronted with the greatest struggle that has visited civilization. To understand it we must first relate it to the nature of the civilization that is threatened.

The backbone of our free society is morality. It is the foundation on which our existence and our mode of life has been erected.

᛬᛬

Robert C. Hendrickson, *United States Senator from New Jersey, begins an address before the Secretary's Conference on Juvenile Delinquency, Washington, D. C.*

GATHERED HERE TODAY, I believe, is more experience and knowledge relative to the problem of juvenile delinquency than has ever before been brought together. This is an auspicious gathering. Yet we can bring to this conference neither pride in past accomplishments nor optimism for the immediate future for we are leaders in the "war this nation is losing"—against juvenile delinquency. Nor have we yet developed a strategy which promises to turn the tide of battle. This can be a momentous conference if we can here propose such strategy. Certainly you, the leaders, have demonstrated the qualities necessary for successful battle. In the face of perplexing difficulties you have not only carried on the fight but you have also maintained the faith and confidence in your fellow-man which is fundamental to democratic social action. The challenge facing us today is not to find new courage or faith, but to devise a plan for action worthy of those qualities.

Mr. Heathcote Amory, *Minister of State, Board of Trade, addresses the American Chamber of Commerce meeting at the Savoy Hotel, London. (Note how Mr. Amory proceeds directly to the subject of his address.)*

I THANK YOU for inviting me here today, and I welcome this opportunity to speak about the United Kingdom's trade prospects before a body of such distinction and experience in business affairs on both sides of the Atlantic. Two years ago, the Chancellor of the Exchequer told you about Britain's determination to regain her economic strength and restore the position of sterling as a world currency. I think we can claim that the period since then has been one of solid and substantial achievement.

Joseph B. Hall, *President, The Kroger Co., Cincinnati, Ohio, begins an address before the Women's Advertising Club of Washington, D.C.*

IT IS A PLEASURE to be here in Washington, where so many national and world problems are under discussion. It is especially pleasant to appear before the Women's Advertising Club of Washington when one's subject relates to selling—for selling in our economy is ineffective without advertising. Many farmers have learned that truism, for marketing co-operation with aggressive advertising support often has assisted the wide distribution of many farm products.

The farm problem has become one of the greatest single issues facing our nation today. Experts who have devoted their lives to agriculture have expressed their opinions. National farm organizations have announced their positions. Special commissions have been studying the farm situation for many months, and their findings have been incorporated in the program submitted by President Eisenhower to the Congress. There are complex overtones involved, both economic and political, which cannot be ignored. But the basic question is, "Do we want our economy controlled by actions of the government or by the action of the marketplace?" Do we want continued price supports, acreage controls and price regulations, or do we want prices and production to reflect the will of all the people as expressed in their day-to-day buying of food products?

⌒

General Alfred M. Gruenther *responds to an introduction before the English-speaking Union of the Commonwealth, London, England.*

YOUR ROYAL HIGHNESS, Sir Winston Churchill, Your Excellencies, my lords, ladies and gentlemen:

I am deeply grateful for the generous introduction which Your Royal Highness gave me. I should like to say to you that during the trip which the Queen and you took, we at SHAPE watched your progress carefully, and with a great deal of interest. We felt that your journey was an event of great significance for the entire Free

World. I hope you will be kind enough to convey to Her Majesty our sincere admiration and gratitude for her devotion to the concepts of liberty and freedom for which we are all working.

I regret very much that Mrs. Gruenther could not be here this evening, but it happens that we have two sons and seven grandchildren. Some of you will be old enough eventually to have grandchildren. And you will then learn that complications develop in the lives of grandchildren, especially when one of the sons happens to be in Korea, and his wife is left with four children between the ages of eight months and five-and-a-half years. That was the situation which developed in our family and Mrs. Gruenther had to go back to the United States last night.

But it's about the future of those grandchildren that I would like to talk to you tonight—not about the toys that they play with, but about the kind of world to which they must look forward.

⸺

Lester B. Pearson, *Secretary of State for External Affairs of Canada, begins an address on "Canada—Nation on the March," New York City.*

It is always a pleasure for me to visit Town Hall. Its very name evokes nostalgic memories of an earlier and more tranquil day when across Canada and the United States town hall meetings were in a very real sense the cradles of democracy. Freedom of discussion and debate, the honest exchange of conflicting ideas and argument—these things which we cherish were born of such meetings.

Since those days the democratic community has immeasurably increased in size and complexity. This is one reason why the importance of freedom of thought and discussion is greater than ever before. Therefore I welcome the chance of initiating this series of talks on Canada, which has been planned (like so many other projects in which our two countries are concerned) as a co-operative venture on the part of public spirited men from both sides of the border.

⸺

Edmund S. Muskie, *Governor-elect of Maine, responds to an introduction.*

MR. PRESIDENT, distinguished guests and members of the Executives' Club of Chicago: May I say, first of all, that I am very happy, indeed, to be here; not only as your guest, but as Governor-elect of Maine I am in a position to bring to you greetings from that most beautiful of the forty-eight states, the state of Maine.

You know, whenever I get an introduction like that, I am always puzzled as to how I can begin in such a way as to make you forget the introduction. It reminds me of a story concerning a certain Irish ne'er-do-well who had lived a pretty dissipated life.

He loved to gamble, threw away his money, drank to excess, never provided for his family, beat up his wife whenever the occasion seemed appropriate, and finally he died. His relatives and friends, of course, held a good old Irish wake, and as is customary, they had nothing but good to say about the late departed. They spoke about his excellent habits, what a wonderful family man he was, how well he provided for his children, until suddenly the widow called one of the children over to her and said, "Son, would you go look in that coffin and see who's in there?"

If, as in the case of Maine, you are the first Democrat to be elected Governor in two decades, you are assumed to be somewhat of a magician, or at least a rare, though perhaps curious specimen of the *genus politico*. And then if you are unusually fortunate, you are the recipient of an invitation to address the Executives' Club of Chicago.

Seriously, however, I am delighted to be here, and glad to express some of my views from this forum, where so many distinguished public figures have appeared.

I was warned by someone—someone thought it wise to tell me that I was addressing a group predominantly of Republicans. I don't know why it was thought necessary to give me this warning. After all, I'm quite accustomed to that kind of an atmosphere.

Gene Flack, *Sales Counsel and Director of Advertising, Sunshine Biscuits, Inc., responds to an introduction.*

DISTINGUISHED GENTLEMEN, and gentlemen: After that very eloquent introduction, I could hardly wait until I heard myself talk.

It's a real honor to be introduced by Dr. John McDonough, here, whose name is in *Who's Who.* And, incidentally, my picture is in *What's This?*

As the little firefly said as it backed into the electric fan, "I'm delighted, no end." I am delighted to have the privilege of appearing before this keen, alert, intellectual, intelligent, aggressive, select, distinguished, and dynamic audience here today.

John, here, told me that I was a sort of a business consultant for this organization. Of course, I was very much flattered, until I heard the definition of "business consultant." A business consultant is a guy whose business it is to make it possible for you to go wrong—with *Confidence!*

I can certainly prove to you that I am no expert, and, of course, no one of you are. You know the definition of an expert. "Ex" stands for the unknown quantity, as always, and a "spert" is a "big drip under pressure."

I wouldn't presume to tell you how to run your business. Let the government do that.

One time there were two alley cats sitting on a fence, watching a tennis game. One cat turned to the other and said, "My old man is in that racket."

❧

Dr. Nathan Marsh Pusey, *President, Harvard University, responds to an introduction.*

I'M VERY GRATEFUL to your Chairman for that generous introduction. It was a little too generous, perhaps, at many points, but at one point I can't let it go without correcting the record. I didn't really write my thesis in Greek. It was about Greek law, so that it kind of wrote itself in Greek.

I am grateful to all of you for giving me this chance to come here today and talk to you about Harvard and Harvard's affairs. I would also like to express my gratitude to the members of the organization who invited me to come here last year and speak to you; I say to all of you that I regret very much that I was unable to do so at that time. I am happy that my life is so organized that I could be here today.

I have been the president of Harvard just a little more than a year, and every day now I think of a story that I heard our colleague, Morell, tell, when someone came to him (or to another university president) a member of the board of trustees charged with the responsibility of finding a new president, and asked him what the qualifications should be. He said, "Well, it isn't what you think. It isn't scholarship. It isn't teaching ability. It isn't ability to speak. It isn't any of these things. The real fundamental requirement is simply physical endurance." I think there is a great deal in that statement.

I want to talk to you about what goes on at Harvard. I don't have nearly enough time to treat this subject adequately—scarcely to begin on it—and this is complicated further because, before I start on the subject, I want to spend a few minutes talking to you about what does not go on at Harvard. When I have cleared that out of the way, then I will turn to the other, and I hope there will be time to say something about that from the point of view of what kind of people go to Harvard, what kind of people are on Harvard's faculty, and what they are doing. I would also like to say something about what kind of people have gone to Harvard and what they are doing. There are quite a few of them sitting up here, so you can be judging that question for yourself.

◦~◦

Dean Richard H. Armstrong of Portland University, Maine, opens his address after he has received a flowery introduction. His admission of being human makes the audience friendly.

I WOULD NOT BE HUMAN if I denied that the introduction by our good chairman pleases me. There are periods in one's life when one feels pretty good—pretty much satisfied with his lot. Occasionally these feelings of elation are followed by periods of depression—or shall we say getting back to earth—not a bad place to get back to, by the way.

My first trip up and down was early in life—in fact as a twenty-one-year-old lawyer. No one could have felt more elated, and I might add important, than I when I received a notice from the post office that certain law books were there waiting for someone to call for them. I proudly perused the notice: there was no doubt about it; it read, "*Attorney* Richard H. Armstrong, ——Apts., Charlotteville, Virginia." On the way to the post-office I re-read the notice over and over for this was the first time I had been addressed as *Attorney*. At the moment I couldn't think of anyone more important than an attorney. With this elated feeling I pushed the notice over the counter at the post office and a postal clerk produced the books. The clerk handed me the package and then as though explaining to an office boy he advised, "You sign Mr. Armstrong's name right here, and yours right underneath it."

～⁓〜

Dean Richard H. Armstrong *of Portland University, Maine, has used the following response where the toastmaster or chairman not only was flowery in his introduction but gave him titles or offices to which he was not entitled.*

I AM REMINDED of a banquet given to a prodigal son returning home to a small town after many years in foreign lands. Elaborate provisions were made for the occasion. The chairman of the banquet introduced the speaker and guest of honor somewhat as follows: "We are pleased to welcome Ray T. White, affectionately known in his school days as 'R. T.,' who has been in South America for two decades and has amassed a fortune of a million dollars in railroads." R.T. replied, "I am flattered by your introduction, although I must make one or two minor corrections. I'm not sure whether it was affectionately or not, but I was known around town as a kid as "Rat," not "R. T." I have been not in South America but Southern Europe; not for two decades, but three; my interests were in shipping, not railroads; the amount was not a million, but two millions; and I didn't amass it, I lost it."

～⁓〜

Fulton Lewis, Jr., *radio and TV commentator, responds to an introduction.*

THESE REMARKS are not going to be very long because I think you will enjoy a great deal more, and I will too, the question period with which we will close. We ought to be able to assassinate quite a few characters during that time.

Part of what I say some of you will disagree with. To you I say, if this be treason, make the most of it. Part of you will agree with the things I say. To you I say, you are very intelligent people.

*

Ralph D. Paine, Jr., *publisher of Fortune, responds to an introduction at a luncheon of the Executives' Club of Chicago.*

THANK YOU, Mr. President. I didn't realize until I just listened to these remarks that my obituary had already been prepared. And I might also say about this reputation that I have for taciturnity, that in New Hampshire, where I come from, I am regarded as a rather garrulous fellow.

I would also like to say that I am highly honored to be asked to this luncheon. As you probably don't have to be told, it is becoming a nationally known forum.

*

Mr. Gardner Cowles, *publisher, responds to an introduction.*

I AM VERY HONORED to come to speak before this distinguished Club, but I want to assure you that the next time I attempt to come from New York to Chicago, I'm coming by dog team. This is the third time in three years—once by airplane and twice by railroad—that I have been jinxed and have been unable to arrive by the same means with which I left New York.

I want to talk today about world trade, and what I think is wrong with our foreign policy, because I feel this very deeply. Although

I am sure some of you in the audience will not agree with me, I hope, anyway, that I will provoke some thought.

All of you have heard, I am sure, of that ingenious advertisement posted by the owner of a kennel who offered cocker spaniel puppies for sale. Along the highway leading to his kennel, he erected a large sign, illustrated by a fetching portrait of a cocker puppy. Beneath the picture was the message: *The Only Love That Money Can Buy.*

Love is a universal, human need. But there is another human need —equally universal. That need is *freedom*—freedom of conscience, freedom of speech, freedom of press, freedom of trade. All of these aspects of freedom are only parts of a larger whole, for freedom is indivisible.

Economic freedom cannot be divorced from political and religious freedom. Nor can freedom be cornered in the market, like wheat. No nation can conserve political and economic freedom to itself while denying them to others. It is trite, perhaps, but it is true: Freedom is the only thing that we can keep by giving it to others.

~

Mr. Marquis W. Childs, *author and columnist, responds to an introduction.*

I AM DEEPLY HONORED that you have asked me back.

I think you have taken an awful chance in inviting me back again. You survived the last time.

These are very perilous times. Someone told me the other day of the minister who made two files of his sermon material—sacred and top sacred.

One of my kind friends had me to breakfast with some of his railroad friends today in the Chicago Club, and we got to talking about their favorite Republican, who I hardly need to tell you was Calvin Coolidge. It reminded me of a Coolidge story I heard in Europe that I had never heard before, which also got into the railroad field.

It was in another economic era, the Coolidge economic era, and Calvin had forsworn private railway cars. Going to New York from Washington one day, he got on the parlor car of the train and went into the diner with his wife. The steward was overwhelmed by his presence. Lunch was served, and at the first course the steward said, "Is everything all right, Mr. President? Is everything all right?" Mr. Coolidge looked up and sort of nodded. With the second course the steward said, "Are you sure everything is all right?" Finally there was the same thing with the dessert, and old Cal looked up and said, "Say, what's supposed to be the matter with it?" Which was an attitude of healthy New England skepticism that could be carried a very long way in these times in which we are living.

❧

❚ **Bishop Fulton J. Sheen** *responds to an introduction.*

WHEN ONE RECEIVES such an introduction, one always wonders if one is the next speaker.

It reminds me of a Judge Dunn who was seated in court in New York—or, rather, in Brooklyn—while a very, very stupid witness was being interrogated.

The attorney said, "Were you at the corner of Fourth and Elm the day of the accident?"

The witness said, "Who? Me?"

"Yes, you," said the attorney. "Did you notice whether or not the ambulance came to care for the wounded woman?"

"Who? Me?"

"Yes, you. Did you notice whether or not the woman was seriously injured?"

"Who? Me?"

By that time the prosecuting attorney was exasperated. He said, "Certainly—you. Why do you think you are here?"

The witness said, "I came here to see justice done."

Judge Dunn said, "Who? Me?"

I'm sorry that some of you have to stand for this talk. I include those who are seated. I understand that this is the first time the ladies have come to an open meeting, and, of course, that has crowded out some of the men, who have to stand.

It reminds me of when I went up to Rochester some time ago to talk, and I went into a barber shop in the afternoon. The barber said, "Are you going to this lecture tonight?" I said, "No." He said, "Well, you'll probably have to stand."

I said, "You know, it's a peculiar thing, but every time I go to hear that man talk, I always have to stand."

I was talking in Syracuse, where they had built a tremendously large armory. A couple of the ushers were discussing the coming wrestling matches, the boxing matches, roller skating, prize fights, and so forth, and one of the ushers said, "I think we'll have a big crowd next Thursday night. We'll fill the place."

Another usher asked him, "Who's coming?"

The first usher said, "Bishop Sheen."

The other usher said, "Who'd he wrestle?"

⌒⌒⌒

Herbert V. Prochnow, *Vice-President, The First National Bank of Chicago, begins an address on "The International Situation."*

IN AUGUST 1945, World War II ended. The summer sky that year looked down upon a distraught world. There was sad disillusionment and deep weariness in the hearts of men. Thirteen million men lay dead. Great cities were vast piles of rubble. Currencies had been debauched. Nations staggered under debt with their savings dissipated. Millions of people were destitute, hungry refugees. For the second time in a generation, man had watched his social, economic, and political structure crumble.

Into that distress and devastation, the United States poured billions of dollars in aid to prevent dangerous unrest. That assistance took various forms. We propose in these few minutes to see what has happened and what may logically be the next step.

⌒⌒⌒

Herbert Hoover, *former President of the United States, begins an address on the occasion of the State of Iowa's celebration of his eightieth birthday at his birthplace, West Branch, Iowa, August 10, 1954.*

THE LEGISLATURE and the Governor of Iowa did me the great honor of inviting me to a reception by my native State on this, my eightieth birthday.

It is more than difficult adequately to express my appreciation for such evidence of affection.

I am glad to come to West Branch. My grandparents and my parents came here in a covered wagon. In this community they toiled and worshipped God. They lie buried on your hillside. The most formative years of my boyhood were spent here. My roots are in this soil.

This cottage where I was born is physical proof of the unbounded opportunity of American life.

My first paid job was in this community picking potato bugs at one cent a hundred. I was not inspired by altruism to relieve the world of a pest. Such altruism as was attached to that labor was to secure firecrackers with which to commemorate properly the Declaration of Independence. But Iowa is a progressive State. Its mothers, anxious to avoid repairs to small boys, secured a law abolishing that kind of tribute to the Founding Fathers. Moreover, by insecticides, the slave wage of only a cent a hundred has been overcome.

Iowa has made fabulous progress since I left here. I can prove it by statistics—and all speeches must have statistics because nobody can defy a statistic.

Since that time, the people of Iowa have multiplied the wealth of the State nine times over. That statistic is weakened by the decrease in purchasing power of money. In the meantime with the blessing of "the tall corn," you have sent to market enough hogs to cover the Chicago Stock Yards 5,045 feet deep. You can vary that statistic as you like.

Also, you have sent forth a host of men and women who have distinguished themselves in every state in the Union and every foreign country. Their quality is proved by the fact that I have never seen Iowa attributed as the origin of any of our leading bank robbers, gangsters, or Communists.

❧

Erwin D. Canham, *Editor of the Christian Science Monitor, responds to an introduction.*

MR. PRESIDENT, distinguished guests: Of course, it is always a great distinction—and it was a great distinction to me—to be invited to address the Executives' Club of Chicago, but to be invited back again is totally overwhelming. I can only infer that you want to get out of the headlines, because a newspaper editor is—while he makes headlines by writing them—probably least likely of all men to make them by virtue of what he says.

‿

| **Dr. W. O. Ross,** *Professor of English, Wayne University, begins an address at the Annual Swing-In, Senior-Class Program, Wayne University, Detroit, Michigan.*

MEMBERS of the Graduating Class:

When I have spoken previously under such circumstances as this, I have tended, naturally enough perhaps, to deliver some final professional admonitions concerning the uses of an education. Tonight, however, I do not propose to enjoin you to do anything and I do not propose to attempt to prove anything. I am going to do something a little unfashionable in contemporary education: I am going to state some opinions, and some opinions whose truth I admit I cannot prove. But I cannot see why somewhere in their process of being educated students are not entitled to hear the suspicions of their professors as well as demonstrable knowledge. And besides I feel not wholly out of the prevailing fashion in America today when I report to you my suspicions rather than my knowledge.

It is my suspicion, then, that our culture—that *you*—are fundamentally wrong in your understanding of the basic nature and needs of man. You and all of us are wrong, I suspect, because within the last century we have become materialists, whereas man's true humanity lies in his mind, in his spirit, and not in the matter, the material, the body—though for some curious reason the body is necessary if man's mind is to express itself on this earth. Not only, I suspect, do we make a mistake in deciding that man himself is simply an all-but-incredible expression of the possibilities of matter, and nothing more; we also believe, or act as if we believe, that man's *needs* are principally material, whereas his true material needs are few and simple, and his needs for certain mental or spiritual qualities, such as love, selflessness, and knowledge of himself are great out of all proportion with these material needs. In other words, if I may express myself in language which can be very readily understood in a rough way, man's needs are religious, not material. Man, I suspect, is primarily a religious creature, and is best comprehended in religious terms. And the precise error which the intellectuals of the Western world have been making for the last century or two is to deny this fact and insist that men are only complicated pieces of matter, whose true gratifications are ultimately those of the senses. To think thus, I suspect, is an error.

～

Harold J. Drown, D.D., *First Presbyterian Church, Ottumwa, Iowa, responds to an introduction before the Rotary Club of Ottumwa, Iowa.*

I AM MOST SINCERE when I say Thank you for inviting me to speak before your club. I like it because it gives me an opportunity to rub shoulders with men of business. That is one thing I miss since leaving the business world ten years ago for the ministry.

Something has been happening in these past ten years. I entered the insurance business in Erie, Pennsylvania in 1924, and stayed there until 1944. During that time I ate lunch almost every noon with other business men. The conversation revolved around business and politics, seldom around religion. We were not irreligious, but no one thought about mixing religion and business. It just wasn't being done.

Since entering the ministry I have consciously tried to spend lunch hours with businessmen of Ottumwa. And I purposely do not bring up the subject of religion. I want to hear what is going on in the business world. But seldom does a lunch hour go by without some-one bringing it up. And that was not the case ten years ago. Some-thing is happening in our world.

I subscribe to a little magazine called *Vital Speeches*. In it are all the speeches given around the world that the editors think are the most vital. They are speeches by high-ranking politicians, bank offi-cials, and leaders in the various fields of industry. And though I have not taken an exact poll, I am sure that no less than 75 per cent of those speeches include something of a spiritual nature. That, too, was not happening prior to ten years ago. Something is happening in our world that is far more significant than the splitting of the atom. Man is opening up the business side of his life to let in the directives of the spiritual.

↬

Clifford F. Hood, *President of the United States Steel Corporation, responds to an introduction.*

AFTER LISTENING to that introduction, you can realize what it is to be among friends.

When I accepted the invitation extended on behalf of your Club, I suffered from a grave misconception.

Somehow, I had conceived of the Executives' Club as a small group of men who met occasionally to eat their way to a solution of the world's problems. My associates in Chicago hastened to set me right, and to impress me with statistics about your organization.

They did more than impress me—they humbled me as well. I therefore count it a rare honor to be invited to occupy a rostrum that has been graced by so many distinguished Americans. I am further complimented by the presence here this noon of two directors of the United States Steel Corporation—Mr. Avery and Mr. Clarke. Normally, these gentlemen hear me in a different role from that which I am occupying this noon.

Of course, I should have known better than to expect a small gathering in Chicago. To do so was to underestimate the city with the big shoulders. I might have expected that your town, which leads the world in output of so many products, also would have an equally large output of executives.

The diversity of your industrial production, the pre-eminence of your commercial and merchandising organizations, and the wide scope and variety of your educational and cultural interests made that fact immediately apparent.

Certainly, Chicago's rise to the top in all these fields required leaders—managers, or, if you please, executives. Their vision and drive were as basic to the city's development as its favorable geographic location, its proximity to raw material sources and to the rich agricultural midland of the United States. How has the job been done?

↬

Mr. John L. Lewis, *American labor leader, responds to an introduction.*

MEMBERS of the Executives' Club, distinguished guests: I suppose I have been a long time coming to address this club, but it is generally known that I was detained, either by an industrialist or a federal judge.

As I look back on those numerous detentions through the years, I am not right now clear as to how they all came out. At least, however, I am happy that time and circumstances have permitted me to be your guest at this magnificent meeting of your great Club. The Executives' Club of Chicago is one of the nation's great forums, and it has been made so by the interest in public and national affairs, by the vigor and ability of its members, their mobility of thought and their desires constantly to break new ground in the affairs of the nation and of the world. So I come here today by invitation and with gratification that circumstances have permitted me to come on this occasion. I am delighted at your hospitality. I shall speak to you merely as a fellow American.

I am particularly happy to see present here today so many of the towering figures of one of our great basic industries—the coal industry—whom I have valued as friends and adversaries, wise counsellors and earnest men who have been constantly working through the years to make a contribution not only in their own personal well-being but to the public weal. As I look upon them here today and greet them, I am happy to think that they have honored me with their attendance at this luncheon, to join with us in any discussion which may ensue, affecting those problems that are so important to every American.

~

Dr. Grayson Kirk, *President of Columbia University, responds to an introduction before the Executives' Club of Chicago.*

THIS IS INDEED a great privilege and an opportunity for me to meet with you today, because a great many of my friends have had the pleasure of speaking here in the past. I have heard much of the organization and a great deal about the type of individuals here—not only those who compose it but those whom you have asked to be your speakers. Therefore, I appreciate the privilege, and I am delighted to have the opportunity to join that distinguished group.

I suspect that the men who are here in this room today represent an impressive proportion of the corporate enterprises which make up the industrial and financial power of the United States, and it is precisely this industrial and financial strength of our American society which is the one stable, permanent and sure guarantee that the Western peoples, as a whole, will not lose their battles against the forces of Communist imperialism.

I think it is quite likely that future historians of the Western civilization will have just cause to rejoice in the fact that at a critical time in the history of the world, the free enterprise system of the United States had the strength to safeguard the forces of freedom and democracy. Without that power, one wonders if any of the free peoples could have protected and maintained—much less, guaranteed —their freedom.

ॐ

Mayor R. F. Wagner, Jr. *of New York City welcomes the Convention of Lions International.*

THE PEOPLE of New York City—eight million men, women, and children, united in civic pride, united in brotherhood—welcome you with sincerity and enthusiasm to the greatest town in all the world.

We are happy that you are here and we know that you will be equally happy that you selected New York as the headquarters for your convention.

Certainly no group of people is more welcome to this great city than is Lions International. The work which we do every day in our own communities, the program which we have undertaken in extending aid to those in need, and the Creed of Good Fellowship by which we live touch upon the essential roots of the City of New York.

You belong with us and we are proud to have you. And for my part I hereby declare each of you an Honorary Citizen of this city— your city.

It is a thrilling sight, all of you gathered here to deliberate as to the future, undertaking to elect to office those who will be responsible for carrying out the program and to have good, clean, decent fun.

It is wonderful indeed to contemplate that so many of you are dedicated to the furtherance of the business life of your respective communities on the one hand, and also to the fulfillment of your obligations as civic-conscious and socially-minded people.

So long as there are Lions who believe that each man is his brother's keeper, so long will the beacon of hope and faith shine upon the world, and so long will men of good will continue to work for and to serve their neighbors.

I need not review with you delegates the extraordinary achievements of the Lions, the fields of child care, aid to the needy, social welfare, fraternity and patriotism. Your work and your efforts exemplify the noblest calling of man.

I am proud that I am a Lion and New York City is proud to extend its hand of friendship and its heart of affection to this great organization.

May this convention, blessed by God, be the most fruitful in your long history and may all of you find your visit to this city as memorable as I am sure it will be festive.

Thank you for coming here. Congratulations to all of you upon your success. And may you return soon that we may again welcome you to the Capital of the Free World.

⌣৯

M. Maurice Schumann, *then Deputy Foreign Minister of France and head of the French delegation to the United Nations, responds to an introduction.*

A FEW DAYS AGO I was invited to dinner by a British diplomat, together with a Canadian general and a Russian diplomat. After having exchanged a few rather pointed remarks, my two dinner companions decided to steer clear of political subjects. As they had to keep up the conversation and try to find some common ground, they were delighted to discover that their favorite fruits were apples. "Do you grow apples in Canada?" the Russian asked. "Certainly," said the Canadian. "Our apples are the best in the world."

"Really?" wondered the Russian. "And how do you call them?"

"We call them MacIntosh Reds and Northern Spies," replied the Canadian.

"What?" exclaimed the Russian. "Didn't we agree not to talk politics?"

This story, Mr. Chairman and gentlemen, strengthened my conviction that the smartest thing to do is never to shun your difficulties. I shall therefore try to state our problem in the most embarrassing manner for a French citizen, and more particularly for a Frenchman in political life.

ᴗᴥ

Dwight D. Eisenhower, *President of the United States, begins an address at the American Legion Convention, Washington, D. C.*

MY FELLOW VETERANS and friends: For the third time since World War II, I am honored to join a national convention of the American Legion.

With you, I give thanks that—at last—we can come together at a time when the sounds of the battlefields, everywhere in the world, have been stilled.

In such a gathering, made up of those who have served their country in time of war it seems fitting that we turn our attention to our international affairs and our nation's security. Now, in saying this, I do not mean that any group or any section of America has a monopoly either of interest or of wisdom in dealing with complex world problems. The contrary is true. The term "bi-partisan participation" is too narrow to describe accurately the attitude that all Americans should maintain in this great area of vital concern. Rather we should speak of universal or national participation, which would in turn imply serious study, analysis, and debate of every proposal and issue presented.

ᴗᴥ

Celal Bayar, *President of Turkey, begins an address before the American-Turkish Society, New York City.*

DURING THE PAST SIX DAYS I have been in the United States, our friend and ally, as a guest of His Excellency, President Eisenhower. Today,

I have the honor to be in this beautiful city of New York, which is the most perfect symbol of twentieth century civilization. I am deeply moved by the manifestations of friendship and affection shown toward Turkey through my person. I should like to thank your society, which has rendered a great service in the development of that friendship, for its gracious invitation. I have brought you the affection and gratitude of the Turkish people.

❧

Dorothy Thompson, *author and columnist, responds to an introduction before the Executives' Club of Chicago, where she was substituting for Clare Booth Luce, Ambassador to Italy.*

Now, IN SPITE OF ALL these kind and rather embarrassing words in my praise, I realize that I am here under a handicap, having been invited to pinch-hit for my friend, the distinguished, witty, knowledgeable, and very beautiful American Ambassador to Italy.

You know, with Mrs. Luce and me, certain male theories regarding the psychology and temperaments of women are, I believe, exploded. On political issues, Mrs. Luce and I have, on several occasions, had what might be described as knock-down-and-drag-out fights in the best female hair-pulling manner, while remaining from first to last devoted—I might even say mutually admiring—friends. Incidentally, she is in a very, very difficult position in the Western country which, at this moment, is closest to being lost to Christendom, of which it has been for centuries the center, and to the West to which it gave the first rule of law.

But you have invited me to speak on the Middle East. I am concerned at the magnitude of this theme, and the shortness of the time to deal with it.

The globe is *not* one world, and those who think so should get around more. It is not even all living in One Time, and this is particularly true of that area of the world which we call the Middle East.

❧

John L. McCaffrey, *President, International Harvester Company, begins an address before the National Industrial Conference Board, New York City.*

FOR MORE THAN twenty years now, the American people have been fascinated by the idea of stability as a general social goal.

This interest is a natural one, considering the times in which we live. We are about in the position of that old friend of Abe Lincoln who was so fond of gingerbread.

Lincoln said his friend put it this way:

"I don't suppose anybody on earth likes gingerbread better than I do—and gets less of it."

And I don't suppose there has been any recent generation that craved stability more than ours—or got less of it, from wars to depressions, from inflation to atom bombs.

Most of us who now hold responsible jobs in industry, finance, labor and government lived through the great depression. We were horrified by the hardships we saw or experienced then, hardships created by radical changes of prices, employment and incomes. We want to do everything in our power to prevent another disaster of that kind.

So we have probably done more talking, and more thinking, and undertaken more hopeful experiments related to the ideal stabilization than any other generation since the beginning of the Industrial Revolution, two centuries ago.

While we have been concerned about stability as a general goal—and mostly with praiseworthy motives—it remains true that people are people, and therefore to some degree inconsistent and selfish.

Our friends in the labor unions, for example, have been greatly concerned about stabilization of income for employees, but their interest in stabilization of income for share owners—who are frequently the same people—approaches absolute zero.

Businessmen are greatly interested in the stability of prices and costs; that is to say, *their* prices and costs. As to their suppliers, they take a somewhat different view. Government officials, judging by their actions, have certainly had a strong interest in stabilizing taxation and spending.

Yet all these groups—so concerned with stability—are always hope-

.ul that the prices of pork chops, television sets, automobiles, clothing, and other items will somehow go down.

It seems to be an almost universal truth that men are interested in stability only in their capacity as sellers and never in their capacity as buyers.

The one exception to this rule is our common interest in the stabilization of employment, because we all understand that it is to our own interest—whatever our occupations may be—that as many other people as possible be gainfully employed. In this respect, we are all for one and one for all.

◆

W. Alton Jones, *President, Cities Service Company, responds to an introduction.*

MR. PRESIDENT and gentlemen of the Executives' Club of Chicago: I suppose you have heard this from every speaker who has appeared on this platform for years, but I really am glad to be here today. I guess most people who come here tell you that because they really mean it.

I was born in the Midwest, and while they say you can take a boy out of the country, you can never take the country out of a boy, I really feel at home here, and particularly so when I look around and see so many of my old friends. There are some competitors here, too, who'd like to take my pocketbook, but there are a few bankers here, too, who have loaned me money in times past.

When I looked at the house organ of your club, I read something that intrigued me very much. The masthead of this interesting paper reads "The Executives' Club of Chicago stands unalterably for the Constitution of the United States as handed down to us by our forefathers, and under which we have lived for the past 163 years; and affirms that the fundamental principles it asserts form the basis of true Americanism." Gentlemen, that's a very fine masthead and it's something that should be close to the heart of every one of us. It seems to me that a club that has that slogan is on the ball.

That reminds me of a little story that I tell at Lee Wescoat's expense—this "being on the ball." You know, Lee used to be a pretty good golfer, but like some of us, as we get older, we lose our technique and can't do as well. He was out the other day at one of his favorite clubs and had sliced badly into the rough. He got over into the high grass, and after some time with the help of four caddies and three companions and a Geiger counter, he found his ball.

He was teed up on an ant hill, quite high, and Lee looked pretty confused. He finally called his caddie over and after much deliberation he picked the wrong club, squared around, and took an awful hack at this ball and missed it, but he killed 400 ants.

There were two ants over at one side, watching this. It was their rest period and they were having a Coca-Cola in the shade of a blade of grass. They looked a little startled and surprised at the swing Lee had made at the ball.

Well, Lee backed away and changed clubs and took another swing and again he missed the ball, but he killed 9,000 ants. One of the ants who was resting said to the other, "Listen, sister, if we're going to take care of ourselves, we'd better get on the ball!"

༄

Dwight D. Eisenhower, *President of the United States, begins an address before the annual meeting of the Chamber of Commerce of the United States.*

LADIES AND GENTLEMEN, one of the most pleasant duties that falls to the lot of the President is the opportunity from time to time to welcome here in the capital city bodies of Americans. Normally organized according to function or activity in the country or some basic purpose, they come here to meet and consult together, and in so doing they consult with members of the government and bring us counsel, bring us in touch with the areas lying outside of the District of Columbia, and we think greatly to our advantage.

We hope that sometimes this is a two-way road.

༄

Willard W. Wright, *General Sales Manager, Sun Oil Company, begins an address before the Sixth Annual Community Leader Oil Progress Luncheon, Newark, New Jersey.*

YOU CAN ALWAYS COUNT on oil men coming up with a new approach. I notice in the program that this meeting is called a Community

Leader Oil Progress Week Luncheon. I thought at first we were to talk about you fine gentlemen who have won places of leadership in the cities and towns of northern New Jersey. Instead, I found that you were invited here by oil men like me to hear us talk about ourselves and our industry.

We were not always as brash about things like this as we are today. This practice of setting aside a whole week to report to the American people on what we are doing and how we are contributing to the progress of our nation is distinctly a post-World War II development. Some of us who started rather timidly and self-consciously in this business of talking about ourselves seven years ago are now enjoying it.

〜

Dr. J. L. Morrell, *President, University of Minnesota, begins an address at the University of Minnesota.*

BY THIS TIME the new students among you are beginning to be settled down to the new life and learning of the University—encouraged, I am sure, by the thrilling success of your fellow-students on the football team last Saturday.

And by this time—so much talked to, and advised, have you been during Welcome Week and these first days of your classes—by this time doubtless you are ready to believe, indeed, the beatitude that "blessed is he that hath nothing to say, and cannot be persuaded to say it."

And yet you have become one of us in this great University—and thereby a partner in its problems and prospects. Its dilemmas and decisions you are entitled to understand. Some aspects of all this I wish we might think about together this morning—remembering, as it has been said, that "universities are the thinking devices of society."

I have been looking lately at a very important report on "America's Resources for Specialized Talent." It was prepared by an impressive commission of American scholarly and scientific leaders—including one of our own, Vice-President Malcolm M. Willey of the University of Minnesota.

Let me read you the first paragraph:

"With only 6 per cent of the world's land and 7 per cent of its population, the United States publishes 27 per cent of the world's newspapers, owns 31 per cent of all radio and television sets, produces 40 per cent of all electric power, uses 58 per cent of the world's telephones, and drives 76 per cent of its automobiles."

No wonder you can hardly find a place to park!

But the report recites these facts to emphasize the results, and the need, of trained intelligence in a free society; in a society that is enormously inventive and resourceful because it is free and because it has encouraged education.

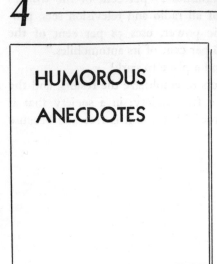

HUMOROUS ANECDOTES

Short Trip

First Space Cadet: "Meet you on Jupiter tonight."
Second Cadet: "But how do I get there?"
First Space Cadet: "When you get to the moon, turn left. You can't miss it."

Courtesy

Policeman: "Hey you, didn't you hear me say, 'Pull over'?"
Driver: "Oh, I thought you said, 'Good morning, Mayor!' "
Policeman: "It is a nice morning, isn't it?"

Education

First student: "Ya like to read, don't-cha?"
Second student: "Sure!"
First student: "Whatcha like to read?"
Second student: "Oh, Li'l Abner, Superman, Terry and the Pirates."

First student: "You like O. Henry?"
Second student: "Not so much. The nuts get in my teeth."

A Little Dry

Two cannibals met in a hut. One was tearing out pictures of men, women, and children from a magazine—stuffing them into his mouth and eating them.

"Tell me," said the other. "Is that dehydrated stuff any good?"

Pot Calling The Kettle

"What funny names those Korean towns have," remarked a man from Schenectady, as he read a Poughkeepsie newspaper while on his way to Hackensack.

Hard To Explain

An absent-minded professor tripped on a staircase and fell all the way to the bottom. Picking himself up, he said, "I wonder what in the world all that noise was about."

Shouldn't Take Chances

"Good heavens, Mr. Druggist, I'm poisoned!" the customer shouted. "It must have been the sandwiches my wife gave me."

"Yes, that's it," agreed the pharmacist. "You're taking a chance every time you eat a sandwich that isn't prepared by a registered pharmacist."

We Did, Too

A householder excitedly reported to the police that he had been struck down in the dark outside his back door by an unknown assailant.

A policeman was sent to the scene of the crime and soon returned to headquarters with a lump on his forehead and a glum look on his face.

"I solved the case," he muttered.

"Fast work," his superior complimented him. "How did you accomplish it?"

The young cop explained, "I stepped on the rake, too."

Honest

The application blank for a new driver's license held the question, "Have you ever been arrested?" The applicant put down "No."

The next question was, "Why?" The applicant put down, "Never been caught."

No Casserole Man

The young minister sitting down to dinner was asked by his wife to say grace. He opened the casserole dish she had prepared from a new French recipe book and an uncounted number of refrigerator left-overs. "Well, I don't know," he said, not being a casserole man himself, "it seems to me I've blessed all this stuff before."

Inquisitive

A child from the city slums was in the country for the first time. Everything he saw on the farm was new and wondrous to him.

Toward sunset of the first day he stood intently watching the farmer's wife plucking a chicken.

After a bit his curiosity grew too great and he asked gravely, "Do you take off their clothes every night, lady?"

It Was His Turn

A stranger, watching a poker game in a tough town out West, saw the dealer give himself four aces. He moved around and whispered to the player opposite.

"Mister, you better git out of here," said the player.

"But," the stranger insisted, "he dealt himself four aces!"

"Say, you don't understand this here game, podner," the player said. "Suppose he did deal himself four aces? Ain't it his deal?"

Legal Advice

Two friends met who hadn't seen each other for some time. One was on crutches.

"Hello," said the other man. "What's the matter?"

"Streetcar accident," said the man on crutches.

"When did it happen?"

"About six weeks ago."

"And you still have to use crutches?"

"Well, my doctor says I could get along without them, but my lawyer says I can't."

Special Delivery

A man was complaining that he had just bought a prefabricated house, and that it had cost him $50,000.

"Fifty thousand!" exclaimed one of his friends. "Isn't that a lot to pay for a prefab?"

"Yes," said the home-owner. "It wasn't so much to begin with, but I told the factory I wanted it right away, and they sent it to me air mail."

Probably

Edgar Bergen: "As Achilles lay dying after being wounded in the heel, do you know what he said?"

Charlie McCarthy: "My feet are killing me!"

Conscience

An anonymous New York taxpayer sent a letter to the State Comptroller's office in Albany, saying that he had cheated on his income tax ten years ago, and had not been able to get a good night's sleep since.

He enclosed twenty-five dollars, and added, "If I still can't sleep, I'll send the balance."

Like Seed Catalogs

A farmer who sent for a book on *How to Grow Tomatoes*, wrote the publisher later: "The man who writ the ad shoulda writ the book."

Couldn't Take It

A man from the East on his first visit West stopped in a Fred Harvey Restaurant for lunch, and took a seat beside a bunch of railroad men.

One of them ordered a bowl of vegetable soup. The waitress bellowed, "Let the garden come in a shower for one."

Another ordered a hamburger steak. Again the waitress let loose with, "Clean up the kitchen for one."

The Easterner figured this joint was a little too rough for him—he would just order a cup of black coffee and two doughnuts, and be on his way. But the waitress yelled, "Draw one in the dark and let a couple of washers come for a nut."

The Easterner did not wait to be served.

Yes And No

A man wanted to buy a riding horse for his wife and was trying one out. Noticing that the horse required a firm hand and constant watching, he asked, "Do you think this is a suitable horse for a woman?"

The owner of the horse was a reasonably honest man, so he answered carefully: "Well, I think a woman could handle the horse, but I wouldn't want to be the husband of the woman who could do it!"

Hard Question

Trying to rest after a hard day, poor father was being annoyed by an endless stream of questions from Willie.

"What did you do all day at your office, Daddy?"

"Nothing!" shouted the father.

After a thoughtful pause, Willie asked, "Dad, how do you know when you're through?"

Hold The Line

A businessman, telephoning a friend at home, was answered by a childish voice.

"Tell your father Mr. Brown called," he said.

"Wait till I get a pencil," the youngster replied. Then, "How do you spell Brown?"

"B-r," the man began. There was labored silence. Finally, the child asked, "How do you make a 'B'?"   *Badger Bell*

Good Solution

Bob Sterling tells of a boy who was behaving badly. His mother said to him: "How do you ever expect to get into Heaven?"

The lad replied: "Well, I'll just run in and out and keep slamming the door until St. Peter says, 'For heaven's sake, come in or stay out.' "

Never Mind The Dictionary

Teacher: "Johnny, how do you spell 'imbecile'?"

Johnny: "I-m-b-u-s-s-u-l."

Teacher: "The dictionary spells it 'i-m-b-e-c-i-l-e.'"

Johnny: "Yeah. But you asked me how *I* spelled it."

Just A Spendthrift

Husband to wife: "What do you say we take this money we've been saving toward a new car and blow it on a movie?"

Why

Teacher: "If you had eight pennies and lost three, how many would you have left?"

Thrifty Lad: "But, teacher, why should I lose three?"

It's Free

"My Dad is an Eagle, a Moose, an Elk, and a Lion," boasted one youngster.

"Yeah?" gasped his wide-eyed companion. "How much does it cost to see him?"

Inexperienced Clerk

A tourist went into a London shop and requested an "E" string for his fiddle. The youthful clerk looked puzzled, but disappeared and returned with a box of strings.

"Would you mind, sir, picking hit hout yourself? Hi'm afraid hi cawn't tell a 'he' string from an 'er' string, an' that's a fact."

Complaint Department

Two spinsters were talking. One remarked, "Last week I advertised in the paper for a husband."

"You don't mean it!" the other exclaimed. "Get any replies?"

"Hundreds of them. And they were all the same. They all said, 'You can have mine.'"   *Sunshine Magazine*

It Ain't Easy

Small boy to father: "Mom says I'm getting more like you every day—how can I stop that?"   *Ohio Motorist*

Of Course

A man was seated on a park bench when a little chap about five sat down beside him and started winding what appeared to be a most prized possession—a dollar watch.

"My, what a pretty watch," the man remarked. "Does it tell you the time?"

"No, sir," replied the little fellow, "you gotta look at it."

Easy Mistake

"Oh, Mother!" cried Jimmie excitedly. "There's a big black bear in the backyard!"

"You know perfectly well it's only a big dog," said his mother. "Now go to your room and ask God to forgive you for telling a lie."

"Did you ask God to forgive you?" she said, when Jimmie came downstairs a little later.

"Yes," he replied, "and He said it was all right. He thought it was a bear Himself the first time He saw it."

Just In Time

The proprietor of a store which had recently been burglarized met a friend on the street.

"I was sorry to hear about the robbery," the friend said. "Did you lose much?"

The storekeeper shrugged. "Some. But it would have been a lot worse if the burglar had broken in the night before."

"Why?" asked the questioner.

"Well, you see," said the storekeeper, "just the day of the robbery I marked everything down 20 per cent."

Sweet

The waitress watched as the customer put eight spoonfuls of sugar into his cup of coffee, and proceeded to drink it without stirring it first.

"Why don't you stir it?" she asked.

The customer regarded her coldly, and said, "Who likes it sweet!"

Sunshine Magazine

Queen For A Day

Sooner or later every woman must take a choice between mother-hood and a career. Should she give the cereal boxtop to Jimmy to send for a compass, or should she keep it herself and enter the $10,000 contest?

To The Head Of The Class

"What," asked the teacher, "was the title for the former rulers of Russia?"

"Czar," replied a student.

"And the title for his wife?" the teacher continued.

"The Czarina."

"That's right," said the teacher, "and for his children?"

The student thought a minute and replied, "Czardines?"

Good Old Days

"Has your husband changed much in the years you've been married?" asked one wife of another.

"No," was the reply, "but he thinks he has. He's always talking about what a fool he used to be."

We Doubt It

Little boy (in woodshed): "Father, you say grandpa spanked you and great-grandpa spanked grandpa, too?"

Father: "Yes."

Little Boy: "Well, don't you think with my help you could overcome this inherited rowdyism?"

Safe

An aged couple was listening to a broadcast church service. Both sat in deep contemplation. Half an hour went by. Then suddenly the old man burst into a fit of laughter.

"Sandy!" exclaimed his wife in horrified tones, "why this merriment on the Sabbath?"

"Ah," said Sandy, "the parson's just announced the collection, and here I am safe at home!"   *Sunshine Magazine*

Easy

"Pardon me, does this train stop at Tenth Street?"

"Yes; watch me and get off one station before I do."

"Thank you."

Now Girls

Mrs. Jones swept into the meeting of the Ladies' Aid society. She was in a huff and she stormed across to Mrs. Smith.

"Did you tell Mrs. Brown I was nothing but a gossip?" demanded Mrs. Jones.

Mrs. Smith's eyebrows raised in mild surprise. "Why, no," she answered. "I thought Mrs. Brown knew."

Not His Idea

"Do you mean to say you worked all night? I wouldn't have dreamed of it."

"Neither would I—the boss thought of it."

Not So Good, Please

Client: "Do you think you can make a good portrait of my wife?"

Artist: "My friend, I can make it so lifelike that you'll jump every time you see it."

Modest

Crosby: "You know what I like about you, Paul? Your great success hasn't changed you one bit."

Douglas: "Why should it? I always knew I was great."

One To A Customer

Doctor: "Now, madam, place this thermometer between your teeth and keep your lips closed for five minutes."

Husband (aside to doctor): "What will you take for that gadget, Doc?"

Ya Gotta Quit It

Coach to football lineman: "You're out of condition again, Jones. What'cha been doing, studyin'?"

Must Have Been From Brother

A woman clerk discovered a youngster wandering forlornly in the lobby of a great building, and in a spirit of kindness, said to him, "Perhaps you'd like to see the forty-foot mural on the floor above. It's really quite interesting."

With an expression of awed anticipation, the small boy hot-footed his way upstairs. A few minutes later there came a despairing call from the Bureau of Animal Husbandry upstairs. "What's the big idea?" a voice demanded. "Who sent a kid up here looking for a forty-foot mule?"

Willing To Help

Over in South London town in Canada during the holiday season an enthusiastic Salvation Army girl-lieutenant was going from door to door with the collection box. She went to the door of a good old lady and asked if she would like to help the carolers.

"I'd love to dearie," replied the old lady, rather croakily, "but I've got the bronchitis something terrible this year, and I couldn't sing a note."

Honest Young Man

Farmer: "Hi there! What are you doing up in my cherry tree?"
Youngster: "There's a sign down there says, 'Keep off the grass.' "

Sorry, Mr. President

Merriam Smith, a Washington correspondent, reveals the "most famous" phone call ever received at the White House. It did not come via the switchboard, but over a pay telephone off the lobby. The voice said, "Ah wants to tawk wi' Miss Mary, please."

"There's no Miss Mary here," said a policeman, "this is the White House."

"Well, pahdon me, Mr. President," was the reply, "Ah sho' diden means to bother you."

Take That And That

"Sir, my stenographer, being a lady, cannot type what I think of you. I, being a gentleman, cannot think it. You, being neither, will understand just what I mean."

Pull Over

The traffic officer ordered the motorist to pull up to the curb and produce his driver's license.

"I don't understand this, officer," the motorist protested. "I haven't done anything wrong."

"No, you haven't," the officer replied. "But you were driving so carefully, I thought you might not have your driver's license."

A Rose By Any Other Name

One of Samuel Goldwyn's associates became a proud father, and Goldwyn heard about it. "What did you name your son?" he inquired.

"John," replied the associate.

"Now, why did you name him John?" declared the perturbed Goldwyn, "every Tom, Dick, and Harry is named John!"

Sunshine Magazine

For Ten Cents And Three Box Tops

The newly engaged kindergarten teacher was justly proud of her sparkling solitaire and enjoyed showing the stone to all who asked to see it. Bruce, one of her pupils, asked to see it one day, and then inquired, "Is it a real ring?"

"Why, certainly," replied the teacher.

"Well, then," he said, "let's see it squirt water."

No Hurry

Manager of the store: "Been to the zoo, yet, sonny?"

New Delivery Boy: "No, sir."

Manager: "Well, you should. You'll enjoy it, and get a big kick out of watching the turtles zip by."

Hired Man

Don McNeill tells about a sign spotted in Rains County, Texas: "Attention Hunters. Don't shoot anything on my farm that isn't moving. It may be my Hired Man."

Correct

Teacher: "If your mother has a package delivered C.O.D., what do the initials mean?"

Bright boy: "Call On Daddy."

She Punctuals Her Typing

Sylvia: "When I applied for a job the manager had the nerve to ask if my punctuation was good."

Mildred: "What did you tell him?"

Sylvia: "I said I'd never been late for work in my life."

Trying Him

A three-year-old boy cried bitterly as a large friendly dog bounded up to him and licked his hands and face. "What is it?" asked his mother. "Did he bite you?"

"No," came the cry. "But he tasted me."

Not So Loud

Harry Morton: "I was out mailing a letter."

Blanche: "Then you didn't hear a word I said."

Harry: "Of course I did. The mailbox is only two blocks away. And anything I missed I can always get from the neighbors."

The Right Time And Place

Louise King: "A woman on the phone wants to know what you think of girls wearing babushkas."

Tom Duggan: "Tell her it's O.K. if they're traveling steerage."

Eatin' In His Eaton Jacket

Irma: "I've got to take Bob shopping and buy him some clothes. What should I get him?"

Kay: "Why not get him an Eton jacket."

Irma: "O.K., but what'll he wear between meals?"

Conscientious

Only a week after he started work, he announced he was quitting. "It isn't the pay," he explained to the foreman. "It's just that I can't help having a guilty conscience."

"What for?" asked the foreman.

"All the time I'm worrying about how I'm cheating some big, strong mule out of a job."

Don't Tell This In California

A company of soldiers was transferred from the East to "Sunny" California and arrived in the rainy season.

The commander of the company, making a night tour of the camp, was challenged by a sentry standing at his post for two hours in a driving rain.

"Who goes there?" called the sentry.

"Friend," replied the C.O.

"Welcome to our mist," said the sentry.

Tend To Business

A lioness saw her young cub chasing a hunter around a bush. The lioness growled and said, "Junior, how often do I have to tell you not to play with your food."

He Had Dad There

A youngster, being scolded for a poor report card, asked:

"Dad, what do you think is the trouble with me—heredity or environment?"

Beautiful Job

Mrs. A to Mrs. B.: "It's a beautiful picture of her, except that the retouch man has made a liar out of the camera."

It Ain't Easy

"Is it possible for a man to make a fool of himself without knowing it?"

"Not if he has a wife."

That's Different

Policeman: "Didn't you hear me call you to stop?"

Driver: "I didn't know it was you. I thought it was someone I had run over."   *Times of Brazil*

No Horse Stealing

Professor: "What is the principal contribution of the automobile age?"

Freshman: "Well, it's practically stopped horse stealing."

We Waited In That Office

After waiting hours in a crowded doctor's office, one patient stood up to go. He said, "Well, I guess I'll just go home and die a natural death."

She Talks A Little

Two housewives chatted as they started off shopping.

"That neighbor of yours is quite a gossip, isn't she?" said one.

"I don't like to say," replied the other. "All I know is that when she came back from her vacation this summer, her tongue was awfully sunburned."

Sounds Reasonable

"Lighthouse no good for flog," says Chinaman.

"Lighthouse he shine; whistle he blow; flog bell he ring; flog he come just the slame. No good."

Not So Good

Golfer (in trap): "The traps on this course are quite annoying, aren't they?"

Second golfer (trying to putt): "They sure are. Would you mind closing yours?"

Complaint

When a diner complained that he couldn't eat the soup that had been brought him, the waiter called the manager.

"I'm very sorry, sir," said the manager, "I'll call the chef."

When the chef arrived, the diner still insisted that he couldn't eat his soup.

"What's wrong with it?" demanded the chef.

"Nothing," calmly answered the diner, "I just don't have a spoon."

Delayed

A doctor asked the woman patient her age.

"I never tell anyone my age," she answered, "but as a matter of fact, I've just reached twenty-five."

"Indeed," said the doctor, "what detained you?"

No Alarm Clock Needed

Husband: "It must be time to get up."
Wife: "Why?"
Husband: "The baby's fallen asleep."

Lucky Break

Woman: "They're playing Beethoven's Fifth Symphony."
Latecomer: "Thank goodness, I've missed the first four."

Also Dictators

"You should marry and let a wife share your life."
"Not for me. Some shareholders become directors."

Too Weak

First boarder: "This cheese is so strong it could walk over and say 'Hello' to the coffee."
Second boarder: "Yes, but the coffee is too weak to answer back."

Short Change

Little Angus, given five dollars for his birthday, had the druggist change the bill into pennies, nickels, and dimes. Then he went to another store and got a five dollar bill for the change, then to a third for change again. Asked by his father to explain, he replied: "Sooner or later somebody will make a mistake in the change—and it won't be me."

What For?

A panhandler approached a prosperous looking man and asked for a dime. "Is this all you have to do?" replied the prospect. "Look at you—you sleep on park benches, your clothes are in tatters, and you're hungry. Why don't you go to work?"

"Go to work?" growled the loafer in disgust. "What for—to support a bum like me?"

Seems Possible

The lawyer was quizzing the witness: "You admit you were seated on the right side of the passenger train. How could you see an extra track? Will you tell the jury how you are so sure there was a double track?"

"Well," said the witness, "occasionally a train, which I could see through the windows across the aisle to my left, would speed by going in the opposite direction from us. So I reasoned it was a better bet that there was a track under those trains than that the engineers were lost."

Such Modesty

"Did anyone in your family ever make a brilliant marriage?"
"Only my wife."

Balance

To be a balanced citizen you must spend some time each day trying to keep up with the national and international news, even though you are more interested in some local scandal.

The Herald, Sauk Centre, Minnesota

Arrived Safely

A Brooklyn gentleman took his wife to the Newark Airport and put her on a plane for Buffalo. After fighting his way through the traffic, he arrived back home and wearily ascended the steps to his home, to find a telegram in his mailbox. He opened it and read, "Arrived safely love Lulu."

Orders Are Orders

Once upon a time the compositors on the old *New York Herald* were negligent in following instructions to italicize the name of the paper. One day the managing editor passed down the order that failure to italicize the word Herald would be cause for dismissal. Later, proofreaders were surprised to find in a Christmas program: "Hark, the *Herald* Angels Sing."

Get Busy

Motorist: "I ran over your cat and I want to replace him."
Housewife: "Well, get busy. There's a mouse in the pantry."

Scram And Eggs

"What makes you think your wife is getting tired of you?"
"Every day this week she has wrapped my lunch in a road map!"

Caterpillar News and Views

Come, Come, Girls

Mrs. No. 1: "That's a very lovely coat your're wearing, Mrs. Jones."
Mrs. No. 2: "Oh, thank you. My husband gave it to me for my thirty-fifth birthday."
Mrs. No. 1: "It certainly wears well, doesn't it!"

He Better Pay His Dues

"Thirty dollars to paint my garage? That's outrageous! I wouldn't pay Michelangelo that much to paint my garage!" "Listen, you," said the painter, "if he does the job for any less, we'll come and picket yer place!"

Good Likeness

It was lunch hour at the plant, and Pat's two buddies decided to play a joke on him during his absence. They drew the features of a donkey on the back of his coat. Pat returned and presently hove in sight bearing the decorated coat.

"What's the trouble, Pat?" asked one casually.

"Not much," replied Pat. "I'd like to know just which one of yez wiped your face on me coat!"

He Was Cautious

A waiter was horrified to see a patron washing his spoon in the fingerbowl. Calling the manager, they hurried to the man's table. "Why," demanded the manager, "are you washing your spoon in the fingerbowl?"

"Because I don't want to get ice cream all over my pocket," replied the diner.

Lost—24 Hours

It was so tough for Bill to get up in the morning that he went to see his doctor, who fixed him up with some pills to cure him of drowsiness. Bill took a pill that night, slept well, and was wide awake before he heard the alarm go off. He dressed and ate breakfast leisurely. Later he told the boss:

"I didn't have a bit of trouble getting up this morning."

"That's fine," the boss said, "but where were you yesterday?"

In Agreement

Two ministers of different faiths were the best of friends, but they often disagreed on religious questions. One day they had been arguing, a little more than usual, on some theological point, when one of them said, "That's all right. We'll just agree to disagree. The thing that counts is that we're both doing the Lord's work, you in your way and I in His."

Aftermath

A prof was retiring after teaching mathematics for fifty years. He was building a lodge in the mountains in which to spend his declining years.

"Have you named it yet?" his friend asked.

"Oh, yes," said the prof. "I'm calling it 'After Math.' "

He Won, Didn't He?

A young man walked into the casino, plunked down a big bet on number thirty-five, and walked out with a roll big enough to choke a horse. "How did you happen to pick that number?" his friend inquired.

"Well, this was the sixth of January and my sixth wedding anniversary. So I multiplied the two numbers together.

"But, look here," said the friend. "Six times six is thirty-six."

"Okay," said the young man. "You should have the education."

Kroehler News

Good Deed

The boy scout remarked at the breakfast table, "I've already done my good deed for the day." His father replied, "You've been very quick about it."

"Yes, but it was easy," replied the boy. "I saw Mr. Smith going for the 7:45 train and he was afraid he'd miss it. So I let the bulldog loose, and he was just in time."

Fair

First Steno: "Yes, the boss is mean all right, but he's fair."
Second Steno: "What do you mean he's fair?"
Third Steno: "He's mean to everyone."

Couldn't Fool Her

Mrs. Jones, enrolling her daughter in an exclusive school, was asked: "Has she had a good musical education?"

"She certainly has," was the mother's reply. "Name any song you like and she'll tell you what's on the other side of the record."

Perfect Toy

Mother (examining toy): "Isn't this rather complicated for a small child?"

Clerk: "It's an educational toy, Madam, designed to adjust a child to live in the world today. Any way he puts it together it's wrong."

Playing Safe

The important man was about ready for his speech when a photographer was observed jockeying for a vantage point, for an action shot. The chairman, fearing that the speaker would be annoyed, called the photographer and said: "Don't take his picture while he is speaking. Shoot him before he starts."

One Must Go

Efficiency Expert: "Mr. Jones, what do you do here?"
Jones: "Nothing."
Efficiency Expert: "And, Mr. Martin, what do you do here?"
Martin: "Nothing."
Efficiency Expert: "Hmmm. Duplication."

Tain't Fair, Teacher

Teacher (patiently): "If one and one makes two, and two and two makes four, how much does four and four make?"

Pupil: "That ain't fair, teacher. You answer the easy ones yourself and leave the hard ones for me."

Modern Education

The teacher played the "Star Spangled Banner" and asked her class to identify it. "That's easy," shouted a pupil. "It's what they play every Friday on TV just before the fights."

Mistake

Officer: "Slow down that truck. Haven't you got a governor on it?"

Driver: "Nawsah, boss. The governor is in the state capitol. That's fertilizer you smells."

There They Is

The Kingfish of Amos and Andy: "Relatives is like radishes. Just when you think you've heard the last of them, there they is again."

That Explains Everything

Mother: "Sit down, Tommy, and tell your sister a story."

Tommy: "Can't sit down, Mother, I just told Daddy a story."

Go To The Head Of The Class

Teacher: "Johnny, can you tell me what a grudge is?"

Johnny: "A grudge is a place where they keep automobiles."

Keep Busy

The recruit was finding his first day of training rugged. Having puffed through the obstacle course to the last lap he fell getting over the last hurdle. The sergeant, noticing the man on the ground, asked what was the matter.

"My leg, sergeant," groaned the man. "I think I broke it on that last hurdle."

"Well, then, don't waste time just lying there—do push-ups until the medics get here."

What Hoppened?

An intoxicated person fell out of a seven story window and landed in the street without any apparent harm.

A crowd gathered and a policeman rushed up and said, "What happened?"

"I don't know," said the intoxicated man. "I just got here myself."

He Ain't Been No Place

According to Senator Lyndon Johnson of Texas, a boy in his state once complained that his brother had been "twowheres and I ain't been nowheres."

Hey, You Can't Do That

One attorney wrote to another, "Sir: I regret to inform you that there is danger of an agreement between our respective clients."

How's That?

A storekeeper had two clerks, Jim and Albert. Albert, whose home was a mile from the store, always arrived on time for the day's work. Jim, who lived in a room above the store, was usually late.

One day the storekeeper remarked to Jim, with some asperity, "It's a funny thing. Albert, who lives a mile away, can always get here on time, while you, who live right here, are nearly always late."

"Nothing funny about that," replied Jim. "If Albert wakes up late, he can always put on a burst of speed. But if I'm late, I'm already here."

He Was Spoiled

A husband, complaining about the food, was met with a strong argument by his wife.

"What's the matter with you?" she demanded. "Monday you liked beans, Tuesday you liked beans, Wednesday you liked beans; now Thursday, all of a sudden, you don't like beans!"

Trouble

Charlie McCarthy: "Bergen, I'm afraid I'm gonna flunk my history test tomorrow on account of illness."

Bergen: "There's nothing wrong with you, Charlie."

Charlie: "No, but the fellow I copy from is home with the mumps."

Information Please

George Jessel told this story at a Cedars of Lebanon hospital benefit.

A nurse answered a phone call: "I vould like to know the condition of Alex Kramer vich has been sick for four months. Tell me, vat is his condition."

She checked his chart and replied: "He spent a restful night. He's improving steadily. Who shall I say called?"

"This is Alex Kramer. My doctors won't tell me a thing."

Inflation

Son: "Pop, what is creeping inflation?"

Father: "It's when your mother starts out asking for a new hat and winds up with a complete new outfit."

Language

Bob Hope tells about two old women who were looking up at a mountain view.

"Isn't the sunset beautiful?" one said. "Every color in the rainbow is gleaming on that snowy mountain peak."

A couple of bopsters were watching it, too. One said to the other: "Man, dig that crazy popsickle!"

Perfectly Legal

He'd driven for miles across sparsely settled territory before he finally came to a little town boasting a hotel of sorts. Sitting down for supper at the single table at which everyone was served, the motorist complained about the condition of the roller towel he had been forced to use. "Besides," he wound up, "roller towels have been prohibited by law for years!"

"Sure," replied the proprietor. "I know about that law. But I had that towel a-hanging there before they passed it."

He Worked For Us

Mechanic: "Which do you prefer, leather or fabric auto upholstering?"

Second Mechanic: "I like fabric; leather is too hard to wipe your hands on."

Curiosity

Dad: "That boy is a nuisance."

Mom: "What's wrong, now?"

Dad: "He wants to know what would happen if he mixed a bottle of ink eradicator with a bottle of ink!"

First Step

Mother made the mistake of leaving the baby in her husband's care while she went out into the back yard to hang up a washing. Father buried himself behind his newspaper, and forgot all about the baby until he heard a series of thumps, and a horrendous wail.

"Martha," called father excitedly, running to the back door. "Come quick! Junior just took his first twenty-three steps!"

Too Much Territory

A man entered a meeting with a piece of paper in his hand, and said, "This is a list of all the men I can whip."

A husky, broad-shouldered boiler-maker exclaimed, "Is my name on there?"

The man said, "Yes."

"Well," bellowed the husky, "you can't whip me!"

"Are you sure?" asked the challenger.

"Bet yer life I'm sure!" yelled the fellow.

"Okay, then," replied the man, "I'll take your name off the list."

Logic

A customer in a Montreal restaurant went to the washroom, turned on the faucet and got scalded. "This is an outrage," he screamed. "Why aren't your faucets properly marked? I turned on the faucet marked 'C' thinking it would be cold, and I got scalding water."

The manager was patient. He led the man back to the washroom. "Look," he said, "the faucet is marked 'C' correctly. That stands for *chaude* and *chaude* means hot! You should know that if you live in Montreal."

The customer stood abashed for a moment. Then he made a discovery. "But look," he cried. "The other faucet is marked with 'C' also! What about that?"

"Ah," said the manager, "that stands for 'cold.' This is a bilingual restaurant, my friend."

Papa Bought The Bicycle

Mama: "Let's buy Junior a bicycle."
Papa: "Do you think it will improve his behavior?"
Mama: "No, but it will spread his meanness over a wider area."

100% In History

Teacher: "Willie, what happened in the year 1732?"
Willie: "George Washington was born."
Teacher: "And what happened in 1776?"
Willie: "George Washington was forty-four years old."

Conceited

The golfer teed up, eyed the distance to the green and announced: "A drive and a putt will do it."

Then he swung—but the ball traveled only a few yards. His caddie handed him the putter, remarking brightly: "This putt will be worth telling the boys about."

Good Question

Then there was the little boy who went to school for the first time. The teacher explained to him that if he wanted to go to the washroom at any time, he should raise two fingers.

Looking very puzzled, the little boy asked: "How's that help?"

You Tell 'Em

The sergeant was drilling raw recruits. It was a hectic job. Finally he noticed one man alone was out of step.

"Do you know, soldier," he said sarcastically, "that they're all out of step except you?"

"Well," replied the rookie, "you're in charge—you tell 'em!"

Correct Amount

The butcher informed a customer: "I can't give you any more credit. Your bill is bigger than it should be."

"I know that," said the customer. "Just make it out for what it should be, and I'll pay it."

It's A Tough Job

"It's becoming increasingly difficult to reach the downtrodden masses in America," a Comrade wrote to his superior. "In the spring they're forever polishing their cars. In the summer they take vacations. In the fall they go to the world series and football games. And in the winter you can't get them away from their television sets. Please give me suggestions on how to let them know how oppressed they are."

That Fixed Him

A pupil was having trouble with punctuation, and was being taken to task by the teacher.

"Never mind, Sonny," said the visiting school-board president, consolingly, "it's foolish to bother about commas. They don't amount to much, anyway."

"Elizabeth Ann," said the teacher, quietly, to a small girl in the class, "please write this sentence on the board: 'The president of the board says the teacher is misinformed.' Now," she continued, "put a comma after 'board,' and another after 'teacher!' "

That Did It

"How did you cure your wife of her antique craze?"

"Oh, I just made her a birthday present of a 1923 model automobile."

He Got Off Easy

Tenant: "The people upstairs are very annoying. Last night they stamped and banged on the floor after midnight."

Landlord: "Did they awaken you?"

Tenant: "No. As it happened, I was still up practicing on my tuba."

Just A Warning

"Joe, I see your mule has 'U.S.' branded on his left hind leg. I suppose he was an army mule, and belonged to Uncle Sam."

"No, suh, dat 'U.S.' don't mean nothin' 'bout Uncle Sam. Dat's jest a warnin'. 'U.S.' stands fo' unsafe, dat's all."

Insurance

In a certain backward community, where shoes were mostly for Sunday wear, a candidate employed an unusual electioneering technique. To each voter who turned a sympathetic ear to his campaign promises, he gave a single shoe, explaining, "You promise to vote for me, but I'm not so certain you will do it. So I'm giving you one shoe only. If I'm elected, I'll come back and give you the other one!"

He was elected by a landslide.

Nobody Home

A young man dashed into the electrician's shop, his face flushed with anger. "Didn't I ask you yesterday morning to send a man to mend our doorbell?" he roared. "And did you not promise to send him around at once?"

"But we did, sir," broke in the manager. "I'm quite sure of it! Hi, Bill!" he called to one of his workmen at the back of the office. "Didn't you go round to Park Lodge yesterday to do that job?"

"Yes sir," replied Bill. "I went round all right, and I rang the bell for over ten minutes, but I couldn't get no answer, so I guessed they must not be at home."

Union Hours

Marge: "If your folks won't consent to your marrying Jack, why don't you elope?"

Minnie: "No chance. Jack's a painter and he won't climb a ladder after 4:30 P.M."

Still There

The father played possum while his youngsters tried their best to rouse him from a Sunday afternoon nap to take them for a promised walk. Finally, his five-year-old daughter pried open one of his eyelids, peered carefully, then reported: "He's still in there."

Logic

A cop stopped a man from jumping off a bridge. "If you jump in," he pleaded, "I'll have to jump in after you, and while we're waiting for the ambulance we'll both get pneumonia and die. Now be a good fellow and go home and hang yourself."

United Mine Workers Journal

That's Enough

Last fall she had dismissed her boy friend, saying she couldn't think of marrying him until he had saved a few thousand dollars. Came spring . . . a gorgeous night and a full moon. Again—how much had he saved?

"About thirty-five dollars," he said.

"Well," said Joan, with a blush, "that's enough."

Indiana Telephone News

Fine

Two psychiatrists met on the street one day, and one said to the other, "You're fine. How am I?"

All Over

Went to the baseball game with my wife. One fellow hit the ball over the fence, and she said, "I'm glad they got rid of it; now we can go home."

Do They Come Hollow?

"Darling," said the bride as she put dinner on the table, "this is my first roast turkey."

"Marvelous! And it looks as if you've stuffed it well, too."

"Stuffed it? Why this one wasn't hollow."

No Piker

"Lady, if you will give us a nickel my little brother will imitate a hen."

"What will the little dear do—cackle?"

"Naw, he wouldn't do a cheap stunt like that. He'll eat a woim."

Not Guilty

Boss: "I wish you wouldn't whistle at your work."

Clerk: "I wasn't working."

Hear! Hear!

The messenger had just caught sight of Birnam Wood marching on Dunsinane. He turned to Macbeth and said, "Your majesty, cheese it! The copse!"

Good Reason

"Those new people across the street seem very devoted. Every time he goes out he kisses her, and he goes on throwing kisses all the way down the street. Albert, why don't you do that?"

"Me? I don't even know her."

Ho Did

Wife: "Didn't I tell you to notice when the soup boiled over?"
Husband: "I did. It was half past four."

He Wanted Real Happiness

"So, Lefty, not content with stealing five thousand dollars in cash, you went back and took a couple of watches, six diamond rings, and a pearl necklace?"

"Yes, Your Honor. I remembered that money alone doesn't bring happiness."

Too Smart For The Boss

The new office boy had neglected his duties and his employer decided to give him a reminder.

"Belsen," he began, "I wrote your name with my finger in the dust on my desk this morning."

"Yeah, boss, I know," the youth replied, "and you spelled it wrong."

Heard On The Radio

Gene Autry: "Why don't you try the Lonely Hearts club?"
Pat Buttram: "I've done that. I sent 'em a lock of my hair and told 'em if they found anybody with hair that matches it, to have 'em get in touch with me."
Autry: "What happened?"
Buttram: "I got pictures from two cocker spaniels and one poodle."

It Fit Well

"Jane," moaned her husband, "you promised you wouldn't buy another new dress. What made you do it?"

"Dear," she replied, "the devil tempted me."

"Why didn't you say: 'Get thee behind me, Satan?' " her husband inquired.

"I did," the woman replied, sweetly, "and then he whispered over my shoulder: 'My dear, it fits you just beautifully at the back.' "

But Figures Do Lie

"Figures can't lie," said the instructor. "For instance, if one man can build a house in twelve days, twelve men can build it in one."

A puzzled student interrupted: "Then 288 will build it in one hour, 17,280 in one minute, and 1,036,800 in one second. I don't believe they could lay one brick in that time."

While the instructor was still gasping, the "ready reckoner" went on: "And again, if one ship can cross the Atlantic in six days, six ships can cross in one day. I can't believe that, either."

Not Enough Pay

A farmer in great need of extra hands at harvest time finally asked Si, who was accounted the town fool, if he could help him out.

"What'll ye pay?" asked Si.

"I'll pay you what you're worth," answered the farmer.

Si scratched his head a minute, then answered decisively: "Don't believe I'll work for that!"

In Trouble

Two businessmen who had both borrowed money from a local bank met on the street. One said, "If the market doesn't go up, I'll have to rob a bank." The other said, "If the market doesn't go up, I *have* robbed a bank."

Caught

The preacher at the wedding was an ardent fisherman and forgetful. He asked the groom: "Do you promise to love, honor, and cherish this woman?"

"I do," said the groom, meekly.

"OK," said the preacher, turning to the bride. "Reel him in."

American Eagle

Sensitive

Little Bobby's mother reluctantly sent her precious child to school when he reached kindergarten age. She took him to school the first day. She gave the teacher a long list of instructions.

"My Bobby is so sensitive," she explained. "Don't ever punish him. Just slap the boy next to him. That will frighten Bobby."

That's The Way It Looks Lady

An elderly Yorkshire couple was visiting an exhibition of domestic appliances in London, and paused to gaze through the glass panel of a demonstration washing machine at a bunch of laundry that was being swirled and splashed. "Well," said the lady, "if that's television, they can have it."

He Had Him There

The manager of a hotel, finding that a guest had departed without paying his hotel bill, wrote him: "My dear Mr. Smith: Will you please send the amount of your bill and oblige." To this Mr. Smith wrote: "My dear Mr. Manager: The amount of my bill is a hundred and ten dollars. Yours respectfully."

She Drove

Mr. Jones and his family had just returned from their vacation. "Did you enjoy your vacation trip?" asked a neighbor of Mr. Jones.

"Very much," Mr. Jones replied. "My wife did all the driving."

"Then you had a chance to enjoy the scenery."

"Yes, indeed," said Mr. Jones. "All I had to do was to hold the wheel."

Lincoln's Wisdom

The novice was not enjoying his first airplane trip, and his more experienced companion regarded him with amusement.

"Say, Bill, what's on your mind?" he demanded.

"I was just thinking about Abraham Lincoln," replied Bill.

"Abraham Lincoln?"

"Yes, I was thinking how truthfully he spoke when he said a man's legs ought to be just long enough to reach the ground."

Just Paw And Maw

"I've been asked plenty of times to get married," said the old maid with a toss of her head.

"Who asked yuh, Daisy?" inquired her boy friend.

"Oh, Pa and Ma."

Death Benefits

Zeke: "Does this lodge yo' belong to have any death benefits?"

Ike: "Yessuh! Deed it does. When yo' dies, yo' don' hab to pay no dues."

Don't Mention It

"Young man, how long have you been with us?" asked the president of the company.

"Six months, sir," was the answer.

"And how long have you been a foreman?"

"One month, sir."

"And what are you paid?"

"One hundred and ten dollars per week, sir."

"Well, I've been watching your work closely, and I'm exceedingly pleased with the progress you have made. We always recognize outstanding ability. Therefore, it affords me great pleasure to advise you that on the first of next month you will assume the post of Vice-President—Operations, and your salary will be $65,000 a year."

"Oh, thank you, Dad!"   *Foreman's Digest*

Very Similar

A Scotchman had been told by his doctor that he had a floating kidney. Disturbed by the diagnosis, he went to the pastor of his church with a request for the prayers of the congregation.

"I'm afraid," the pastor said, "that the mention of a floating kidney would cause the congregation to laugh."

"Only last Sunday you prayed for loose livers," said the Scotchman.

Don't Believe In Signs

Attendant: "I'm sorry, sir, but all business at this service station is strictly cash."

Motorist: "But the sign says plainly, 'Batteries Charged.' "

On A Diet

"Crop failure!" exclaimed the oldtimer. "Lord, I've seen some in my time. In 1898 the corn crop was almost nothing. We cooked some for dinner, and my pa ate fourteen acres of corn at that one meal!"

No Luck

It was Junior's first day in school, and when he got home his mother asked, "Did you learn anything today?"

"No," he replied in disgust. "I have to go back tomorrow."

Perfectly Legitimate

"What was your mother's name before she was married?" the professor was asked.

"Sir," the professor replied in high dudgeon, "I had no mother before she was married."   *Marta Davis from Partners*

Could Be Wrong

A woman was called for jury duty, but refused to serve because she didn't believe in capital punishment. Trying to persuade her, the judge explained: "This is only a case where a wife is suing her husband because she gave him $1,000 to pay down on a fur coat, and he lost the money in a poker game."

Thereupon the woman said: "I'll serve. I could be wrong about capital punishment."

Took Too Long

Eight years working for the firm—never absent, never late—then one morning he came in an hour and a half late, his clothes torn, his face and hands scratched and bloody.

Boss: "Why are you late?"

"I leaned out the window and fell three stories!"

Boss: "That took you an hour and a half?"

Me Too

I always do my hardest work before breakfast.
What's that?
Getting up.

That'll Hold Him

During preliminary inspection at a Boy Scout camp, the director found an umbrella in the bedroll of a tiny Scouter. Since the umbrella was obviously not one of the items of equipment listed, the director asked the lad to explain. The tenderfoot neatly countered with his question:

"Sir, did you ever have a mother?"

Accurate

A memorandum on a phone call was handed to a manager by his secretary.

"I can't read this," he said.

"I couldn't understand him very well," explained the secretary, "so I didn't write it very clearly."

Lucky Discovery

On his way out of the lecture the professor asked if anyone had seen his hat.

"You're wearing it, sir," a student replied.

"Thank you," said the professor. "If you hadn't seen it, I'd have gone home without it."

He Knew

Tom: "Say, Bill, how did you get that swelling on your nose?"
Bill: "Oh, I bent down to smell a brose in my garden."
Tom: "Not brose, Bill, rose. There's no 'B' in rose."
Bill: "There was in this one."

Precocious Boy

A young lad of thirteen was waiting to get into the play, *South Pacific*, when he was spied by one of his father's friends.

"Hello, Paul," said the man. "How did you happen to get here tonight, you lucky kid!"

"Oh, I came on my brother's ticket," said the boy.

"And where's your brother?"

"Home looking for his ticket, I suppose," said Paul.

Just Fill It Up

The old engineer pulled his engine up to the water tank and briefed the new fireman. The fireman got up on the tender and brought down the spout all right, but somehow his foot got caught in the chain and he stepped right into the tank.

As he floundered around in the tank, the engineer regarded him with a jaundiced eye.

"Just fill the tank with water, Sonny," he drawled. "No need to stamp the stuff down."

Progress

At a village store in the Blue Ridge country the old proprietor was trying to sell a wastebasket to a hillbilly. Sales resistance was in the set of the bearded man's chin. "How come I need a basket? It'll need emptyin' every month or so."

"Not this one," said the proprietor. "Ain't got no bottom to it. Just move it a jot."

Smart Boy

An old mountaineer and his son were sitting in front of the fire smoking their pipes, crossing and uncrossing their legs. After a long period of silence, the father said, "Son, step outside and see if it's raining."

Without looking up, the son answered, "Aw, Pop, why don't we jest call in the dog and see if he's wet?"

With Kind Regards

An executive had occasion to write to a Chinese friend in San Francisco. Mindful of the Oriental's appreciation of flowery language, and of his own duty to the cause of good public relations, he ended his letter with the wish: "May Heaven preserve you always."

The Chinese responded with: "May Heaven pickle you, too."

Lucky

"I was so cold last night I couldn't sleep. I just lay there and shivered."

"Did your teeth chatter?"

"I don't know—we don't sleep together."

Say That Again

A small boy went to a Sunday school picnic, but it hardly lived up to his expectations. He was stung by a bee; he fell into a creek; a little girl pulled his hair; he got badly sunburned. Late in the afternoon he reached home in an extremely disheveled state. As he limped up the front steps his mother greeted him and said:

"Well, son, what sort of a time did you have at the picnic?"

"Mama," slowly replied the little lad, "I'm so glad I'm back I'm glad I went."

That's What We Found

While his birthday party was being planned, little Jimmie was asked for a list of friends he would like to invite to the party.

"I want Aunty Mills, Grandpa Smith, Uncle Dick, and Grandma Jones, and—"

"But wait a minute, Jimmie. Every one of those you have mentioned is an older person," said mother.

"Well," replied Jimmie. "They're the only ones who ever seem to have any money."

Happy Home

It was the first day of school, and the teacher was going from desk to desk making the acquaintance of her new class. Stopping in front of the desk of little Mehitabel, she asked, "What is your father's name?"

"Daddy," replied Mehitabel.

"Yes, I know that," said the teacher, "but what does your mother call him?"

Little Mehitabel thought for a moment, then said, "She don't call him anything—she likes him."   *Sunshine Magazine*

Smart Family

Mother was helping Sonny with his homework, and asked, "How much is seven and four?"

"Twelve," said the son.

"Not bad for a little shaver," said his dad, who was listening; "he only missed it by two."

Whatsinaname?

Sandy McPherson had just started to write a telegram to his wife, when a girl at the desk told him there was no charge for the name.

Putting down his pencil, Sandy said, "I may not look like one, but I am an Indian, and my name is 'Iwontbehometillsaturdaynight.' "

Heard On The Radio

Irma: "My cabin on the ship was nice, but I didn't like the washing machine on the wall."

Kay: "Washing machine? That was a porthole."

Irma: "No wonder I never got my clothes back."

State Of Transition

Tommy: "Mom, is it true that we come from dust and will return to dust?"

Mom: "Yes, dear, that's what the Bible says. Why?"

Tommy: "Well, I just looked under my bed and there's somebody there, either comin' or goin'."

We Saw The Picture

Then there was the gunman who walked up to a theatre cashier, stuck a gun in her face, and growled: "The picture was horrible—give me everybody's money back."   *Photoplay*

Bang! Bang!

The TV repairman was trying to find the trouble in a set. Just then the six-year-old came home from school. "I'll bet," he said, "if you'd clean out the dead cowboys from the bottom of the set, it would work again."

His Brother Is Standinthecorner

Little Rosalie, a first-grader, walking with her mother, spoke to a small boy. "His name is Jimmy, and he is in my class," she explained.

"What is the little boy's last name?" her mother asked.

"His whole name," said Rosalie, "is Jimmy Sitdown—that's what the teacher calls him."

To The Head Of The Class

A teacher in Brooklyn said, "Joey, give me a sentence using the word 'bewitches'." After deep thought, Joey replied, "Youse go ahead. I'll bewitches in a minute."   *Gosport, USNAS, Pensacola*

Not Appreciated

The office manager was greatly disturbed when one of the most efficient young ladies under his command announced she was going to quit.

"Don't you like your job?" he asked.

"Oh yes. I like it very much."

"Is your salary satisfactory?"

"Yes."

"Do you like working conditions here?"

"Yes."

"Then why are you leaving?"

"I was off a whole day last week, and nobody took up a collection for me."   *Phoenix Flame*

Trade Is Good

Friend: "Why do you have such misspelled and ungrammatical signs in your front window?"

Sharp Merchant: "People think I am a dunce, and come in to swindle me. Trade's just fine!"   *Abundant Living*

Ambitious Youth

The teacher asked his pupils to write an essay telling what they would do if they had a million dollars.

Every pupil except little Willie began writing immediately. Willie sat idle, twiddling his fingers and watching the flies on the ceiling.

The teacher collected the papers, and Willie handed in a blank sheet.

"How is this, Willie?" asked the teacher. "Is this your essay? All the other pupils have written two sheets or more while you have done nothing!"

"Well," replied Willie, "that's what I'd do if I had a million dollars!"

Sunshine Magazine

Youth

An old man heard about some pills that would restore his youth. He bought a box, but instead of taking one every day, he swallowed the whole boxful in a single dose the next night.

When morning came, the family had great difficulty waking the old man. At last he rolled over, rubbed his eyes, and said, "All right, all right, I'll get up, but I'm not going to school!"

Too Busy At The Depot

A mountaineer took a trip to New York City—his first to a large city. On his return, a friend asked him how he liked New York.

"Well," said Zeke, "to tell the truth, I never did get to see the town—there was so much going on around the depot."

He Had Teacher There

"If your mother gave you a large apple and a small apple and told you to divide with your brother, which one would you give him?" asked the teacher.

"Do you mean my little brother or my big brother?" asked the pupil.

Unable To Speak

An after-dinner speaker rose to speak. "After partaking of such a meal," he continued, "I feel, if I had eaten another bite, I would be unable to speak." From the far end of the table came an order to the waiter: "Give him a sandwich."

College Humor

At a large eastern college Professor Davis was talking to a small group of students after class one day, and the name of a colleague was mentioned.

"I understand," he said, "that the boys have a nickname for Professor Brown. I think that is a great sign of affection and friendship. Someone told me they call him 'Maxwell House'. Is that correct?"

"Yes, it is," one of the boys replied.

"I wish they had one for me," said Professor Davis. "I'd take it as a high compliment."

"Oh, they have one for you already," said another boy. "They call you 'Sanka'."

Shortly afterward, Professor Davis happened to see advertising displays of the coffees named and examined them carefully. On the first he found the words, "Good to the last drop," and on the second, "More than ninety-eight per cent of the active portion of the bean has been removed."

The New Age

Backfire

A party of New Yorkers was hunting in the piney woods of Georgia, and had as an attendant an old Negro with a fondness for big words. One of the hunters, knowing the old man's bent, remarked to him, "Uncle Most, the indentations in terra firma in this locality render traveling in a vehicular conveyance without springs decidedly objectionable and painful anatomically. Don't you think so?"

Uncle Most scratched his left ear a moment, then replied with a slow shake of his woolly head, "Mistah Gawge, de exuberance ob yo' 'ambulatin' wurds am pas' mah expicious jurydiction."

Sunshine Magazine

Make An Offer

Edgar Bergen: "Are you all right?"

Mortimer: "No, I'm sick as a dog. Call a veterinary. Oh, my stomach! I better take something."

Bergen: "That's a good idea. What'll you take for your stomach?"

Mortimer: "I dunno—make me an offer."

Probably A Drum

The horn-tooter in traffic was squelched by a lady pulling up alongside his car and inquiring, very sweetly, "What else did you get for Christmas?"

We Use Casaba Melons

"Hilda, what on earth are you taking those avocado peels home for?"

"Well, ma'am, they make my garbage look so stylish."

Naturally

Small boy scowling over his report card said to his dad: "Naturally, I seem stupid to my teacher; she's a college graduate."

Lucky Guy

When the defendant's name was called in court, to everyone's amazement, he stood up in the jury box. "What are you doing there?" barked the clerk.

"I was called to serve on the jury," came the meek reply. "But you must have known," the clerk snapped, "that you couldn't sit on a jury and judge your own case."

"Well, I suppose not," the defendant admitted. "I did think it was a bit of luck."

Practically Unused

An antique collector, passing through a small village, stopped to watch an old man chopping wood with an ancient ax.

"That's a mighty old ax you have there," remarked the collector.

"Yes," said the villager, "it once belonged to George Washington."

"Not really!" gasped the collector. "It certainly stood up well."

"Of course," admitted the old man, "it's had three new handles and two new heads."

Those Oysters Rockefeller

Blonde in restaurant as her escort studies check: "You look ill. Is it something I ate?"

Lost Golfer

Golfer (in a thicket): "Never mind about my ball, caddie. Come and find me!"

Watch Out For A Cadillac

"Last week a grain of sand got into my wife's eye, and she had to go to a doctor. It cost me three dollars."

"That's nothing. Last week a fur coat got into my wife's eye, and it cost me eight hundred."

Are You Kidding?

The Bohlman kids are rabid baseball fans, and everybody who knows the old man can understand why. Well, one day a kid in the neighborhood asked this question: "Suppose, Johnny, your father and the leading batter in the National League were both hanging from a cliff, about to drop off. Which one would you rescue first?"

"Are you kidding?" exclaimed little Johnny. "Why my father never hit .300 in his life!"

No Need For It

Mother: "Did you thank Mrs. Jones for the lovely party she gave?"

Mary: "No, mummy. The girl leaving just before me thanked her, and Mrs. Jones said, 'Don't mention it,' so I didn't."

It Was Strange

A kangaroo sat down at a drug counter and ordered a lemonade. The clerk served the drink. The kangaroo reached for it, then dropped his paw suddenly.

"Where's the red cherry?" asked the unusual customer.

The clerk supplied it promptly.

"Strange, isn't it?" a man whispered to the clerk.

"Yes, it is," said the latter. "It's the first time in five years that I forgot to put a red cherry in a lemonade."

He Should Know

"They say brunettes have sweeter dispositions than redheads."

"That's a lot of hooey. My wife's been both and I can't see any difference."

We Heard Him Too

During a pause in a long, tiring speech, one guest said to another: "What follows this speaker?"

Second guest: "Wednesday."

Education

The teacher had asked the class to list, in their opinion, the eleven greatest Americans. After a while she stopped at one desk and asked:

"Have you finished your list yet, Bobby?"

"Not yet, teacher," Bobby replied. "I can't decide on the full-back."

Elementary Education

Sally, a kindergarten pupil, was learning the alphabet. "What comes after T?" asked the teacher.

The little girl didn't hesitate a minute. "V," she replied.

A Demagogue

"Father," said a small boy, "what is a demagogue?"

"A demagogue, my son, is a man who can rock the boat himself and persuade everybody else that there is a terrible storm at sea."

That'll Fix Him

"I'm warning you," said the exasperated piano teacher to the young boy. "If you don't behave yourself, I'll tell your parents you have talent!"

Smart Boy

Golfer: "You must be the worst caddy in the world!"

Caddy: "Oh, no sir. That would be too much of a coincidence."

Needed A Rest

"You are very run down," said the doctor to his patient. "I suggest you lay off golf for a while and get a good day in now and then at the office."

The Note Was Clear

An orchestral arranger, wanting to get together with a fellow musician, wrote him the following note: "Luncheon at the same place—key of G."

His friend was there—at one sharp.

Good Neighbors

A finance agency was having trouble collecting from a man named Jones. Finally, they wrote him: "Dear Mr. Jones: What would your neighbors think if we came to your town and repossessed your car?"

A week later they received their letter back. Scrawled on it was this message: "I took the matter up with my neighbors and they think it would be a lousy trick. Sincerely, L. Jones."

To Be Specific

A safety sign read: "School—Don't Kill a Child."
Beneath this admonition was written in a childish scrawl: "Wait for a Teacher."

Cheap

Then there was the man who appeared in a newspaper office to place an ad offering $500 for the return of his wife's pet cat.
"That's an awful price for a cat," the clerk commented.
"Not for this one," the man snapped. "I drowned it."

In The Freezer

The modern man comes home from work and greets his wife with: "Hi-ya, honey, what's thawing?"

Hard Job

The son of a Harvard professor, recently inducted into the army, sneaked off to sit behind the barracks and rest. He was discovered by a grizzled old sergeant who demanded: "What are you doin' back here?"
The guilty recruit stammered, "I'm procrastinating, sir."
The sergeant thought about this for a time and barked, "Well, O.K., just keep busy!"

That's Different

A man walking down the street on a dark night passed an alley. Two thugs jumped on him, and though he put up a terrific fight, they got him down. After they searched him, they were amazed at the small sum of money they found in his pockets. "You mean you put up that fight for sixty-seven cents?" they asked.
"Shucks, no," answered the victim, "I thought you were after the $500 in my shoe."

It Ain't There

"Folks," said the old colored minister, "the subject dis evenin' is 'Liars.' How many in the congregation has done read the 69th chapter of Matthew?"

Nearly every hand in the audience was raised.

"Dat's right," said His Reverence. "Yo' is de folks I wants to preach to. Der ain't no 69th chapter of Matthew!"

Hard To Fool 'Em

"Jack, dear," said the bride, "let us try to make the people believe we've been married a long time."

"All right, honey," came the reply, "but do you think you can carry both suitcases?"

Fragile

A little old lady handed the post office clerk a package containing a Bible.

"Anything breakable in this?" he asked.

"Nothing but the Ten Commandments," the little lady replied.

No One

"They tell me your wife is outspoken."

"By whom?"

We Met These Guys

Two cavalry rookies were each given a horse, and they wondered how to tell them apart. Joe cut the mane off his horse, but in time it grew out again. Then Tom cut the tail off his horse, but it grew back. Finally Joe said, "Why don't we measure them? Maybe one horse is larger than the other." So they did, and sure enough, the black horse was three inches taller than the white one.

Easy

Patient: "How can I ever repay you for your kindness to me?"

Doctor: "By check, money order, or cash."

He Needs Horse Sense

To the city-bred youngster animals on the farm can be confusing. Some cows grow horns, some don't, some get them early and some get dehorned—and others don't have any because they are horses.

Record-Argue, Greenville, Pa.

We Do Too

A lady was entertaining her friend's small son.

"Are you sure you can cut your meat?" she asked, after watching his struggles.

"Oh, yes," he replied. "We often have it as tough as this at home."

Extraordinary

Professor: "Didn't you have a brother in this course last year?"

Student: "No, sir; it was I. I'm taking it over."

Professor: "Extraordinary resemblance, though . . . extraordinary."

Maryland Old Line

He Knew

The policeman stopped the man going down the street clad only in a barrel. "Are you a poker player?" the voice of the law demanded.

"No, I'm not," the culprit replied, "but I just left a group of fellows who are."

Time Marches On

Be patient with the girl who walks to the front seat late for church in order to show off a new hat. In a few years she will drop into the back seat, to get out quickly if the baby cries.

Globe, Atchison, Kansas

Didn't Have Time

"Why did you fire that secretary you had?"

"She couldn't spell—kept asking me how to spell every other word when she took dictation."

"And you couldn't stand the interruptions?"

"It wasn't that. I just didn't have time to look up all those words."

Smart Boy

Neighbor: "You say your son is only four, and he can spell his name backwards? What's his name?"

Proud parent: "Otto."

Nice Come Back

Waitress: "This is your fifth cup, sir; you must like coffee!"

Diner: "I do; that's why I am willing to drink all this water to get a little of it."

A Blank

A clever young lady was asked to attend a public function. She was given a place between a noted bishop and an equally famous rabbi. It was her chance to break into high company, and she meant to make use of it.

"I feel as if I were a leaf between the Old and the New Testament," she said during a lull in the conversation.

"That page, Madam," said the rabbi, "is usually a blank."

He Had Dinner

Joey Adams tells of a fisherman who met a friend on his way home.

"Where are you going with that lobster under your arm?" the angler asked.

"I'm taking him home to dinner." Just then the lobster piped up: "I've already had my dinner; how about a movie?"

Heredity

"Dad, why did you sign my report card with an X instead of your name?"

"I don't want your teacher to think that anyone with your grades could possibly have a father who can read or write."

Correct Weight

The professor stopped at the penny scales, took off his overcoat and put it over his arm. Then he dropped a penny in the machine to get his "true weight."

Pretty Bad

Two sharpshooters hadn't seen each other in a long time.

"How's business?" asked one. "Rotten," replied the other with a sigh. "If it keeps up, my income tax report will be just about correct."

Make Him Happy?

Judge: "I think you might as well give your husband a divorce."
Wife: "What! I lived with this bum for twenty years and now I should make him happy?"

That's All

Salesman: "This model has a top speed of 120 miles per hour, and she'll stop on a dime."
Prospect: "What happens then?"
Salesman: "A little putty knife comes out and scrapes you off the windshield."   *Tappa News*

Courtesy Please

Two hoboes headed south of town and settled down on the fairways of a country club to eat their food. Along came one of the members. "Get out of here, you bums," he shouted. "This is private property! It costs hundreds of dollars to belong to this club!"

"OK, OK," said one of the bums, pulling himself up to his full height and brushing the crumbs away. "But let me warn you, this is no way to get new members."

Don't Do As I Do

Mother (trying to induce little daughter to go to bed early): "Why, even the little chickens go to bed at sundown."
Daughter: "Yes, but the old hen goes with them."

Not Me

The children were in a free-for-all when Dad entered the room. "Billie, who started this?" he asked the nearest boy.

"Well," replied Billie, "It all started when Frank hit me back."

Careful James

The despondent gentleman emerged from his club and climbed stiffly into a limousine.

"Where to, sir?" asked the chauffeur respectfully.

"Drive off a cliff, James. I'm committing suicide."

Cornell Widow

Not Too Bright

Jane Haley on the "Travelers" show:
"Mother Glowworm and Father Glowworm
"Watched Baby Glowworm fly by night.
"Said Papa Glowworm to Mama Glowworm—
" 'I fear our child is not too bright!' "

Could Be

There is not much to see in a small town, but what you hear makes
up for it.   *The Hardy Herald, Hardy, Nebraska*

Logical

Margie: "Why do you keep stamps in the medicine cabinet?"
Freddie: "Why not? I buy them at the drug store."

Reckless

A reckless driver is a fellow who passes you on the highway in
spite of all you can do.   *Lincoln Parker, Lincoln Park, Michigan*

That's Different

Overheard on the beach: "Mother, may I go for a swim?"
"Certainly not, my dear, it's far too deep."
"But Daddy is swimming."
"Yes, dear, but he's insured."

Taking Care Of It

Teacher: "Are you doing anything for your cold?"
Boy: "I sneeze when it wants me to."

Better Be Careful

Teacher: "Yes, Johnny, what is it?"
Johnny: "I don't want to scare you, but Papa said if I don't get
better grades someone is due for a licking."

He Had Experience

The woman autoist posed for a snapshot in front of the fallen
pillars of an ancient temple in Greece.

"Don't get the car in the picture," she said, "or my husband will think I ran into the place."

Smart Lad

Teacher: "Jimmy, are you eating candy or chewing gum?"
Jim: "Neither. I'm soaking a prune to eat at recess."

Might Work In Other Lines, Too

University dean: "Why do you want to be a pharmacist?"
Student: "Well, my dad is one. He works seven days a week and it's our family ambition to give him a day off."

Fair

Freshman: "How about a battle of wits?"
Senior: "Sorry, I never attack an unarmed man."

Persistence

Teacher: "Why does your father put up storm windows every Fall?"
Tommy: "Well, Mother keeps at him until he finally gives in."

Lost Every Battle

The driver of a sightseeing bus who was describing a Southern battlefield of the Civil War told of many Southern victories. Finally a Northerner in the car asked him, "Didn't the North win any battles in the Civil War?"

The Southern driver said, "No sir, Mister. They ain't won a battle and they ain't going to as long as I'm drivin' this sightseeing bus."

Ham

Ralph Bellamy tells about the cannibal chief who sent his men out after a radio actor.

"I'm just dying," he said, "for a good ham sandwich."

That's How It Was

Two men were talking about how they came to get married. "Where did you meet your wife?" asked one.

"In a travel bureau," came the reply.

"Were you going somewhere?"

"No, but she was looking for a vacation and I was the last resort."

He Should Know

"It's raining cats and dogs outside."

"I know—I just stepped into a poodle."

Generous

Neighbor boy: "That candy you're eating looks good."

Small boy: "It is good."

Neighbor boy: "It makes my mouth water."

Small boy: "To show what a good sport I am, here's a napkin."

Ain't It The Truth

Don McNeill tells about the woman who was filling out an application for credit. When she came to the space for age she hesitated a long time. Finally the clerk leaned over and said: "The longer you wait the worse it gets."

Loaded

A Father, his arms filled with groceries, got on a bus with his son, about five.

The son had the fare and dropped it in the box, then seemed to feel he should explain. "I'm paying the money," he told the driver in a voice that carried clearly through the bus. "My father is loaded."

Just Made It

George Gobel: "As the old fellow who was knitting a sweater for a camel said—'at last I'm over the hump.' "

It Certainly Does

Henry Morgan offers a household hint for helpless housewives: Use a tablespoonful of soap powder to every recipe. It won't help the flavor, but it certainly makes the dishes easier to wash.

Inferiority Complex

She: "The man I marry must be as brave as a lion, but not forward; handsome as Apollo, but not conceited; wise as Solomon, but meek as a lamb; a man who is kind to every woman, but loves only me."

He: "How lucky we met."   *Purdue Rivet*

One Definition

Marriage: That something that begins when you sink into his arms and ends with your arms in the sink.   *Purdue Rivet*

No Fooling

You may be able to make some people think you are younger than you are, but you can't fool a hamburger, just before bedtime.

How About It, Dad?

Someone the other day was telling me about a youngster who asked his mother this question: "If the *Lord* gives us our daily bread and *Santa Claus* brings the Christmas presents and the *stork* brings the babies, then what's the use of having Daddy around?"

Or Woman?

The rocking chair was invented for the man who doesn't need to work, can't sit still and likes to make a noise.

Sounds Like Propaganda

While the young suitor was waiting for his girl, the latter's little sister sidled into the room.

"Did you know my sister's got three other boy friends?" she asked coyly.

"Really," he said in surprise. "I haven't seen any of them."

"Neither have I," said the little one, "but she gave me a quarter to tell you."   *Louisville Courier*

Humor At Harvard

A famous physician named Bungi
Had a knife-sharp and venomous tongue. He
Refused all nutrition
With this admonition:
I fear there are fungi among ye.

Indubitably

Ralph Paul says: "Procrastination is the thief of time—and so is every other big word."

Confused

The professor had his hat on backwards. A student told him about it.

"Are you certain?" asked the professor. "How do you know whether I'm going or coming?"

What Time You Got?

A passenger on a fast train hailed the porter with "What time do we get to New York, George?" The porter replied thoughtfully, "We is due in New York at 1:15, unless you has set your watch by Eastern time, which would make it 2:15, an' then if you is goin' by daylight savin' time, it would be 3:15, unless we is an hour an' fifteen minutes late, which we is. What time you got?"

They Were Leading

What a day, I lost my job, I lost my bill fold, my wife ran away with the electric light man, the Yanks lost to the Senators. It's unbelievable, leading by three in the eighth and they lost to the Senators.

Perfect

Fan: "How about your team? Are they good losers?"
Coach: "Good? Heck, they're perfect."

What's In A Name?

Before I married Maggie dear I was her pumpkin pie, her precious peach, her honey lamb, the apple of her eye. But after years of married life this thought I pause to utter; those fancy names are gone, and now I'm just her bread and butter.

Good Reason

"How does it happen that you are five minutes late at school this morning?" the teacher asked severely.

"Please, ma'am, I must have overwashed myself."

Why Hurry?

Recently I asked a Georgia friend why Southerners were always so slow and deliberate.

"I asked my great-grandfather that same question once," he replied, "and I'll never forget his answer: 'Son, it just doesn't pay to be in a hurry. You always pass up much more than you catch up with.' "

He Who Works

He who works with his hands is a laborer.

He who works with his hands and head is a craftsman.

He who works with his hands and head and heart is an artist.

He who works with his hands and head and heart and feet is a salesman.   *Sunshine Magazine*

Water

Asked to write an essay on water, little Tommy, after chewing his pencil for a long time, wrote: "Water is a colorless liquid that turns dark when you wash in it."   *Sunshine Magazine*

A Long One

A Virginia kennel with dachshund puppies for sale advertises, "Get along little doggie."   *Sunshine Magazine*

We Saw This Show

Mort Lawrence says television is a device that lets folks who haven't a thing to do watch people who can't do a thing.

Lawrence also insists that many TV shows keep you wondering— wondering what's at the movies.

Not A Bad Idea

All that keeps some people from having a home of their own is a popular teen-age daughter.

The Cat

The following essay on cats was turned in by a grade school pupil:

"Cats and people are funny animals. Cats have four paws but only one maw. People have forefathers and only one mother.

"When a cat smells a rat he gets excited—so do people.

"Cats carry tails, and a lot of people carry tales, too.

"All cats have fur coats. Some people have fur coats, and the ones who don't have fur coats say catty things about the ones who have them."

Point of View

Casey and Murphy were admiring a large building.

"It's surprisin'," said Casey, with a knowing air, "how mortar binds all those hundreds of bricks together."

Murphy gave his companion a supercilious sneer.

"Whinever are ye goin' to learn a bit of sense, Casey," he replied.

"Sure and whatever d'ye mean?" queried Casey.

"Bricks aren't kept together by mortar," Murphy explained. "Mortar keeps them apart."

No Trespassing

An irate landowner came in the other day to have a sign printed for posting on his property. It was all we could do to talk him out of wording it like this: "No Hunting or Fishing. Survivors Will Be Prosecuted."

Proper Credit

Bishop Fulton J. Sheen was on the air receiving a special award for the excellence of his program. In acknowledging it, he stated that he thought writers often deserved credit for TV programs but rarely got it. So he gave credit to—Matthew, Mark, Luke, and John.

Impartial

The only persons who will gladly listen to both sides of an argument are the neighbors on the party line.

Pretty Bad

Ernie Simon says: "Some political speeches are so bad they actually sound like the candidate had written them himself."

Daylight Saving

Daylight-saving time started with an old Indian, out in Arizona. He cut a foot off one end of the blanket and sewed it onto the other end—to make it longer.

Correct

Teacher: "How old would a person be who was born in 1899?"
Billie: "Man or woman?"

Only 39 Cents

"See this jewelry?" said the sorority pledge. "It once belonged to a millionaire."

"Gosh," gasped an impressed sister, "what was his name?"

"Woolworth," the pledge replied.

5

SHORT VERSES

Is There a Doctor Syntax in the House?

If for a single noun the verb be plural,
Forgive the man,—he's unrefined and rural;
And if his writing show a variant tense,
Just pass it as a lack of bookish sense;
Excuse mixed metaphors and scrambled cases,
Such errors oft are writ in learned places.
But, don't forgive the man with brain diminutive,
Who, cold and cruel, splits a poor infinitive!

William A. Philpott, Jr.

If Mother Could Only See Us Now

In the year 1488, a little old lady penned a prophetic poem which has since become known as Mother Shipton's Prophecy. Her clairvoyance proved to be extremely remarkable with phenomenal accuracy on every count but the last. If mother could only see us now . . .

Carriages without horses shall go
And accidents fill the world with woe.
Around the earth thoughts shall fly
In the twinkling of an eye.
Under water men shall walk,
Shall ride, shall sleep, shall talk.
In the air men shall be seen,
In white, in black, in green.
Iron in water shall float
As easily as a wooden boat.
The world to an end shall come
In 1881.

The Southern Banker

Terse Verse

Mary had a little lamb,
'twas awful dumb it's true.
It followed her in a traffic jam
And now it's mutton stew.

Wilton (Wisconsin) Star Herald News

Loss and Gain

Old Bill had all the sense there is,
He gained (and kept) great wealth;
The advantageous breaks were his—
They called him Mister Super Whiz—
Alas, he lost his health!

William A. Philpott, Jr.

Calling All Gardeners

Here's some advice it'll pay you to heed ...
Don't plant more than
Your wife can weed.

National News

He Listened

His thoughts were slow, his words were few,
And never formed to glisten,

But he was joy to all the clan—
You should have heard him listen!
Sunshine Magazine

'Tis Midnight

'Tis midnight; and the setting sun
Is slowly rising in the west;
The rapid rivers slowly run,
The frog is on his downy nest,
The pensive goat and sportive cow,
Hilarious, leap from bough to bough.
Anonymous

To Fathers Who Do Not Own the Book of Knowledge

"The wind goes where? How come snow's white?
"What makes the sky so high?
"Why is it dark without a light?
"Please tell me, daddy, why?"
"I'm busy, can't you see—now run
"And bother me no further—
"Your questions are quite silly, son—
"Why don't you ask your mother?"
William A. Philpott, Jr.

The Fool and the Poet

Sir, I admit your general rule,
That every poet is a fool,
But you yourself may serve to show it,
That every fool is not a poet.
Alexander Pope

As To the Weather

I remember, I remember,
Ere my childhood flitted by,
It was cold then in December,
And was warmer in July.
In the winter there were freezings—
In the summer there were thaws;

But the weather isn't now at all
Like what it used to was!

Anonymous

Be Careful

I'm careful of the words I say,
To keep them soft and sweet,
I never know from day to day
Which ones I'll have to eat.

Seydell Quarterly

Money

They call it legal tender,
That green and lovely stuff—
It's tender when you have it.
But when you don't it's tough!

Orlando Sentinel

Shortest Poems

While lecturing, Strickland W. Gillilan quoted his poem

Adam
Had 'em

as the shortest ever written. Yet Elmer E. Keeler, a Pennsylvania
country schoolmaster, thereupon wrote

Little Lambs
They
Play
Preachers
They
Pray
Industrious Hens
They
Lay
Greatest Day in Year
Pay
Day

Ye Occasional Idler, by John J. Corell

Baby on Vacation

And you don't need to tell me,
That he will always sneeze
When loaded with a mouthful
Of cereal or peas.

The Mo-Hawker

Drive a Tractor

When it's ninety in the shade
Drive a tractor
When a seed bed must be made
Drive a tractor
For its hamestrings never burst
And when dogdays are the worst
It will hardly have a thirst
Drive a tractor
When the ground is hard and dry
Drive a tractor
It will plow when horses die
Drive a tractor
Laughs at hornets, flies, and bees,
Never known to have disease
Saves you veterinary fees
Drive a tractor.

Caterpillar News and Views

How's Tricks—and Trade

When a man's chief concern
Is in making the grade,
He starts out to learn
All the tricks of his trade;
But he's soon in a fix,
Though he head the parade—
While learning the tricks
He neglected the trade!

William A. Philpott, Jr.

On a Hill

A safety jingle from Jimmy Nelson's radio Highway Frolics:
There was once a fellow named Bill
Who just loved to pass on a hill—
Till he met with another—
A smash—and, O, brother!
Now his lawyer is checking his will.

Happy Old Santa

I'm a happy old boy, dressed in red,
Who just comes when you're tucked into bed.
So don't make a sound,
For I'll soon be around
With my reindeer, and gifts in my sled.
Western Union Santagram

Patient's Dilemma

The doc says I'm as sound as a dollar
And I know he's wise in his ways,
But this is the thing that disturbs me,
How sound is a dollar these days?
Uncle Mat in Bagology

The Frog

What a wonderful bird the frog are—
When he stand he sit almost;
When he hop, he fly almost.
He ain't got no sense hardly;
He ain't got no tail hardly either.
When he sit, he sit on what he ain't got almost.
Anonymous

A Is an Apple

A is an apple, sour and green,
Working in Tommy but cannot be seen.
Anonymous

On the Democracy of Yale

Here's to the town of New Haven,
The Home of the Truth and the Light,
Where God talks to Jones in the very same tones
That he uses with Hadley and Dwight.

Frederick Scheetz Jones

On the Aristocracy of Harvard

And this is good old Boston,
The Home of the bean and the cod,
Where the Lowells talk only to Cabots
And the Cabots talk only to God.

John Collins Bossidy

The Humorist

He must not laugh at his own wheeze:
A snuff box has no right to sneeze.

Keith Preston

As I Was Laying on the Green

As I was laying on the green,
A small English book I seen.
Carlyle's *Essay on Burns* was the edition,
So I left it laying in the same position.

Anonymous

Pater Patter

Ah! life is sweet with naught to bother
If there be those to call one father;
And then a man is always glad
To have a youngster dub him Dad;
His heart will glow and never stop
When his fine lad refers to Pop—
. . . . .
He irks us as none other can
Who calls his father "my old man!"

William A. Philpott, Jr.

Risk

A certain young gourmet of credition
Took some pâté de foie gras and spread it on
  A chocolate biscuit,
  Then murmured, "I'll risk it."
His tomb bears the date that he said it on.

Rev. Charles Inge

Waiter, Please

An epicure, dining at Crewe,
Found quite a large mouse in his stew.
  Said the waiter, "Don't shout,
  And wave it about,
Or the rest will be wanting one, too!"

Anonymous

Perfume

The bottle of perfume that Willie sent
Was highly displeasing to Millicent;
  Her thanks were so cold
  They quarrelled, I'm told,
Through that silly scent Willie sent Millicent.

Anonymous

Sounds Silly, Sisister

There was a young lady of Woosester
Who usest to crow like a roosester;
  She usest to climb
  Two trees at a time,
But her sisester usest to boosest her.

Anonymous

An Economist

John Stuart Mill,
By a mighty effort of will,
Overcame his natural bonhomie
And wrote "Principles of Political Economy.

Edmund Clerihew Bentley

Woman

Two things make woman slow, we find,
In going any place;
For first she must make up her mind
And then her face.

Keith Preston

Music

A squeak's heard in the orchestra
As the leader draws across
The intestines of the agile cat
The tail of the noble hoss.

George T. Lanigan

Fresh Air

I'm glad the sky is painted blue;
And the earth is painted green;
And such a lot of nice fresh air
All sandwiched in between.

Anonymous

The Arch Villain

List all the ills that you can mention,
There's nothing as hyper as hypertension!
Take cancer, ulcers, various tumors;
There's chicken pox, fermented humors;
T.B. and asthma, flux, pneumonie—
A thousand pains both real and phony—
Name all the ills on which Docs tinker—
Old hypertension is the stinker!
There's nothing as deadly that you can mention,
  There's nothing as hyper—
  As much like a viper—
There's nothing as hyper as hypertension!

William A. Philpott, Jr.

I Do Not Love Thee, Doctor Fell

I do not love thee, Doctor Fell,
The reason why I cannot tell;
But this alone I know full well,
I do not love thee, Doctor Fell.

Thomas Brown

Probably

I am the captain of my soul;
I rule it with stern joy;
And yet I think I had more fun,
When I was cabin boy.

Keith Preston

How Are You?

Don't tell your friends about your indigestion:
"How are you!" is a greeting, not a question.

Arthur Guiterman

Traffic

The manner of her death was thus:
She was druv over by a Bus.

Anonymous

Straight From the Horse's Mouth

A teen-age lass adds to her lure
(She thinks) with pony-tail coiffure;
An older gal ties up her knot
In manner of a Hottentot.
The mode we really can't endorse—
It looks much better on a horse!

William A. Philpott, Jr.

Epitaph on His Wife

Here lies my wife: here let her lie!
Now she's at rest—and so am I.

John Dryden

Soap

You may live without faith,
You may live without hope;
But civilized man cannot
Live without soap.

Saintsbury

Good Reason, Too!

She was peeved and called him Mr.
Not because he went and Kr.
But the thing that made her sore
Was that on the night before
This same Mr. Kr. Sr.

Armstrong Trap

Time to Rise

A birdie with a yellow bill
Hopped upon the window sill,
Cocked his shining eye and said:
"Ain't you 'shamed, you sleepy-head?"

R. L. Stevenson

Baby

Baby said
When she smelt the rose,
"Oh! what a pity
I've only one nose!"

Laura E. Richards

Silver Lining

Every cloud
Has its silver
Lining but it is
Sometimes a little
Difficult to get it to
the mint.

Don Marquis

The Time Has Come

"The time has come," the Walrus said,
"To talk of many things:
Of shoes—and ships—and sealing wax—
Of cabbages—and kings—
And why the sea is boiling hot—
And whether pigs have wings."

Lewis Carroll

Weather

It hain't no use to grumble and complain,
It's jest as easy to rejoice;
When God sorts out the weather and sends rain,
Why rain's my choice.

J. W. Riley

Work

And only the Master shall praise us, and only the Master shall blame;
And no one shall work for money, and no one shall work for fame;
But each for the joy of working, and each, in his separate star,
Shall draw the Thing as he sees It, for the God of Things as
    They Are!

Kipling

Window

The window has four little panes;
But one have I—
The window panes are in its sash;
I wonder why!

Gelett Burgess

Sight

My sense of sight is very keen,
My sense of hearing weak.
One time I saw a mountain pass,
But could not hear its peak.

Oliver Herford

June

How softly runs the afternoon
Beneath the billowy clouds of June!
Tom Treanor

Embarrassment

He scratch'd his ear, the infallible resource
To which embarrass'd people have recourse.
Lord Byron

Condemnation

Let me consign to utter ruin
The lads who ask me "How'm I doin'?"
Anonymous

Cotton

Behold the pretty cotton plant
With blossom white and full!
They pick the down stuff and, lo!
They make us suits of wool!
Anonymous

Nothing Right

We men have many faults;
Poor women have but two;
There's nothing good they say,
And nothing right they do.
Anonymous

Public Speaking

Begin low, speak slow;
Take fire, rise higher;
When most impressed
Be self-possessed;
At the end wax warm,
And sit down in a storm.
Rev. Dr. Leifchild

True or New

Some things that you have said are true,
And some things you have said are new;
But what are true, alas! they are not new,
And what are new, they are, alas! not true.
*Said to be founded on a criticism
of Voltaire by Lessing*

Not Enough

Heavenly Father, bless us,
And keep us all alive;
There's ten of us to dinner
And not enough for five.
Anonymous

A Wise Bird

A wise old owl lived in an oak;
The more he saw the less he spoke;
The less he spoke the more he heard:
Why can't we all be like that bird?
Punch

For the Album

This space is mine
Wherein to write;
Remember me
When out of sight.
All I ask is one small spot
In which to write, "Forget me not."
Remember me when this you see
And think of one who thinks of thee.

Only a Little More

A little more kindness, a little less creed;
A little more giving, a little less greed;
A little more smile, a little less frown;
A little less kicking a man when he's down;

A little more "we", a little less "I";
A little more laugh, a little less cry;
A little more flowers on the pathway of life;
And fewer on graves at the end of the strife.

The Choice

The man who on his trade relies
Must either bust or advertise.

Anonymous

Fame

Of all the cocks that greeted dawn today
How many will be heard a year from now?
How many preen their feathers on the heap,
How many strut the yard? How many crow?

Monk Gibbon

This World

This world that we're a-livin' in
Is mighty hard to beat;
You git a thorn with every rose,
But ain't the roses sweet!

Frank L. Stanton

6

UNUSUAL STORIES AND UNUSUAL SELECTIONS

Doctor

I remember when I grew up in the little town of Woodville, just north of Beaumont in the pine woods of eastern Texas, when we needed a doctor for a member of the family, we called Dr. So-and-So. If a cow was sick or one of the horses or even a pig, we usually called the same doctor.

But now when you go to see your family physician, you probably will wind up having a specialist recommended to you. A friend of mine did that, in this changing world, a few days ago, and the specialist recommended was a skin specialist. And he went over to the specialist who said, "Let me see your hands."

And he looked at them and said, "Yes, yes, yes, I see. Have you ever had that before?"

And the man said, "Yes."

And the specialist said, "Well, you've got it again."

Allan Shivers,
Governor of Texas

Good Neighbors

As for us, we know all about you, because we live under your friendly, if at times, overwhelming, shadow. Because of this, and because of our close and our intimate relationship, Canadians watch with a very special interest everything that you do, with a mixture of admiration, anxiety and awe, but always, I hope, with friendly understanding.

This intense preoccupation on our part with your policies and your practices is perfectly natural, because we know that there is no way by which we can escape their consequences, political or economical, and if at times we may seem to be a little critical or worried, our reactions are the same as yours would be if the situation were reversed. But if we may, at times, seem to be anxious about your policies and even of your power, I can assure you that we would worry far more if you didn't have that power, or if your policies were concerned solely with continental matters.

I wonder if I can put it this way without being misunderstood: Our relationship is, in a sense, that of a happily married man to his wife. He finds her possibly, at times, a little difficult to live with, but he knows it would be impossible to live without her.

Lester B. Pearson,
Canadian Secretary of State for External Affairs,
discusses United States-Canadian relations

Words

I wonder if you heard the story I told the other day about the two fellows at three o'clock in the morning, talking about the use of words and how people get them balled up.

One of them said, "Let me show you the difference between three similar words—irritation, aggravation, and frustration. You watch me."

So he went over to the phone booth and put a dime in it. First he picked a number at random out of the book, just any number. Then he dialed that number, and a sleepy voice answered, "Hello?"

He said, "Is Winterbottom there?"

The fellow at the other end said, "What number do you want?"

He said, "Superior 1-2345."

"No, you have the wrong number. There's nobody here by that

name. Now, do you mind letting me get back to sleep?" And he hung up.

The guy said, "See? That's irritation. That's what you call irritation."

Twenty minutes later he went back to the phone and dialed the same number. This other guy answered the phone and said, "Hello!"

"Is Winterbottom there?"

The fellow said, "Look, I told you there isn't anyone by that name here at this number. Now, go to sleep, and let me go to sleep, you dumb jerk." And the guy hung up.

He said to his friend, "That's aggravation."

Then about a half hour later he dialed the same number again. This time the fellow answered the phone and said, "HELLO!"

The guy said, "This is Winterbottom. Have there been any calls for me?" That's real frustration.   *Arthur Godfrey*

Money is Not the Kernel

We all know that money is a relative matter. Do you recall what Ibsen said about money? "Money may be the husk of many things, but not the kernel. It brings you food, but not appetite; medicine, but not health; acquaintances, but not friends; servants, but not loyalty; days of joy, but not peace or happiness."   *Lionel Crocker,*
Professor of Speech, Denison University

Traffic Light

I wonder if you heard about Pat and Mike, who just came over from the Auld Sod? They were stopping at a street corner in New York when the traffic light was red; then it changed to orange and then it turned green. First it was red, then it turned very briefly to orange, and then it turned green. Pat looked at Mike and said, "Faith, you know, they don't allow much time for the Protestants here, do they?"   *Arthur Godfrey*

Wisdom of This Kind

There are certain things that we can accomplish by law and there are certain things that we cannot accomplish by law or by any process of government. We cannot legislate intelligence. We cannot legislate morality. No, and we cannot legislate loyalty, for loyalty is a kind of morality. We cannot produce these things by decrees or commissions or public inquisitions. The proverbs teach us that

"When wisdom entereth into thine heart, and knowledge is pleasant unto thy soul,

Discretion shall preserve thee, understanding shall keep thee:

To deliver thee from the way of the evil man . . ."

Wisdom of this kind is born in man. It is awakened in him by the fear of God. It is cultivated in him and through him put to the uses of society by true religion and liberal education. What was John Adams' charge to the government of Massachusetts? It was not that the government should take it upon itself to organize and manage this process but that the government should respect and give all possible support and encouragement to the schools and colleges and churches whose proper function that was.   *A. Whitney Griswold*
President, Yale University

The Good Life

What, after all, is the object of political society? Its end and purpose says Aristotle, "is the good life, and the institutions of social life are means to that end." He defines that good life as "a life of true felicity and goodness"; and he goes on to say, "It is therefore for the sake of good actions, and not for the sake of social life, that political associations must be considered to exist."   *A. Whitney Griswold,*
President, Yale University

The Greatness of Our Time

Some of us don't know it yet, but this is a great time to be alive. It is the greatest time humanity has ever experienced. First of all we must get the contagion of the greatness of our time. Cynicism and confusion are as out of place today as they were in the great time of the Renaissance. They are signs of weakness. This is no time to be weak. As in the Renaissance, mankind is embarking today on a new and fantastic adventure—its third great venture: the moral unification of the world.

It took the whole of history so far to unify the world in body and mind—now we must unify it in spirit. To be exact, counting history from the beginnings of Egypt about 4000 years before Christ, it took fifty-five hundred years to unify the world in body, and five hundred years to unify her in mind. If the ratio keeps on in the same proportion it will take forty-five years to unify the world in spirit and bring-about peace—just about one generation, yours and mine. By 1990 we should have peace and many of us will see the day.

Two consecutive ventures integrated the world's body and mind. Before Columbus the body of the world did not exist for mankind. There were at least three worlds, mutually unknown to one another, and even undreamed of: The European, the Asiatic, the American. Each of these worlds had its empires and beliefs, and there was less conscious intercommunications between all three than there is today between the planet Mars and this earth. Mars is an object of continuous observation and interpretation; America was not even imagined. Columbus, venturing into the dark unknown of the ocean, fearing to be blown off the terrestrial disk with every new blast of wind, triumphantly proved the roundness and wholeness of the earth. Though he did not reach the Indies he opened the gates through which later Magellan, Drake and other circumnavigators could safely travel.

When the earth was known man turned toward his second great task. This time he did not venture into new realms of the earth but new regions of the universe. He plied the dark ocean of space, not with ships that carried his body, but with telescopes and spectro-scopes that carried his sight. He advanced into the unknown land of electronics, of chemistry, of molecular and nuclear physics. His scientific discoveries contracted and integrated the physical body of the earth. Today the world is one. It is as big as ever, but small in comparison with man. Man's body and mind have outgrown the earth. He is virtually omnipresent; his voice can be heard—and soon his picture seen—at one and the same moment all over the globe. His mind can communicate with every other mind on earth in a flash. His body can move around the globe in less time than it used to take to traverse a large city. Man's body and mind span the earth.

But man is more than body and mind. The two great ventures of the past were not enough. Now a third great venture has to be undertaken. Now the soul of man has to span the world.

Man integrated the body of the world, in the geographical revolution of Columbus. He integrated the mind of the world, in the scientific revolution from Copernicus to Einstein. He must now integrate the con-science of the world. This is the moral Revolution

of our time. Instead of delving into and ordering the chaos of material nature man must now delve into and order the chaos of his own nature.   *Robert S. Hartman,*
Department of Philosophy,
The Ohio State University,
Columbus, Ohio

The Significance of the Commonplace

The relating of the ordinary to the ordinary creates the significant and makes life beautiful and worth living. A young man and his bride from New York on a trip south stopped at a typical Kentucky creek-bottom road, one of those roads that follows the creek bottom and at points leaves the creek bed for drier land and after the bad spot has been passed, returns again to the creek bottom. Walking up the road for a short distance they came to a cabin on the side of the hill. Sitting on the front stoop was a native of the region. Feeling a bit superior to the native, the young man said, "Stranger, isn't it a bit lonely back here in this God forsaken country?" Immediately the man answered, "Lonely, my son? No, not lonely. When I look to yon hills from whence cometh my strength, I understand the poet who said, 'only God can make a tree.' When I look into the green valley, I know each blade of grass holds the secret of life. When I look into the heavens, blue of the blue, I see the clouds etch in white the outline of the eternal city. When I hear the babbling brook, voices speak to my soul. And then I feel the head of my dog on my knee and see in his eyes loyalty, confidence and faith. And suddenly I seem to see, as of yesterday, my children coming up the path, dirty, dishevelled but with a smile on their lips and shouting the old familiar greeting of Hi, Pop! And then I feel two hands on my shoulders, the hands of my faithful wife, the hands that have sustained me in my hours of trouble and difficulties. And then I know that God is good. Lonely, my son? No, not lonely."   *Charles L. Ansbach,*
President, Central Michigan
College of Education

How Well Informed Are You?

The average citizen devotes not more than four minutes a day to reading news of national and international affairs, Dr. George H.

Gallup said recently in an address at the State University of Iowa. . . .

In a survey of U. S. daily newspaper readers made for the International Press Institute in the spring of 1953, Gallup found that 40 per cent of those questioned could not name Malenkov as Stalin's successor. Fifty-six per cent could not identify Syngman Rhee, and 49 per cent could not name Chiang Kai-Shek as leader of the Chinese nationalists. Seventy-nine per cent did not know the meaning of NATO, 54 per cent said they were not familiar with any of the work of the United Nations, and 47 per cent could not identify John Foster Dulles.   *Prof. Leslie G. Moeller,*
Director of the School of Journalism,
State University of Iowa

What Do You Read?

Entertainment features have such a strong pull that it is not by accident that U. S. dailies run tremendous quantities of comic strips. And make no mistake about it; reading of comic strips is *not* confined to youngsters. Readership studies show consistently that in a given issue at least one comic strip, and usually several, will have better readership than the most important story on page one.

The amount of time devoted to the comics, to the sports page, to the society page, to local news, and to other service and entertainment items, is, in general, at least ten times as great as that given to national and international news.   *Prof. Leslie G. Moeller,*
Director of the School of Journalism,
State University of Iowa

Benjamin Franklin

Aside from human liberty, Benjamin Franklin's great design of American life or his ideology, as we would call it nowadays, had its central idea in frugality, thrift and hard work. He conducted a propaganda campaign on that subject for over sixty years. His slogans sunk so deep into the American mind that we practiced at it for quite a while. However, that was before we discovered the theory of spending ourselves into prosperity.

Franklin had definite ideas on the conduct of governments. His opinion of governmental borrowing and debts appear in his abundant command of the language. To him they were the road of sorrow and in general the destroyers of liberty. He knew none of the joys provided by Lord Maynard Keynes.   *Herbert Hoover*

The Whole World Was Hanging On

In considering the place of the Suez Canal in world affairs, I think of the little girl who was struggling to uproot a large weed. When she finally succeeded, her father patted her on the head and said, "My, that was hard, wasn't it?" "Yes," she replied, "and the trouble was, the whole world was hanging onto the other end!"

John S. Badeau,
New York City, President Near East Foundation,
Formerly President, The American University at Cairo

Growing Up

We should have grown up far enough to have learned the difference between liberty and license. The very possession of liberty imposes a necessity for discipline, which respects the liberty of others, in their person, in their property and in their intellectual attainment.

I hope we will some day grow sufficiently mature to know that possession of material superiority is in no way associated with cultural superiority. We will never gain the friendship or understanding of the uncounted millions of free Asia until we recognize in our hearts and in our minds that their ancient culture is as richly entitled to our respect as we believe our culture and achievements to be entitled to theirs. I hope we will indeed learn that we cannot make the world over into our image. This is a lesson we must learn before we try it once too often, disastrously.   *Thomas A. Dewey*

Freedom

Educators quite properly are concerned with preserving academic freedom, and deplore the fact that laymen are too often indifferent or misinformed on the subject. Businessmen quite as properly are concerned with preserving freedom of enterprise, and certainly deplore the ignorance and apathy on this subject in other circles. Are the two areas so different? I do not think so. Both certainly are based on the same premise. Through free competition in business we

achieve material progress. Through the free competition of ideas we arrive at truth.   *Robert E. Wilson,*
Chairman of the Board, Standard Oil Co.
(Indiana), from an address before the Associated
Colleges of Indiana Dinner, Indianapolis

Living Life Richly

It is a truism that we are living in a world in which we have tremendously increased our information without having appreciably increased our wisdom. We are living in a world in which we have fantastically multiplied our riches without having fully learned to use those riches wisely. We have developed our natural resources without having developed correspondingly greater resources of the spirit.   *Robert E. Wilson*

Education

It is my belief that stressing ethical concepts should be a basic part of education. It is one of the glories of the Christian college that, while open to all faiths and tolerant of all beliefs, it has throughout its history emphasized the relationship of man to his Maker and the final accounting that each individual must render for his actions. Such emphasis, it seems to me, recognizes a fundamental educational truth: that culture in its highest sense is moral as well as intellectual and esthetic.   *Robert E. Wilson*

How This Republic Was Founded

Nothing is more important, more contributive to the American achievement, than the spiritual foundation on which the republic is based. Men "are endowed by their Creator," wrote the founders, "with certain inalienable Rights . . . Life, Liberty and the pursuit of Happiness." The men who wrote these words were the greatest political scientists of their and perhaps of any time. They read and understood the political thinkers of the 18th century: they transcended them all. And their republic was founded on a recognition of man's debt to God. It was spiritually buttressed.
Erwin D. Canham,
Editor, Christian Science Monitor

The Importance of Europe

Europe is important for many reasons. It is strategically located and it has industrial power. But above all, Europe is important because of its people. They possess to a unique degree the qualities which ennoble a civilization which bears the deep imprint of Christianity.

What are those qualities? In individuals they are minds trained to reason clearly and serenely; vision to see far and truly; hearts which comprehend the Fathership of God and the fellowship of man, and finally capacity to act rather than to be merely contemplative.

John Foster Dulles,
United States Secretary of State

Education

The men who framed the Constitution would not today be called a highly educated group, by academic standards. There was not a professor of government among them. Benjamin Franklin had only three years of formal schooling. George Washington was tutored in Latin until he was fourteen and later taught himself mathematics. James Madison was one of the few college graduates there. I daresay that most of the men who drafted the Constitution could not have met the entrance requirements for college.

Still, despite their lack of formal education, the men who met in Philadelphia in 1787 were well-educated in the true meaning of the term. First, and most important, they knew how to think.

Second, although they lacked access to the well-stocked libraries so common today, they were well-read in the classics, and had learned how to blend living experience with the lessons of history. They had also studied those pioneering works of political philosophy which appeared in the 18th Century. From Montesquieu's "Spirit of the Laws," for example, they drew the concept of separating the executive, legislative and judicial powers, fitting it into the American experience in a novel way.

The fathers of our country were well-educated in still another sense—they were deeply imbued with moral values. Their minds drew a clear distinction between good and evil, between principle

and expediency. They were not uncertain of the values they believed in and were determined to uphold.   *Bernard M. Baruch,*
Statesman

Competition

Let us take a look at capitalism as it works in the United States and see where it differs from capitalism abroad.

Competition has kept our producers on their toes to the delight of the buying public. Most of them realize the futility of conspiring among themselves. They do not try to crush or freeze out their rivals. Instead they seek to out-do each other in technical advances, and in advertising, merchandising, repair and replacement. American entrepreneurs plow an ever mounting percentage of their profits back into their business to improve their products, for they know that the consumer is the final judge. In our economy the slogan: "The Customer Is Always Right," has rich and real meaning.

I am not implying that American businessmen are so lofty that they welcomed competition from the outset. Who ever does? Yet, faced with rivalry, our entrepreneurs have made the most of it. Indeed, they have improved because of it to a point where American management, production and salesmanship have few, if any, equals anywhere.

Now why should Americans enjoy virtually unchallenged industrial and commercial leadership in the modern world? Our country was not the mother of the Industrial Revolution. That honor belongs to Great Britain. We cannot lay undisputed claim to superior craftsmanship, nor do we have a monopoly on managerial brains.

The fundamental answer, it seems to me, is that our economy is sparked by competition and we thrive on expanding markets. In most other societies, the economy is restricted, production is rigged, prices are fixed and the markets are captive.

When consumer demand falls off in the United States, our producers make strenuous efforts to gain new customers and to hold old ones by cutting prices and by making products more attractive.

In other lands, the general practise is to match falling markets with curtailed production and maintained prices. Without competition there is a premium on scarcity. With it, the accent is on growing markets.

In the light of this important difference between capitalism as

Americans know it and capitalism as it is practised abroad, is it surprising to learn that American manufacturers, to keep up with their rivals, feel compelled to replace plant machinery on the average of once every four and a half years, while in France, for example, industrial equipment has a normal operating life of something like seventeen and a half years?

In our country enlightened managers and forthright labor leaders have also played key roles in establishing the kind of buyers' economy we have today.

The pressure of rising wages has forced producers to expand their markets. As profits decreased on each unit through rising costs, the entrepreneur increased the volume of his sales to assure his undertaking of adequate returns.

Moreover, higher wages have also meant increased mass purchasing power—one very practical way of expanding markets. For a mass production society, it means mass consumption—without which such an economy could not flourish.

From an Address by Eric Johnston,
President, Motion Picture Association of America

We Can Build a House, But a Home Must Grow

The traditional fountain on which the individual drew for wisdom and character was the home—the centre and inspiration of every Christian community. The modern trend is to take the training of the citizen out of the home and make it a public responsibility. Much, of course, can be done by collective action by the State—but by no means all. We can build a house, but a religion and morality are founded in parental love and care. All home life is not good, but beyond question the good home is a sure foundation for the good society.

The Earl of Home,
Minister of State for Scotland

Advice

I kind of like the advice of the old fellow in Kansas who was asked by reporters how he lived to be a hundred. He said, "Just keep breathing, keep breathing."   *Arthur Godfrey*

The Secret of America's Greatness

This sovereign faith of ours in the freedom and dignity of the individual is infinitely more than a dry and lifeless philosophic doctrine. It is the nerve and the fiber of our very laws. This supreme ideal—not merely the votes of so many Congressmen or Senators—is what sends aid to drought-stricken areas, guarantees a decent income to the farmers, banishes needless restrictions on individual enterprise, guards the free union of workers, extends the protection of social insurance to the aged and the needy.

This sovereign ideal we believe to be the very source of the greatness and the genius of America.

In this, we proclaim nothing very new. It was seen clearly by a wise French visitor who came to America considerably more than a century ago. He patiently sought the greatness and genius of America in our fields and in our forests, in our mines and in our commerce, in our Congress and in our Constitution, and he found them not. But he sought further and then he said:

"Not until I went into the churches of America and heard her pulpits flame with righteousness did I understand the secret of her genius and power.

"America is great because America is good—and if America ever ceases to be good—America will cease to be great."

I have read those words to such an audience as this once before. It was here in Boston. The utter truth they held for me then, they hold today.   *From an address by Dwight D. Eisenhower,*
President of the United States, in Boston

The Garden of Eden

After the Fall in the Garden of Eden, Adam was out walking with his two boys, Cain and Abel. They passed by the wrecked ruins of the once beautiful Garden of Paradise, and Adam pulled the two boys to him and looked in and said, "Boys, that's where your mother ate us out of house and home." We almost ate the Hilton Hotel out of house and home today.   *Bishop Fulton J. Sheen,*
speaking at a luncheon at the
Conrad Hilton Hotel, Chicago

He Looked Him Up and Down

You might be interested in how our employees speak their minds. I would like to tell you a little personal story.

I remember very well a visit to our sales branch in Philadelphia. I barged in the place when all the salesmen were out selling goods (I hoped), and I couldn't find anybody to talk to there. I wandered into the warehouse, and met one of our employees, a large Negro who was about twice my size. I introduced myself to him, and he broke out into a great big grin and said, "I thought I knew you. I saw your picture in the paper this morning." He looked me up and down and said, "Well, Mr. Humphreys, you ain't as big a man as I thought you was."   *From an address by H. E. Humphreys, Jr.,*
Chairman of the U. S. Rubber Company

Two Great Tasks

It is inherently true in all the material affairs of life that an individual faces two great tasks: First, to acquire something or accomplish something; and second, to try to keep it. And that's the obligation upon America today. Can we keep this nation of ours? Can we retain free enterprise? Can we offset and resist the rising, threatening tide of World Communism? Can we resist the tendency in a Republic such as our own, to adopt the devices of the more absolute forms of government, seeking to justify ourselves in so doing that we are saving the basic concepts of the Republic? That's the job that we face today.   *John L. Lewis*

Weak Boom

A businessman was asked several years ago how the recession had affected his business. He answered, "We have no recession in my business, but I will admit we are having the worst boom in many, many years."   *Edward T. McCormick,*
President, American Stock Exchange

Popular Phrases

According to a recent survey, the six sweetest phrases in the English language are: *I love you, Dinner is served, All is forgiven, Sleep 'til noon, Keep the change, Here's that five.* The saddest: *Buy*

*me one, Out of gas, Dues not paid, Insufficient Funds, External use
only.*

How's That?

Sign on hotel in New York State resort area: "Open to take tourists."

Progress

The old narrow trails where two cars could barely move without
colliding are being replaced by splendid wide roads where six cars
at a time can collide easily.   *Herald-Tribune, Sarasota, Fla.*

The Town Crier

"List, good people all!
Past ten o'clock the houre I call.
Now say your prayers and take your rest,
With conscience clear and sins confessed.
I bid you all good night! Good night!"
Sunshine Magazine

Christmas

At Christmas be merry and thank God of all,
And feast thy poor neighbors, the great
and the small,
Yea, all the year long have an eye to the poor,
And God shall send luck to keep open thy door.
Thomas Tuser

What is a Child

Often I look at their angelic faces and marvel at the miracle God
has wrought and the blessings He has given me in the persons of a
six- and four-year-old. I contemplate the wonder of it all as I muse
to myself: "Just what is a child?"

And the answer comes out—a child is something that stands half-
way between an adult and a television screen.
Public Opinion, Westerville, Ohio

Language

I never know whether to lift my hat to a lady in the elevator or to elevate my hat to a lady in the lift.

A University

The university is the archive of the Western mind, it's the keeper of the Western culture, * * * the guardian of our heritage, the teacher of our teachers, * * * the dwelling place of the free mind.

Adlai Stevenson,
defining a university at the fourth bicentennial
Conference of Columbia University.

Luck

Stephen Leacock, the novelist, covers the ponderous subject of luck most admirably and completely in his single-line comment: "I am a great believer in luck, and I find the harder I work the more I have of it."

"We Texans"

We Texans believe in progress; we do not want to repeal the Twentieth Century. But neither do we want to be led down the disastrous road to socialism, a close first cousin of Communism. Because of our Constitution, we Americans have no one to whom we must account except our fellow citizens. Our government is always subject to the will of the people. We must keep it that way, always, by continuing to make regular payments—the amortization of freedom.

This amortization, although it never ends, is one of the most satisfying processes in which a citizen can participate. Regardless of material wealth, any man who contributes to the cause of liberty and the pursuit of happiness is rich indeed.

America will never be liquidated if it continues paying on a debt to freedom that is never liquidated. As long as we continue to preserve, protect and defend the Constitution of the United States, as long as we are alert and vigilant, America will continue to be the greatest country on earth.

Allan Shivers,
Governor of Texas

Ode to Customers

OUR CUSTOMERS are the most important persons in this business—in person, by mail, or by telephone.

OUR CUSTOMERS are not dependent on us—we are dependent on them.

OUR CUSTOMERS are not an interruption of our work—they are the purpose of it. We are not doing them a favor by serving them—they are doing us a favor by giving us the opportunity to do so.

OUR CUSTOMERS are not outsiders to our business—they are a part of it.

OUR CUSTOMERS are not cold statistics—they are flesh-and-blood humans with feelings and emotions like our own, and with biases and prejudices.

OUR CUSTOMERS are persons who bring us their wants. It is our job to handle them profitably—profitably to both the customer and ourselves.

That is what customers are—in our business or in any business. Some people seem to have forgotten a few of these basic truths in recent years, but it is high time to be remembering them again. *Tomorrow may be too late.*   *Paul Talbot,*
The Management Review

Profits

We must preach and teach that adequate profit is something to be proud of, and not a subject matter for which to apologize, inasmuch as an adequate profit is the lifeblood of our economy. This problem was stated very succinctly recently by a Chicagoan who wrote to the Bureau of Internal Revenue at Washington. "Please help me with my problem," he said. "My problem is that my income is less than my outcome." One of the requirements for the executive of today is that he so divide the "outcome" as to have something left from the income.

Out of the money we take in, of course, we must first meet our operating costs—the cost of labor, the cost of goods and services we buy, the cost of replacing worn-out tools, and the heavy and inevitable cost of taxes. But that is not enough. After these obligations have been met, there must be something left of our income not only

to provide dividends for those who have invested their savings in our business, but also to finance the further modernization and expansion of our facilities.   *Clifford F. Hood,*
President of the United States Steel Corporation

Two Brothers

Two brothers in Ohio believed that they could fly craft heavier than air. They were ridiculed and scorned. They still elected to exercise the right of choice. Their genius has remade the world. Decision always implies choice.   *Dr. Charles L. Anspach,*
President, Central Michigan College of
Education, Mount Pleasant, Michigan

The Right of Decision

An old legend describes the formation of the universe. The legend I think has considerable point for us. According to the legend, when the world and other planets were formed, the good Creator gave each planet to a guardian angel. The earth was placed in charge of the archangel Michael. Michael decided that in the supervision of the earth he would give the people who lived on the earth the right to make decisions. From time to time reports were to be given him as to the progress the people were making. For many years the reports dealt only with the bickerings of people and the many disagreements over trivial things. Finally the archangel Michael decided that he would give the people on the earth something which would make the earth either a paradise or a literal hell. He gave the earth nuclear fission and the atom bomb. With his gift he gave the right of decision.   *Dr. Charles L. Anspach,*
President, Central Michigan College of
Education, Mount Pleasant, Michigan

An Ivory Tower

The scholar has a right to his study if he can keep it sacrosanct. But it must have great windows looking out upon the contemporary world ... The man of culture who lives in an ivory tower easily becomes a pathetic angel of learning ineffectually beating his wings as he moves about a world in which he lives like an alien mind. The very men of the mighty past whose companionship he so deeply prizes can be truly seen and adequately understood only as they are allowed to come forth upon the very arenas of the modern world.

Dr. Lynn Harold Hough
in the Congregational Quarterly,
London, April 1952

If I Condemn You

In a cathedral at Lubeck, Germany, there is an inscription that could well be written large over the portals of many churches today:

Thus speaketh Christ our Lord to us:
Ye call me Master and obey me not,
Ye call me Light and see me not,
Ye call me Way and walk me not,
Ye call me Life and choose me not,
Ye call me Wise and follow me not,
Ye call me Fair and love me not,
Ye call me Rich and ask me not,
Ye call me Eternal and seek me not,
Ye call me Noble and serve me not,
Ye call me Gracious and trust me not,
Ye call me Might and honor me not,
Ye call me Just and fear me not,
If I condemn you, blame me not.

Dr. John S. Wimbish

Opportunity or Calamity

Our Father, when we long for life without its trials and work, without difficulties, remind us that oaks grow strong in contrary winds and diamonds are made under pressure. With stout hearts may we see in every calamity an opportunity, and not give way to the pessimism that sees in every opportunity a calamity.

Peter Marshall (1902-1949)

Make No Little Plans

Make no little plans. They have no magic to stir men's blood and probably themselves will not be realized. Make big plans; aim high in hope and work, remembering that a noble, logical diagram once recorded will never die, but long after we are gone will be a living thing, asserting itself with ever growing insistency. Remember that our sons and grandsons are going to do things that would stagger us. Let your watchword be order and your beacon beauty.

Daniel H. Burnham,
distinguished architect. (From a speech
delivered at a Town Planning Conference
in London, England in 1910)

The Responsibility of Parents

The best defense against juvenile delinquency is still prevention.

Restore the home to its rightful place as a center of living, learning and parental love. Parents should realize that they have the basic responsibility of teaching their children to be good citizens.

Parents should give their children close but sympathetic guidance. This means understanding their problems, teaching them hobbies. Parents should know where their children are at night.

Citizens should exercise their civic responsibility. This means supporting youth-serving agencies, taking an interest in juvenile problems, trying to help youngsters in need.   *J. Edgar Hoover*

Industry

I do not despise genius—indeed, I wish I had a basketful of it. But yet, after a great deal of experience and observation, I have become convinced that industry is a better horse to ride than genius. It may never carry any man as far as genius has carried individuals, but industry—patient, steady, intelligent industry—will carry thousands into comfort, and even celebrity; and this it does with absolute certainty.   *Walter Lippmann*

Valuable Information

Fed up with the fancy descriptions he had to set in type day after day, a printer on the *Mena (Ark.) Star* added this on his own to the end of one wedding story: "The linotype operator, while he set this, wore a pale blue shirt with pants to match and a silver wrist watch on his left wrist."

Opportunity

The reason so many people never get anywhere in life is because, when opportunity knocks, they are out in the back yard looking for four-leaf clovers.   *Walter P. Chrysler*

Prayer

Lord, make me an instrument of Your peace.

Where there is hatred, let me sow love; where there is injury, pardon; where there is doubt, faith; where there is despair, hope; where there is darkness, light; where there is sadness, joy.

O Divine Master, grant that I may not so much seek to be consoled as to console; to be understood as to understand; to be loved as to love; for it is in giving that we receive; it is in pardoning that we are pardoned; and it is in dying that we are born to eternal life.

Saint Francis

He Didn't Like to be Annoyed

Month after month a firm sent bills to a customer and finally received this reply:

Dear Credit Manager: Once a month I put all my bills on the table, and pick at random five, which I pay. If I receive any more reminders from you, you won't get a place in next month's shuffle.

Mill Whistle

You Can't Lose

Socrates' marital difficulties are well known. Out of them he coined this sage advice: "By all means marry. If you get a good wife, you will become very happy; if you get a bad one you will become a philosopher."

Where Are You Going?

Dwight W. Morrow was unable to find his railroad ticket one day as he was on a train leaving New York City. While the conductor stood waiting beside him he searched in vain. "I must find that ticket," he said.

"Don't worry about it, Mr. Morrow," said the conductor. "We know you had a ticket. Just mail it to the railroad when you find it."

"That's not what's troubling me," replied Mr. Morrow. "Where am I going?"

That's a good question for any man to ask.

It's Up to You

If you want your father to take care of you, that's paternalism. If you want your mother to take care of you, that's maternalism. If you want Uncle Sam to take care of you, that's Socialism. If you want your comrades to take care of you, that's Communism. But if you want to take care of yourself, that's Americanism.   *Rotamoor*

Today's Seven Wonders

The seven wonders of the world in 1954 have been listed by Dr. Leonard Carmichael, head of the Smithsonian Institution in Washington, D. C., as follows:

1. The atom—not as a bomb but as a source of power.
2. The supersonic jet airplane.
3. Man's ability to manipulate the wave impulses, as in radio, to extend his knowledge of the universe.
4. Antibiotic drugs.
5. The high-speed electronic calculator.
6. The Coelacanth Fish, which has remained unchanged for 300 million years. Several living specimens have been caught off Madagascar and they are identical with fossil remains. This fish had long been believed extinct.
7. The Smithsonian Institution. Of it Dr. Carmichael said, "Here are 34 million catalogued objects. There is no other place in the world like it, so far as I can discover."

Depends on Location

The City National Bank of Binghamton, New York, sent flowers recently to the management of the Binghamton Savings Bank, congratulating the latter institution on the opening of its new facilities. But, unfortunately, the card with the flowers read, "Deepest sympathy."

Later, the florist who made the mistake called the bank to apologize. What really worried him, he said, was that the other bouquet, intended for a funeral, carried the message intended for the bank: "Congratulations on your new location."   *Sunshine Magazine*

A Community of Conservatives

Provided with strong unions that raise wages faster than productivity increases, guarded in most cases from layoff by some years of seniority, protected from want during unemployment by high unemployment compensation, and protected from arbitrary treatment on the part of management by an elaborate system of trade agreements, shop stewards, and grievance machinery, American workmen will be fundamentally conservative on issues of social policy.

Give men hope, let them become adjusted to their environment and successful in realizing their ambitions, and you have a community of conservatives. Even more in the future than in the past, therefore, it is imperative that the economy expand at a good rate, that it avoid serious recessions, and that it succeed in giving people the steady increases in their standard of consumption that they have learned to expect.   *from an address by Sumner H. Slichter*
before the Labor Relations Council,
Wharton School of Finance and Commerce,
University of Pennsylvania

The Thinker

Let us admit the case of the conservative: if we once start thinking, no one can guarantee where we shall come out, except that many objects, ends, and institutions are doomed. Every thinker puts some portion of an apparently stable world in peril, and no man can wholly predict what will emerge in its place.   *John Dewey*

Man Will Live

In the Twentieth Century war will be dead, the scaffold will be dead, hatred will be dead, frontier boundaries will be dead, dogmas will be dead; man will live. He will possess something higher than all these—a great country, the whole earth, and a great hope, the whole heaven.   *Victor Hugo*

Success

If you succeed in life, you must do it in spite of the efforts of others to pull you down. There is nothing in the idea that people are willing to help those who help themselves. People are willing to help a man who can't help himself, but as soon as a man is able to help himself, and does it, they join in making his life as uncomfortable as possible.   *E. W. Howe*

Education

Education does not mean teaching people what they do not know. It means teaching them to behave as they do not behave. It is not teaching the youth the shapes of letters and the tricks of numbers, and then leaving them to turn their arithmetic to roguery, and their literature to lust. It means, on the contrary, training them into the perfect exercise and kingly continence of their bodies and souls. It is a painful, continual and difficult work to be done by kindness, by watching, by warning, by precept, and by praise, but above all—by example.   *John Ruskin*

The Great Voice of America

The great voice of America does not come from the seats of learning. It comes in a murmur from the hills and woods and farms and factories and the mills, rolling and gaining volume until it comes to us from the homes of common men. Do these murmurs echo in the corridors of the universities? I have not heard them. The universities would make men forget their common origins, forget their universal sympathies, and join a class—and no class can ever serve America. I have dedicated every power there is in me to bring the colleagues that I have anything to do with to an absolutely democratic regeneration in spirit, and I shall not be satisfied until America shall know that the men in the colleges are saturated with the same thought, the same sympathy, that pulses through the whole great body politic.

Woodrow Wilson

Children

I love children. They do not prattle of yesterday: their interests are all of today and the tomorrows—I love children.

Richard Mansfield

Grumbling

Nothing is easier than fault-finding; no talent, no self-denial, no brains, no character are required to set up in the grumbling business.

Robert West

Life

Fear not that thy life shall come to an end, but rather fear that it shall never have a beginning.   *Cardinal Newman*

A Gentleman

A man asked to define the essential characteristics of a gentleman —using the term in its widest sense—would presumably reply, "The will to put himself in the place of others; the horror of forcing others into positions from which he would himself recoil; the power to do what seems to him to be right, without considering what others may say or think."   *John Galsworthy*

Slavery and the Machine

The fact is, that civilization requires slaves. The Greeks were quite right there. Unless there are slaves to do the ugly, horrible, uninteresting work, culture and contemplation become almost impossible. Human slavery is wrong, insecure, and demoralizing. On mechanical slavery, on the slavery of the machine, the future of the world depends.   *Oscar Wilde*

These Intimate Conversations

Then, and indeed for many years after, it seemed as though there was no end to the money needed to carry on and develop the business. As our successes began to come, I seldom put my head upon the pillow at night without speaking a few words to myself in this wise:

"Now a little success, soon you will fall down, soon you will be overthrown. Because you have got a start, you think you are quite a merchant; look out, or you will lose your head—go steady." These intimate conversations with myself, I am sure had a great influence on my life.   *John D. Rockefeller*

Circumstantial Evidence

Even the cleverest and most perfect circumstantial evidence is likely to be at fault after all, and therefore ought to be received with great caution. Take the case of any pencil sharpened by any woman; if you have witnesses, you will find she did it with a knife, but if you take simply the aspect of the pencil, you will say she did it with her teeth.   *Mark Twain*

Sweet Valleys of Silence

Society, as we have constituted it, will have no place for me, has none to offer; but Nature, whose sweet rains fall on unjust and just alike, will have clefts in the rocks where I may hide, and sweet valleys in whose silence I may weep undisturbed. She will hang the night with stars so that I may walk abroad in the darkness without stumbling, and send the wind over my footprints so that none may track me to my hurt; she will cleanse me in great waters, and with bitter herbs make me whole.   *Oscar Wilde*

Alone

I love to be alone. I never found the companion that was so companionable as solitude.   *Thoreau*

What is Music

What is music? This question occupied my mind for hours last night before I fell asleep. The very existence of music is wonderful, I might even say miraculous. Its domain is between thought and phenomena. Like a twilight mediator, it hovers between spirit and matter, related to both, yet differing from each. It is spirit, but it is spirit subject to the measurement of time. It is matter, but it is matter that can dispense with space.   *Heinrich Heine*

One Good Old Man

I think that to have known one good, old man—one man, who, through the chances and mischances of a long life, has carried his heart in his hand, like a palm-branch, waving all discords into peace —helps our faith in God, in ourselves, and in each other more than many sermons.   *G. W. Curtis*

The Body
of
Benjamin Franklin, Printer
(Like the cover of an old book,
Its contents torn out,
And stripped of its lettering and gilding,)
Lies here food for worms.
Yet the work itself shall not be lost,
For it will (as he believes) appear once
more
In a new
And more beautiful Edition
Corrected and Amended
By
The Author
"Franklin's self-written epitaph"

An Executive

No man will ever be a big executive who feels that he must, either openly or under cover, follow up every order he gives and see that it is done—nor will he ever develop a capable assistant.

John Lee Mahin

Life

Every man's life is a fairy-tale written by God's fingers.

Hans Christian Andersen

Inconsistency

Do I contradict myself? Very well, then, I contradict myself; (I am large. I contain multitudes).

Walt Whitman

But If

If a friend of mine ... gave a feast, and did not invite me to it, I should not mind a bit.... But if ... a friend of mine had a sorrow and refused to allow me to share it, I should feel it most bitterly. If he shut the doors of the house of mourning against me, I would move back again and again and beg to be admitted, so that I might share in what I was entitled to share. If he thought me unworthy, unfit to weep with him, I should feel it as the most poignant humiliation, as the most terrible mode for which disgrace could be inflicted on me ... he who can look on the loveliness of the world and share its sorrow, and realize something of the wonder of both, is in immediate contact with divine things, and has got as near to God's secret as any one can get.

Oscar Wilde

Prayers

Certain thoughts are prayers. There are moments when, whatever be the attitude of the body, the soul is on its knees.   *Victor Hugo*

Hope, Pray and Work

Several years ago in a ramshackle area in Philadelphia, a little Negro boy had a passion to play baseball. He played the game at every opportunity. When he wasn't practicing, he glued his eye to a knothole in the fence behind which the Philadelphia Athletics played, watching their every move. He longed for the day when he would be a member of a big league baseball club. Yet what chance had he, a Negro boy, ever to play in the big leagues?

Nevertheless, he kept hoping, praying and believing—and he continued to practice. In the course of time a Christian gentleman by the name of Branch Rickey lifted the color bar in the big leagues. "There is no color to a home run," said Branch Rickey. This Negro boy got his chance. Roy Campanella became one of the finest catchers in either league.

Even when it seems impossible to achieve your goal, refuse to give way to despair. Believe, hope, pray and *work* toward its fulfillment. Who knows what kindly Providence may hold in store for you?

Dr. Kenneth Hildebrand,
minister, The Central Church of Chicago,
Chicago, Illinois

Silent Partners

A father and son were discussing the importance and significance of success. The son finally said, "It must be great to be famous and have people remember you. Now, there was Paul Revere. He was a great man." The father responded, "Yes, Paul Revere was a real man, but do you know the name of his horse?" Of course the boy did not know the name of the horse and we do not know, for tradition or history does not record its name. The father then said, "Did you ever stop to think that Paul Revere could not have taken the ride if it had not been for the horse?" Like the boy we do not often give much consideration to the horse, with the result that we do not completely understand success, or develop true appreciation for the ladder by which we climb.

The world is full of silent partners and unknowns. We have forgotten to record the names of the horses on which we have ridden. The architect who designs the Cathedral is known; the names of the contractors are recorded, but the names of those who also toiled are unknown—they are the silent partners. We look into the sky and bring the mysteries of other worlds into the range of our vision without a thought as to the makers of the telescope. Those who aided in the construction of the telescope are our silent partners.

The tendency to forget, to fail to recognize our silent partners is not confined to governments, societies and organizations. It is a

peculiarity of human behavior. As individuals, we forget our silent
partners.   *Dr. Charles L. Anspach,*
President, Central Michigan College of
Education, Mount Pleasant, Michigan

The Legend of the Dogwood

There is a legend that, at the time of the Crucifixion, the dogwood
had been the size of the oak and other forest trees.

So firm and strong was the tree that it was chosen as the timber
for the cross.

To be used thus for such cruel purpose greatly distressed the tree,
and Jesus, nailed upon it, sensed this, and in His gentle pity for all
sorrow and suffering said to it:

"Because of your regret and pity for My suffering, never again
shall the dogwood tree grow large enough to be used as a cross.

"Henceforth it shall be slender and bent and twisted and its blossom shall be in the form of a cross—two long and two short petals.

"And in the center of the outer edge of each petal there will be
nail prints, brown with rust and stained with red, and in the center
of the flower will be a crown of thorns, and all who see it will
remember.   *from The Calvary Pulpit*
published by the Calvary Baptist Church,
New York City

You Don't Mean It, Dearie!

If he doesn't marry, he's a Bachelor, a glamorous word. If she does
not marry, she's an Old Maid.

What he hears at the office is News. What she hears at the bridge
club is Gossip.

If he runs the family, he is the Head of the House. If she runs it,
she Wears the Pants of the family.

In middle-age he is in the Prime of Life, or the Peak of his Career.
At the same age she is No Spring Chicken.

If he is an easy spender, he "Does Not Deny His Family Anything." If she does not count the pennies, she's a Poor Manager and
Extravagant.

If he keeps an eye on her at a party, he is an Attentive Husband.
If she sticks close to him, she is a Possessive Wife.

If he hasn't any small talk, he is the Quiet Type. If she hasn't any, she is just Dumb.

If he is over-solicitous of her, he is a Devoted Husband. If she is over-solicitous of him he is Henpecked.

When it's his night out, he's Out with the Boys or At a Meeting. When it's her night out, she's at a Hen Party.

It just seems to depend upon the point of view.

Sheboygan Press

That Explains It

A distinguished visitor, upon paying a visit to the late George Bernard Shaw, expressed surprise that the famous author had no flowers on display at his home. "I thought," declared the visitor, "that you were exceedingly fond of flowers."

"I am," answered Shaw abruptly. "I am very fond of flowers. I am very fond of children, too. But I don't cut their heads off and stick them in pots all over the house." *Conveyor, Australia*

A Man and His Job

...I don't want any fellow who has a job, working for me; what I want is a fellow whom a job has. I want the job to get the fellow and not the fellow to get the job. And I want that job to get hold of this young man so hard that no matter where he is, the job has got him for keeps. I want that job to have him in its clutches when he goes to bed at night, and in the morning I want that same job to be sitting on the foot of his bed telling him it's time to get up and go to work. And when a job gets a fellow that way, he'll amount to something. *Charles F. Kettering*

Can't Be Too Bad

When people start waiting to get out of this country instead of waiting to get in—we can start worrying about our system.

Herald, Bradenton, Fla.

Work

America is not a land of money but of wealth—not a land of rich people but of successful workers. There is only one thing that makes prosperity, and that is *work*. *Henry Ford*

Who Is It?

A friend of mine has the following verse hanging on the wall of his study:

> "Always when I pass a church
> I drop in for a visit
> So that when I'm carried in
> The Lord won't say, "Who is it?"

Eldon S. Dummit,
former Attorney General of Kentucky

The Search for Peace

The search for peace has its high hopes and its deep frustrations. But after the frustration, there is always renewed hope. On behalf of the United States I would say in my closing words that we believe that international peace is an attainable goal. That is a premise that underlies all of our planning. We propose never to desist, never to admit discouragement, but confidently and steadily so to act that peace becomes for us a sustaining principle of action.

from an address by John Foster Dulles,
Secretary of State of the United States
before the United Nations General Assembly

His Old Man Didn't Know Either

Visiting our high school, I stopped at a history class for juniors. The history of the Roman Empire was under discussion and when one of the students was unable to answer a rather simple question the teacher asked: "Bill, just why do we study history?" and Bill promptly came back: "That's what my dad wants to know."

J. L. Brenn,
President, Huntington Laboratories, Inc.,
Huntington, Indiana

It Pays to Advertise

An occasional disgruntled person in one or two foreign nations got into the habit of painting signs here and there, saying "Americans Go Home." One of our enterprising American airlines took

good advantage of this by hiring a sign painter to go around and
add the phrase "Via TWA."

J. L. Brenn,
President, Huntington Laboratories, Inc.,
Huntington, Indiana

Mercy

¶ **We** ministers have our sins. Everybody has. It reminds me of a
minister who came out and found his car outside of a New York
church tagged with an illegal parking ticket. When in the traffic
court his case came up and his name was called, he stood before the
judge, and the judge said, "Have you anything to say, sir?" The
clergyman said, "Yes, one thing, Your Honor, 'Blessed are the merciful, for they shall obtain mercy.'" And after the uproar had
quieted down in the court, the judge said to the clergyman, "You
know, I've waited a long time for this moment, when I could say to
a parson, 'Go thy way and sin no more.'"

from a sermon of Dr. Lewis Evans
as reprinted in the Congressional Record

The Right Side

General Jackson, the great Confederate general, sent a letter home
to his pastor during the Civil War. The parishioners gathered on the
church steps expecting the missive would carry some word of Missionary Ridge or Lookout Mountain; but there was not a mention of
matters military. It read, "Dear Pastor: I remember that this is Foreign Missionary Sunday. Enclosed find my contribution to the same.
May this war soon be over, and may the right side win, that we may
go back to our main task of saving men and the Kingdom of God."
Not until a man has been conquered by the supreme aim of "The
Kingdom of God and saving men" could he ever subordinate his
military and personal reputation by saying, "May the right side win."

from a sermon by Dr. Lewis Evans
as reprinted in the Congressional Record

The Secret

I met God in the morning,
When my day was at its best
And His presence came like sunrise,
Like a glory in my breast.

All day long the Presence lingered;
All day long He stayed with me;
And we sailed in perfect calmness
O'er a very troubled sea.
Other ships were blown and battered,
Other ships were sore distressed,
But the winds that seemed to drive them
Brought to us a peace and rest.
Then I thought of other mornings,
With a keen remorse of mind.
When I too had loosed the moorings
With the Presence left behind.
So, I think I know the secret,
Learned from many a troubled way;
You must seek Him in the morning
If you want Him through the day.

Anonymous, printed in Partners

Every Hour

Approximately one hour ago we entered this room. During that one hour it became necessary for the transportation facilities of America to move at the rate of an additional two million ton-miles of freight per year. And the need goes on at that rate, every hour of every day and every night. For, in this hour the population of our country increased by 320 persons. And for each of these new Americans 7,000 tons of freight—food, clothing, machinery for increased production, household equipment, etc.—must be moved one mile each year.

Are these astonishing statements? Can they be true? They may be astonishing to some of you—yet they *are true*.

Let me picture what is meant by a ton-mile of freight. Of course you know that it means one ton of freight, moved one mile. But let's examine it.

Undoubtedly, you could carry a 50 pound bag of cement on your shoulder, if it were necessary. But—could you carry it a mile? Now make forty such trips, carrying a bag each time, and you have moved a ton-mile of freight. If you could do this job in one day and keep it up for 22 years and 4 months, resting only on Sunday, you would have transported the amount of freight that is moved each year, for *each and every* person in the United States, and for each of the 160 odd million persons who make up our total population. So if you want to play around with what are sometimes called "box car figures," you can take it from there.

All of this is merely to illustrate that there is a direct relationship of ton-miles of freight to population. In round numbers this amounts to 7,000 ton-miles *per capita, per annum.* And each time that our population *increases* by *one* it involves an obligation on the transport facilities of the country to move 7,000 tons one mile each year.

G. Metzman,
Chairman American Railway Car Institute,
New York City

What is Business Administration

Administration, as I define it, is the leadership and accomplishment of work by, through, and with people. It is the purposeful organization of men and things. In business this work is partly the manufacture and distribution of products and services in competition with other producers of products which consumers demand. Administration embraces, therefore, the *business competence* that enables the executive to balance costs, production efficiencies, product ideas and marketing skill against the know-how of his competitors within available markets or those he may create and, above all, produce profits.

But administration is more than competence, even though we never have enough of that. Business leaders, who wish to preserve and strengthen the kind of society in which we believe, must run a business organization which, beyond being competitive, is a satisfactory social entity for those who work in it and a constructive entity in the national whole. To this basic purpose there must be added the study of the *responsibilities* of management. The sense of obligation which management must undertake is at least twofold. On the one hand, it extends to the people who make up our thousands upon thousands of companies; it means providing for them not only the conditions essential to the effective performance of work but the realizing of their potentialities as persons so that freedom need not be futile or purposeless for any person. The community, which a company itself comprises, must be a *healthy* community, satisfying the noneconomic as well as the economic needs of the individuals who make it up and enabling them to consider their work a way of life as well as a livelihood.

But another responsibility, sometimes in apparent conflict with our commitments inside our companies, extends to the businessman's public responsibilities to the community, to the nation and the world comprised of all such communities. As we attempt to clarify what we mean by social responsibilities, we become aware of the legal, economic, and political environment within which business decisions are made. We must learn how to think about the impact of our behavior as individual businessmen and as members of the business world upon our community. We need to formulate our own ideas of vigorous competition and to consider what businessmen, as distinguished from government administrators, can do to contribute to the stability of our economy. We would like to be able to discriminate between practices which are in the public interest and those which are not. We must define the scope of the public responsibilities which businessmen must fulfill as the corollary to the freedoms in making business decisions which our economic system affords.

So administration, we believe, includes not only the relationships among people in a given company but the relationships between individual businesses and our society as a whole. The operation of our economic system demands of management more than mere technical competence in the various functions of business.   *Donald K. David,*
Dean, Graduate School of Business
Administration, Harvard University

It is Difficult

As Sam said, "You can't no more explain what you don't know, than you can come back from where you ain't been."

My Good Friend

Franklin D. Roosevelt once described William Allen White as "my good friend—three and a half years out of four."

Smart Youngsters

In a certain school in New York there was a teacher, an energetic advocate of "Safety First," who opened her class each morning by rising and asking, "Children, what would you do if fire were to break out in this building?" The children would reply in chorus, "We would rise in our places, step into the aisle, and march quietly out of the building."

One morning when the children arrived at school they found themselves honored by the presence of the well-known and beloved Dr. Henry van Dyke. The teacher stepped before the class and instead of the usual fire drill question, said, "Children, what would you say if I were to tell you that Dr. van Dyke is to speak to you this morning?"

Instantly from the class came the resounding chorus, "We would rise in our places, step into the aisle, and march quietly out of the building."

Some Malapropisms

Jane Ace has created many malapropisms on radio. For example, "Everything," she says, "is so Topsy Eva!"
Other examples:
"I can explain it in words of one cylinder."
"I was sound awake all night."
"It was like looking for a needle on a hayride."
"There's no use crying over spoiled milk."
"Why don't you just come out flat-headed and say so?"
"In a pig's sty, they would!"
"Well, I've got that out of my cistern."
"Once I get started on a thing I'm completely uninhabited."

My Creed

I do not choose to be a common man. It is my right to be uncommon—if I can. I seek opportunity—not security. I do not wish to be a kept citizen, humbled and dulled by having the state look after me. I want to take the calculated risk; to dream and to build, to fail and to succeed. I refuse to barter incentive for a dole. I prefer the challenges of life to the guaranteed existence; the thrill of fulfillment to the stale calm of utopia. I will not trade freedom for beneficence nor my dignity for a handout. I will never cower before any master nor bend to any threat. It is my heritage to stand erect, proud and unafraid; to think and act for myself, enjoy the benefit of my creations and to face the world boldly and say: This I have done. All this is what it means to be an American.   *Dean Alfange*
in Voiceways (New York Telephone Co.)

Prayer

The following is said to be an "Irish Prayer":
Take time for work—It is the price of success.
Take time to think—It is the source of power.
Take time to play—It is the secret of youth.
Take time to read—It is the foundation of wisdom.
Take time to be friendly—It is the road to happiness.
Take time to dream—It is hitching your wagon to a star.
Take time to love and be loved—It is the privilege of the gods.
Take time to look around—It is too short a day to be selfish.
Take time to laugh—It is the music of the soul.

Sunshine Magazine

Illusions

Illusions commend themselves to us because they save us pain and allow us to enjoy pleasure instead. We must therefore accept it without complaint when they sometimes collide with a bit of reality against which they are dashed to pieces.   *Freud*

Life

Surgeons should be very careful
When they wield the knife!
For underneath their fine incisions
Lurks the culprit—Life!

Emily Dickinson

Modern Confucius

The superior man understands what is right; the inferior man understands what will sell.

The superior man loves his soul; the inferior man loves his property.

The superior man always remembers how he was punished for his mistakes; the inferior man always remembers what presents he got.

The superior man blames himself; the inferior man blames others.

The superior man is always candid and at ease with himself or others; the inferior man is always worried about something.

A man who has committed a mistake and doesn't correct it is committing another mistake.

History

History is simply a piece of paper covered with print; the main thing is still to make history, not to write it.   *Bismarck*

Anybody can make history; only a great man can write it.

Oscar Wilde

Inspiration

The bird I heard today, which, fortunately, did not come within the scope of my science, sang as freshly as if it had been the first morning of creation.   *Thoreau*

Money

As a cousin of mine once said about money, money is always there but the pockets change; it is not in the same pockets after a change, and that is all there is to say about money.   *Gertrude Stein*

Academic Scribblers

The ideas of economists and political philosophers, both when they are right and when they are wrong, are more powerful than is commonly understood. Indeed, the world is ruled by little else. Practical men, who believe themselves to be quite exempt from any intellectual influences, are usually the slaves of some defunct economist. Madmen in authority, who hear voices in the air, are distilling their frenzy from some academic scribbler of a few years back. I am sure that the power of vested interests is vastly exaggerated compared with the gradual encroachment of ideas.   *J. M. Keynes*

The World of Tomorrow

What then is to be the design of the economic world of tomorrow? Will it be a world in which national life is dominated by highly organized groups which use the government in a struggle for group advantage; in which national policies are not really national; a world of parochialism and restrictions? Or will it be a world in which economic life is pretty much dominated by bureaucrats through the control of expenditures, sources of information, and power to grant or withhold favors to industries, enterprises, localities, and groups; in which the government is jealous of private enterprise, careful not to encourage it lest it challenge the power of the bureaucrats; careful to maintain tax laws that penalize initiative and daring? Or is it to be a world in which each individual thinks of himself first of all as a member of the commonwealth, highly conscious of the interests which he has in common with all other members of the commonwealth; in which individuals regard public officials of all ranks as their servants and hold them all, from President down, to strict accountability for actions and failure to act; in which public policy undertakes, not only to provide some minimum of security against the vicissitudes of economic life, but also to stimulate more vigorously than ever a wide dispersion of initiative, a vigorous spirit of enterprise, and a large amount of innovation?

Doubtless the world will be a mixture of all three. Doubtless the struggle to mould it in different directions will continue indefinitely. I like to think that victory will gradually go to those who are striving to get common interests, concern for the well-being of the other fellow, placed higher and higher in the scales of value of more and more people and who believe that the encouragement of the innovator, the experimenter, and the enterpriser is one of the most important interests which all members of the community have in common. In fact, it is difficult for me to believe that the outcome of the struggle can be otherwise. At any rate, we can feel fortunate that we live when we do; that we have an opportunity to help mould events when things are in such a state of flux; when decisions so momentous are being made. When I was a small boy, I used to think that I had missed the boat; that the men who lived at the time of the Revolution were the lucky ones. Now I know that isn't so. Of all generations we are the most fortunate. We live in an epic age. We play in by far the greatest drama the human race has ever staged; and we determine whether the outcome is tragedy.

Sumner H. Slichter

Partners

Labor and management are not economic competitors, as some would have us believe. Nor are they social rivals. Nor can they afford to be ideological enemies. The fact is, they are teammates—partners in production—working together on the same job that is vital to each.   *from Partners, by Lester R. Shaw,*
President of Local 1503, IAM, Keller
Tool Company, Grand Haven, Mich.

How to Become Great

If men are to achieve greatness in this life they must be certain their beginnings are obscure. Apparently, it is necessary that the future statesman be born in a log cabin, that the great artist arise from the squalor of an orphanage, that a giant in the banking field begin as a barefooted boy on a worn-out farm, that the merchant prince be the seventh son of ignorant (but always honest) parents who could not afford to send him to school. In compounding genius there seems no other *first* ingredient save obscurity. In building the foundation for a great man there seems no better stone than hard knocks, no more dependable mortar than poverty. To mix up a few metaphors, those blueprints for greatness, those formulas for achievement, those specifications for world leadership all emphasize the angle of a *lowly* beginning.   *William A. Philpott, Jr.*

It's Easy

If you are curious about her age, please pursue the following simple recipe, written by E. V. Durling for the New York Journal-American:

"Suppose you want to find out how old a woman is without asking her. Say: 'I'll bet I can guess the first number in your auto license.' If she has no auto, make it the first number in her house number. Then say: 'Write the number down. Don't let me see it. Conceal all figuring I ask for.' Say the first number in her auto license is nine. She writes it down. You say: 'Double it.' That makes 18. You continue: 'Add five.' That makes 23. You say: 'Multiply by 50.' That makes 1150. You continue: 'Add 1704.' That makes 2854. You conclude: 'Subtract figures of year you were born.' She subtracts 1917. Keep in mind she has concealed all her figures from you. You ask, 'What is your final answer?' She says '937.' You say, 'First number in your auto license is nine.' But you don't mention the last two figures in her answer, the 37. That is the lady's age."   *From Bagology*

Definitions

Lawyer: A person who helps you get what's coming to him.

District Attorney: A man who suffers from an acute prosecution complex.

Jury: Twelve men who are chosen to decide which of the parties before the bar has the better attorney.

Juvenile Delinquents: Other people's children.   *Edward Arnold*

Youngsters

"School days are the happiest days of your life—provided, of course, that your children are old enough to go."

"You know what summer is? It's the season when kids slam the doors they've left open all winter."   *Dave Garroway*

Boston English

A woman visiting Boston was reprimanded by a policeman when she failed to halt for a stop sign at an intersection and protested that in her home "we just slow down and look in both directions." "In Boston, Madam," the policeman said, " 'Stop' means an absolute cessation of forward movement."   *Miami Daily News*

Thirty-five Servants

In the average American home today, electricity does the work which would require the labor of 35 servants, each working a 40-hour week.   *Spark and Flame (Arizona Public Service Co., Nov. 1954)*

Opinion of the Public

People come in three classes: the few who make things happen, the many who watch things happen and the overwhelming majority who have no idea what happened.   *News, Woonsocket, S. D.*

O God

Give me clean hands, clean words, and clean thoughts.
Help me to stand for the hard right against the easy wrong.
 Save me from habits that harm.
Teach me to work as hard and play as fair in thy sight
 Alone as if the whole world saw.
Forgive me when I am unkind, and help me to forgive
 Those who are unkind to me.
Keep me ready to help others at some cost to myself,
 Send me chances to do a little good every day,
  And so grow more like Christ.   *A Boy's Prayer*

God is Love

Once, while riding in the country, I saw on a farmer's barn a weather vane on the arrow of which was inscribed these words: "God is Love." I turned in at the gate and asked the farmer, "What do you mean by that? Do you think God's love is changeable; that it veers about as that arrow turns in the winds?" "Oh, no," cried the farmer, "I mean that whichever way the wind blows, God is still Love."   *Charles Spurgeon*

Business Advice

Thrift—no frills! What you make must be needed. It must be as good as or better than the best in competition. Put all the money you can save back into the business. Never stop improving. If your customers don't grow, you won't. Unless your men are treated fairly, you won't be. In danger, get there first. The company is your business, and you can't run it from the deck of a yacht.   *E. I. Dupont*

Inseparable

We know that the only alternative to private competition is Government monopoly of enterprise. We know that when Government monopolizes production, distribution and employment, it is no longer the servant of men—it is their master. And, therefore, we know that economic liberty and political liberty are inseparable parts of the same ball of wax—that we must keep them both, or we shall lose them both.   *Benjamin F. Fairless,*
Chairman of the board, United States Steel Corporation,
addressing the seventh annual conference of the
Public Relations Society of America, Inc.

Overlooked Completely

In his thirst for revolution, Marx overlooked completely the only economic system on earth under which it is possible for the workers themselves to own, to control and to manage directly the facilities of production. Shocking as the news may be to the disciples of Karl Marx, that system is capitalism . . .   *Benjamin F. Fairless*

Abraham Lincoln

Years ago Homer Hock of Kansas had this to say of Abraham Lincoln: "There is no new thing to be said of Lincoln. There is no new thing to be said of the mountains, or of the sea, or of the stars. The years may go their way, but the same old mountains lift their granite shoulders about the drifting clouds, the same mysterious sea beats upon the shore, and the same silent stars keep holy vigil above a tired world. But to mountains and sea and stars men turn forever in unwearied homage. And thus with Lincoln. For he was mountain in grandeur of soul; he was sea in deep undervoice of mystic loneliness; he was star in steadfast purity of purpose and of service. And he abides." *from an address by Dr. Robert L. Kincaid,*
President of Lincoln Memorial University,
Harrogate, Tennessee

The Humblest Has An Opportunity

Lincoln first of all stands out as the most inspiring example in American history of the opportunity which our nation gives to its humblest citizens. I think that is important to review in this day, when so many people are accustomed to look to society and the state for an easy road to personal achievement. So swiftly have world events piled upon us, our national leaders have been forced to improvise and inaugurate departures from the time-tried principles which had made our nation great. In this process, we have set in motion new forces and embraced new philosophies, which, if continued unchecked, may paralyze our nation and lead to its ultimate destruction. In this atmosphere our present generation has grown up, and it is but natural for our young people to assume that this new trend, so radically different from the old ways, is all good and will lead them to the happy haven in which there is abundance and security for all. That would be good if all worked for it and produced for themselves the heritage they are to enjoy. However, this present philosophy neglects emphasis upon work, personal initiative, and individual thrift.

None of us would want our children to be born into the poverty which faced that frontier child of Kentucky on February 12, 1809. We want to spare them the hardships of the lad who had less than a year's formal schooling. We want them to be clothed, housed,

schooled, and given reasonable advantages, which were denied Lincoln. But none of us can follow the career of the young Lincoln, who strode his solitary way to greatness, without a warming glow in our heart. He asked no favors of a benevolent government; he sought no easy road to achievement; he travelled no shortcut to success. All he had was within himself, not without,—a great mind, a keen ambition, and an earnest and humble heart. But he had something more than that, something which most of us today accept with little measure of gratitude. He had citizenship in a free land, where he could rise to the fullest extent of his abilities and efforts. He lived in the atmosphere of true freedom and his life blossomed into greatness because of that rich heritage.   *Dr. Robert L. Kincaid,*
President of Lincoln Memorial University,
Harrogate, Tennessee

Love of Country

I covet for all American youth an appreciation of Lincoln's deep and abiding love of country. Look at him as a youth literally devouring Weems' "Life of Washington." Feel with him as he read the great documents of American history. Listen to him when he talks about the Declaration of Independence and the Constitution of the United States. Hear him at the age of 29, as a young lawyer, extolling the importance of obedience to the laws of our country: "Let every American, every lover of liberty, every well wisher to his posterity, swear by the blood of the Revolution, never to violate in the least particular, the laws of the country." Follow him through his early political career, slowly developing a philosophy of freedom and equality for all men. Witness his passion for human rights in his debates with Douglas. Then, at last, echo with him the immortal words he spoke at Gettysburg.

Can it not be said we can truly vitalize the meaning of democracy by making Lincoln's words live in the hearts of our American youth?
Dr. Robert L. Kincaid,
President of Lincoln Memorial University,
Harrogate, Tennessee

A Pilgrimage

Did you ever make a pilgrimage over the trail of Abraham Lincoln, from his birthplace at Hodgenville, Ky., to his burial place in

Springfield? If you have not, you have missed a rich experience. It has been my privilege to do that more than once.

Several years ago I made that journey from Long Run in Kentucky to Oak Ridge in Springfield. I visited the unmarked grave of his grandfather, Capt. Abraham Lincoln, at the Long Run cemetery. I stood beside the grave of his grandmother, with its modest headstone chipped away by souvenir collectors. I waited with bared head in the marble building housing the birth cabin in Hodgenville. I walked the paths along Knob Creek in Kentucky where he had played as a boy. I followed his trail to Indiana, and to the quiet forest of Spencer County where the grave of Nancy Hanks is the central point of interest. I went to the Tom Lincoln home in Coles County, Illinois, and looked up the grave of the father of the martyred president.

Then I came to the New Salem State Park in Illinois where young Lincoln emerged from oblivion, where he "read and studied, and got ready." Perhaps no period of Lincoln's life is fuller of interest than these quiet years when he was growing to full manhood. Then came Springfield, and the scenes of his twenty-three years of political and professional life. His modest home; the court houses in which he practiced law; the scenes of his debates with Douglas; all the small and intimate things which made up his simple and modest career as a citizen of a new state, and as an emergent leader of a great cause.

I went to all these little shrines, marked by appropriate legends of a grateful people, and lived again in the spirit of the man who had left his footprints on his path to greatness. Then I recalled the scenes in Washington during the presidential years,—heavy years which he carried so nobly and uncomplainingly upon his broad shoulders of sacrifice and devotion. Finally, I came to the Oak Ridge cemetery where all that is mortal of Lincoln is entombed.

That visit to the Lincoln tomb was an unforgettable experience. I joined the throng of casual visitors, listening to the words of a guide describing nine replicas of famous statues of Lincoln placed in the circle inside the tomb. The climax was reached when we stood before a plaque containing the words of the Gettysburg address. Here we stood as the guide was speaking this tribute:

"This address has been read and re-read, recited and re-recited, in all our schools, from the turbulent waves of the Atlantic to the peaceful slumbers of the Pacific, from the pineries of Maine to the everglades of Florida, and will be read and re-read, I dare say, until time shall be no more. It is considered the masterpiece of the world. By many, it is rated on a parity from the standpoint of perfect English, religious and Christian thought, with Paul's letter to the Ephesians. Men and women who are classical scholars, readily agree it is perfect English and masterminds of the world declare it is the greatest speech that ever emanated from a human mind or fell from the lips of man."

Dr. Robert L. Kincaid,
President of Lincoln Memorial University,
Harrogate, Tennessee

The Difference

Actually there's only a slight difference between keeping your chin up and sticking your neck out, but it's a difference worth knowing.   *News, Milford, Massachusetts*

Tough Guy

The big husky brute who used to swagger about town bragging that he could walk a barbwire fence in his bare feet with a wildcat under each arm married a little redhead who makes him do the dishes twice a day.   *Iron County Miner, Hurley, Wis.*

Important Words

Five most important words: "I am proud of you." Four most important words: "What is your opinion?" Three most important words: "If you please." Two most important words: "Thank you." The smallest word (can you guess?): "I."   *Sunshine Magazine*

Peculiar

Isn't it peculiar that the human brain begins to function from the moment you are born, improves as you grow older, then stops completely when you stand up to talk?   *News-Leader, Arcadia, Wis.*

Righto!

A man has to be an acrobat to amount to anything these days. He has to put his shoulder to the wheel, keep his eye on the ball, an ear to the ground with his back to the wall. At the same time he must have both feet on the ground, keep a level head, a stiff upper lip, whistle while he works, and stay in there pitching as he looks for the silver lining with his head in the clouds.

Prayer

Do not pray for easy lives; pray to become stronger. Do not pray for tasks equal to your powers; pray for powers equal to your tasks.

Phillips Brooks

Half a Mind

One of the commonest of modern expressions is, "I have half a mind to do it." Not much spirit or drive behind that phrase. A man with half a mind never painted a picture, scaled a mountain, made a discovery, or built a house. A man with half a mind never accomplished anything.

Dr. Archer Wallace
in Sunshine Magazine

Same Opinion

When Calvin Coolidge was president, his wife had a portrait painted of him as a surprise. When it was finished she had it hung in his study.

The President was sitting studying it one day when a senator entered. Coolidge indicated the portrait with a nod of his head and the senator sat down and studied the portrait too.

Neither said a word for 15 minutes. Then Coolidge turned to the senator and said: "I think so too."

Uncle Mat.

Love Your Enemies

There is such a destructive reflex action in the soul of a man who allows himself to hate another that it is surprising any sensible person would allow himself to be subjected to it. Hate is a poison which vitiates all character, and brings about the degeneration of personality.

This story was told of General Robert E. Lee: Hearing General Lee speak in the highest terms to President Davis about a certain officer, another officer, greatly astonished, said to him, "General, do you not know that the man of whom you speak so highly to the President is one of your bitterest enemies, and misses no opportunity to malign you?"

"Yes," replied General Lee, "but the President asked my opinion of him; he did not ask for his opinion of me." *Sunshine Magazine*

Choice Bits

Many people owe the grandeur of their lives to their tremendous difficulties.

The real tragedy of life is not in being limited to one talent, but in the failure to use the one talent.

When saving for old age, be sure to lay up a few pleasant thoughts.

Do not stop with doing necessary kindnesses; the unnecessary ones are of far greater importance.

True statesmanship consists in changing a nation from what it is to what it ought to be. *Sunshine Magazine*

California

Being a native son of California, I shall not fail to weave into the tapestry of my remarks a few golden threads of reference to the achievements of that commonwealth, which has been characterized by persons from other and more desolate areas as not a state but a state of mind. I promise you, however, that I shall not say a word about Los Angeles. I come from San Francisco.

Dr. Robert G. Sproul,
President, University of California

It All Depends on How You Look At It

A man bought a new retriever and took him out duck hunting. He was standing in his blind that morning, shot at a duck and the duck fell down. The dog skipped right out on the water, tiptoed over, picked up the duck and brought it back in again. He looked at the dog and thought, "I couldn't have seen that right."

So he shot again, and another duck fell. The dog just skimmed out over the water, tiptoed, and came back with the duck. The man thought, "Boy, that's something!"

A friend of his was in a blind near there, so he went over to see him and said, "Jim, come here. I want to show you something." Jim came over, and they stood there. More ducks came over, the man shot, and this time two ducks fell into the water. The dog just skipped out in the water, picked up the ducks and tiptoed back in.

The guy looked at Jim and said, "How about that? How about that? Don't you notice anything remarkable about the dog?"

Jim said, "Yes, he can't swim."

That's the way it is—it all depends on how you look at it.

John P. Carmichael,
Sports Editor, The Chicago Daily News

Intelligence

Confucius made a remark about intelligence that is worth preserving. He said, "Mankind differs from the animals only by a little, and most people throw that away." When asked, "What is that little thing by which they differ from the animal?" he said, "Intelligence."

Descartes put it better. Descartes said, "There is only one good thing in the world of which everyone thinks he has enough, and that is intelligence."

Dr. Will Durant,
philosopher and author

The Great Learning

In the little book called "The Great Learning," which Confucius is believed (though it is not certain) to have dictated to his grandson, the first paragraph reads like this: "The wise men of antiquity, (that is an astonishing thing—he thought he was a modern, you see, and he talks about Chinese philosophers a thousand years before him) when they wished to make the whole world peaceful and happy, first put their own states into proper order." That is a message to the United Nations. "Before putting their states into proper order, they regulated their own families." That is a message to somebody that I know. "Before regulating their families, they regulated themselves." That is a message for every one of us. "Before regulating themselves, they tried to be sincere in their thoughts, they tried to see things exactly as they really were." An astonishing definition of intellectual sincerity and intellectual conscience, to get your wishes out from between your eyes, and the facts, and see things as they are.

And then the clincher: "And when they learned to see things as they really were, then they became sincere in their thoughts. When they became sincere in their thoughts, their own selves were regulated. When they, themselves, were regulated, their families were in proper order." That is an astonishing statement. It reminds me of my father, who couldn't write his name, but his very presence regulated us because he was all that he was supposed to be, and, looking at him, you had to be decent.

Well, "When they, themselves were regulated, their families were in proper order, and when their families were in proper order, their states were in proper order." As if to say that not all the legislation of a thousand Congresses could make up for the decay of the family organization, and morality. "And when their states were in proper order, the whole world was peaceful and happy."

It sounds too good to be true, but there is a marvelous lesson there —that the faults of society begin in ourselves. We are guilty. We are responsible. And I sometimes marvel that we have so good a government, considering what we are.　　　　　　*Dr. Will Durant,*
philosopher and author

Plato

In the year 372 B.C., Plato issued one of the very finest books ever written, called "The Republic." You will be amazed, if you pick it up, to see how contemporary all the problems are—monarchy, democracy, aristocracy, dictatorship, psychoanalysis, woman suffrage, vegetarianism, Communism, everything is in there, and in the most delightful dialogue form.

He says, for instance, "All forms of government destroy themselves by carrying their basic principle to excess. The first form is monarchy, whose principle is unity of rule. Carried to excess, the rule is too unified. A monarch takes too much power. The aristocracy rebel and establish an aristocracy whose main principle is that selected families rule. The principle of selection is carried to excess, somewhat large numbers of able men are left out, the middle class join them in rebellion, and they establish democracy, whose principle is liberty." That is interesting—it doesn't say "whose principle is 'every man voting,' but 'whose principle is liberty.'"

Then, says Plato, "that principle, too, is carried to excess in the course of time. The democracies become too free, in politics and economics, in morals, even in literature and art, until at last," he says, "even the puppy dogs in our homes rise on their hind legs and demand their rights."

And then disorder grows. Plato says, "Disorder grows to such a point"—and here is the history of the last 25 years—"that a society will then abandon all its liberty to anyone who can restore order."

That is exactly what happened in Italy with Mussolini, and perhaps what happened in Russia, perhaps in Germany.

"And then"—says Plato, in one of the tragic sentences—"comes the fourth form of government, tyranny," or what we call dictatorship. "And then," he says, "monarchy may be restored, and the process begins all over again."

That paragraph gives more light to the events of the Twentieth Century than all the newspapers ever published in my life-time.

Dr. Will Durant,
philosopher and author

Isaac Newton

Isaac Newton was an absorbed, absent-minded student of the mechanism of the world. His wife, going out one day, asked him whether he thought he had brains enough to cook his own lunch? He was not sure, so she told him, "You can boil a couple of eggs."

He asked her, "How do you do that?"

"Well," she said, "bring the water to the boiling point, which will take about two minutes, and then drop the eggs in the water and let them stay there a few minutes."

He brought the water to the boiling point, dropped his watch in the water, and held the eggs carefully in his hands for two minutes, then took out the watch.

One of the inventors of differential and integral calculus, in 1686 he published a second most important book in modern science, perhaps the most important, if you consider the book of Copernicus as rather narrowed to astronomy. This was called "Philosophiae Naturalis Principia Mathematica"—"Mathematical Principles of Natural Philosophy." It attempted to show that the whole universe was a mechanical and mathematical system. It was rather a strange enterprise for so religious a man, because Newton was a very pious man, and wrote books on religion, but as a result of that book of his on natural philosophy, there came the mechanical conception that the world is a machine, that all the operations of it are subject to the laws of physics and chemistry, including the operations of the mind and the heart.

We are just recovering now, I think, from that Newtonian era, both in its literal sense, through the operations of Einstein, and in the philosophical sense that we are abandoning mechanism as a

theory sufficient in itself to understand the universe. We perceive that the organic is something more than the mechanic, and that the world is a scene of growth rather than a mere operation of mechanical law. *Dr. Will Durant,*
philosopher and author

Voltaire

No thinker ever so dominated his age as Voltaire did. Kings and queens courted him. Frederick the Great, having come to Potsdam, supported him, dined with him almost every midnight. The only trouble was that generals came, too, and Voltaire couldn't stand the generals. It seems that they couldn't stand very well, either. They were almost all under the table by 1 A.M. So Voltaire got in the habit of coming late, waiting for the generals to subside.

Frederick didn't like to be left with the generals for a whole hour, so one day (according to an apocryphal story) when Voltaire was late, Frederick put on Voltaire's plate a little card saying "Voltaire ist ein Esel," and signed it "Frederick" with a great big Roman "II."

Voltaire came in and put the little card aside as though it were a platitude, a truism, and Frederick said, "Read that." Voltaire arose and took the card and read, precisely as it was, "Voltaire ist ein Esel; Frederick der Zweite." "Voltaire is one ass, Frederick is the Second." *Dr. Will Durant,*
philosopher and author

Academic Freedom

Academic freedom is not a license to substitute one bias for another. It is not freedom to distort or propagandize, but to inquire and to form judgments. Society quite rightly asks that educators exercise their academic freedom within a framework of acknowledged responsibility and social obligation, just as it quite rightly asks its businessmen to exercise their economic freedom within the same sort of framework. Aside from this qualification, however—which, in essence, is simply requiring the educator to possess moral integrity as well as intellectual competence—the scholar should feel at liberty to examine all ideas critically, and to look at any subject from all viewpoints. But when the truth is found, it should be proclaimed and vigorously defended. *Robert E. Wilson,*
Chairman, Standard Oil Co. (Indiana)

British Quips

1. The First Law of Gravity—never to laugh at your own jokes.
    Almanack 1853
2. The Modern Teacher of Geography—War.   *Almanack 1862*
3. Matrimony—better never than late.   *Almanack 1867*
4. Punctuality is the thief of time.   *Almanack 1864*
5. *Amateur Tenor:* I shall sing just one more song, and then I shall go. *Friend:* Couldn't you go first?   *Almanack 1890*
6. Of all kindnesses it must be confessed that lending books is the one which meets with the least return.   *Almanack 1847*

Daylight Saving Time

In some sections of our country the authorities legislate daylight saving time, and then start the business of the day at 9 o'clock because 8 o'clock is too early. It ain't easy to figure out, son.

The Years of Achievement

The 30's are man's most creative time of life in the arts and sciences, but greatest leadership comes in the 50's, concludes Harvey C. Lehman in his book *Age and Achievement*. The typical creative thinker produces valuable work during most of his life, with his creativity declining only slowly from its early peak.

The time gap between creativity and leadership appears to be increasing, says Mr. Lehman. A study of Cabinet members from 1789 to 1824 shows a median age of 46; from 1925 to 1945 it was 60. The greatest number of top-ranking Civil War generals were between 40 and 44; in World War II the peak ages were 57 to 61. Most college presidents are 50 to 54, and most U. S. senators are 60 to 64.

Commerce

The Majority

Think on this, you salesmen who are timid about going forward against opposition. One time the majority said "The world is flat, and death lies at its edge."

Columbus said "No, it isn't and I'll prove it." And because of him, you and I live in a magnificent land.

Once the majority said, "You can't drive a boat with steam."

Fulton said "Yes you can. And I'll prove it." And civilization took a tremendous leap upwards.

Once the majority said "Man cannot fly." Orville Wright said "Yes he can, and I'll prove it." And business took a mighty surge forward.   *Dr. Harold J. Drown,*
pastor, First Presbyterian Church,
Ottumwa, Iowa

Needed Top Dressing

Those of you who have been in Ireland (in Ulster) may know a place called Clogher. It is rather like Aberdeen, Scotland. There was a railway at one time that ran down that valley.

There was a lady in one carriage with two farmers, and before she got out at a certain station called Aughnacloy, she pulled out her bag and put a little cement filling on, a little of the other ingredients that go on, and put a little on the cheeks and a little on the lips and eyelashes, and these two old boys watched her for some time. The minute she got out, one of them turned to the other and said, "I say, John," says he, "yon lassie puts me in mind of some land a man bought a few years ago. She needs an awful lot of top dressing."

Sir Basil Brooke

Our Opportunities and Our Responsibilities

I believe that essentially what we've got to achieve is an expanding, dynamic balance between productive power and purchasing power. If we will gear our economic capacity to the tremendous unfilled needs of the American people, and make a contribution to other free peoples, in helping them to develop their own resources, then there is enough work to keep the American economy in high gear for many, many years into the future.

Take the housing question. We need to wipe out the slums of America and we ought to start right here in this wonderful city that we call Detroit. Just go down on Skid Row. Just go in any direction from this hotel and you will find slums unworthy for human habitation. There is a tremendous job there.

We need to move to overcome the deficit in our educational system. Millions of American children are being denied their rightful educational opportunity. All of them—made in the image of God—are entitled to an educational opportunity so that they can grow intellectually, spiritually and culturally, limited only by their own individual capacity. We are robbing our nation of the tremendous creative contribution that these young people will make later in life, because we are denying them their educational opportunity.

Our hospitals need to be expanded, so that we can make good health available to every citizen of our great country.

Our roads and our parking problem present a tremendous challenge. There is probably between thirty and forty billion dollars worth of work just on highway construction and parking facilities.

Detroit turns out millions of new cars, but unless Detroit gives some leadership to see to it that our road system, our parking facilities, keep abreast with the progress that we make in the production of automobiles, we are going to be in difficulty.

The St. Lawrence Seaway and many other such projects, will open up whole new areas for economic development, expand job opportunities, develop greater markets and afford our free economy new frontiers of economic expansion.

In the field of consumer goods, you can draw up a monumental list of the needs of the American people for goods needed to provide modern, decent living.   *Walter P. Reuther*

Freedom

Freedom is not a luxury that you can enjoy like membership in the golf club. Freedom is a weapon to fight with. Freedom is a tool to build with. I am confident that if free management and free labor can find a way to cooperate and work together with men of good will in other segments of our society, that working together we can build the kind of a world in which peace will be possible among peoples and nations; a world in which freedom can be made secure; a world that we can make in the image of justice, of human decency, of human dignity, and human brotherhood.   *Walter P. Reuther*

When Flying Was Young

When the art of flying was very young, most of us thought that men on wings would soar over mountains and oceans to bring countries close together in peaceful understanding. We assumed that easy contact between peoples would simplify diplomacy, and decrease war. Now, at the end of the first half century of engine-driven flight, we are confronted with the stark fact that the historical significance of aircraft has been primarily military and destructive. Our bombs have wiped out, in minutes, an inheritance of life and labor which centuries created. Aviation is having its greatest effect on the force-influence of nations, and factors of survival, while diplomatic relationships are floundering in a strange new frame-work of power, time, and space. *from an address by Charles A. Lindbergh before The Institute of the Aeronautical Sciences Honors Night Dinner, New York, N. Y.*

The Character of Man

Survival has a time dimension which says that power consists of more than strength of arms. Short-term survival may depend on the knowledge of nuclear physicists and the performance of supersonic aircraft, but long-term survival depends alone on the character of man. Our scientific, economic, and military accomplishments are rooted in the human quality which produces them. In the last analysis, all of our knowledge, all of our action, all of our progress, succeeds or fails according to its effect on the human body, mind, and spirit. While we concentrate our attention on the tools of economics and war, we must not neglect the basic means of surviving, the basic reason for survival, man himself.

What will this modern environment of ours create in the future character of man? Here, rather than in the atom is the power which will establish our wisdom and decide our fate. And here we pass beyond clear-cut scientific frontiers. Our clocks, weights, measures, and mathematics become inadequate when we discuss the basic qualities of man. We can mark down human efficiency in figures of mass production, but how are we to evaluate mass production, say in such spiritual elements as faith and joy, compassion and courage? We know when we have won a victory in war, but how can we subtract our losses and find the product of that victory in terms of future cultural and hereditary strength? *Charles A. Lindbergh*

Accomplishments and Problems

This mid-century generation we represent stands on amazing accomplishments, but faces alarming problems. We have wiped out a city with a single bomb, but how can we use this fact to heighten our civilization? We build aircraft by the tens of thousands in our factories, but what will our factories build in the character of their personnel—not only in our generation, but in our children, and their children? We tie all countries close together, put each doorstep on a universal ocean, but how are we to direct these accomplishments to improve the basic qualities of life? In emphasizing force, efficiency, and speed, are we losing a humility, simplicity and tranquility without which we cannot indefinitely hold our own, even in worldly competition?   *Charles A. Lindbergh*

Correct

Some people are as confused as that kid who asked his teacher what a cannibal was. She told him, "If you were to eat your father and your mother, what would you be?" The kid replied, "An orphan."   *Gene Flack*

Economists

Probably the most confused people in America are the economists. You've heard it said that if all the economists in the world were laid end to end, it wouldn't be a bad idea. If all the economists in the world were laid end to end, they wouldn't reach one conclusion.

Gene Flack

Me Too

A number of years ago, down in Los Alamos, New Mexico, there were two Navajo Indians standing on hilltops opposing each other, with a beautiful valley down below. They were communicating with each other very quietly, with smoke signals, when all of a sudden, down in the valley below, the first atomic bomb in the history of the world was detonated, with an earth-quaking, shattering sound; a great big mushroom of smoke ascended into the heavens. With that, one of these Navajo Indians dropped his blanket, put his hands on his hips and said, "I wish I'd said that."   *Gene Flack*

Try

A man ran into a doctor's office and said, "Doc, I have a common cold. What do you suggest?"

The doctor said, "If I were you, I'd try for pneumonia. We've got a cure for pneumonia, but we can't do a thing with the common cold." The important thing is to try—try.   *Gene Flack*

Ideas

There is no ceiling in ideas. I think that's the great thing about American business—the fact that there is no ceiling on ideas. Everything goes.

I was down in Florida the other day, and ran into a saltcellar without holes in it, for people on a saltless diet. You get all the exercise and psychological reaction, but you get no salt.

Now they've got a deodorant on the market which kills the odor of deodorant. What a future, what a product!   *Gene Flack*

He Had

Once at Atlantic City there was a man sitting in front of me who kept looking at his watch. I had only been talking about an hour and a half, and wasn't anywhere near through with my talk. Now, I don't mind if someone keeps looking at his watch; it's when they put it up to their ears and shake it that gets me.

Well, he kept looking at his watch, and finally he got up and started to walk out. I said to him, "Where are you going? Why are you leaving?"

He said, "I'm going home to shave."

I said to him, "You should have shaved before you came here." He said, "I did."   *Dr. William H. Alexander*

Not the Whole Load

Once very early in my ministry I went down to the church, expecting a pretty good crowd. I had worked hard on my sermon. When I got there, there was only one man in the audience. I waited, thinking someone else would come in to fill up the church. My wife was ill, or she would have been there. No one came, and finally I said to this man, "Look, I'm just a young preacher, starting out; do you think I should preach my sermon, or dismiss the service now?"

He said, "I'm just a cowhand. All I know is cows. Of course, I do know that if I were taking a load of hay down to the pasture to feed the cattle, and only one cow came up, I'd feed it." So I went ahead and preached, and it took me about an hour and a half, and I kept looking at him as he sat there, with no change in facial expression at all. He just sat there. Finally I went down to him and said, "Look, my friend, was the sermon all right?"

He said, "Well, I ain't very well educated, and I wouldn't know about that. All I know is cows. Of course, I do know if I were taking a load of hay down to the pasture to feed the cattle, and only one cow came up, I'll be hanged if I'd give her the whole load."

Dr. William H. Alexander

Impossible

Someone once told me America was made up of Texas and the outlying states. I knew he was wrong, because no state can outlie Texas.

Dr. William H. Alexander

Should be Interested

Two cats were sitting on the sidelines, watching a tennis game. One cat said to the other, "Who's ahead?" The second cat replied, "I don't know."

"Well, if you don't know what the score is," said the first cat, "why are you watching the game so closely?"

"Oh," said the second cat, "my old man is in that racket."

Dr. William H. Alexander

That Will Hold Him

A guy came up to me and said, "I wouldn't vote for you if you were St. Peter himself." I told him, "If I were St. Peter, I wouldn't need your vote, because you wouldn't be in my district."

Dr. William H. Alexander

"Thank You, Mr. Atkins"

We are a perverse people. The better our American business enterprises, the more proliferous become the attacks upon them from certain of our political leaders and legislators who should, or do, know better but who appear unable to forego minor political advantages even in time of national crises. If it weren't so serious, this continuous attack on American business would be funny.

One is reminded of Kipling's description of the doughboy of Great Britain, Tommy Atkins. You all remember it.

"O it's Tommy this, an' Tommy that,
    an' Tommy, go away;
But it's 'Thank you, Mr. Atkins,' when
    the band begins to play."

And those other lines:

> "O it's Tommy this, an' Tommy that,
>   an' 'Chuck him out, the brute';
> But it's 'Saviour of 'is country,' when
>   the guns begin to shoot."

So it is with American business. We serve, and try to serve well, and yet, over and over again, in the halls of Congress and in our state legislatures, we see these large institutions set upon by thoughtless men.

W. Alton Jones,
President, Cities Service Company

A Stable and Peaceful World

In this critical period, world leadership is clearly in our hands. Our machine civilization is irresistibly pushing its way into every corner of the world. At a thousand crossroads in the world today there are radios, soap, corn flakes, fountain pens, batteries, elevators, road machinery, tractors, automobiles, trucks and refrigerators that came from American factories. Our machines are weaving the economic life of the world into a single fabric. Perhaps America's businessmen and not her politicians hold the key to the solution of the world's problems. Perhaps the 140,000 people that are added every week to the population of Southeast Asia and the two-thirds of the world's people with an income of only $30 to $150 per person each year, will eventually be fed, clothed, and sheltered through the genius of American business leadership.

While the jungles of Africa may not go down tomorrow before an avalanche of American automobiles; while the people of Peru may not eat an American breakfast food tomorrow that pops and crackles as they pour on the cream; and while the people of India may go through life ignorant of the social advantages of Listerine and Lifebuoy, nevertheless, balanced world trade—imports and exports—is imperative to a stable and peaceful world, where Americans and others are not to be called upon to die in wars every twenty-five years, but where people can exchange their goods freely, raise their standards of living, and work and hope with faith in the future.

Herbert V. Prochnow,
Vice-President, The First National Bank of Chicago

Danger and Opportunity

The Chinese long ago learned that a crisis has two parts: the Chinese character for "crisis," I am told, is made of two separate characters—one stands for "danger," and the other for "opportunity."

Louis B. Lundborg,
Vice-President, Bank of America, San Francisco

Poor Judge

There is a story told of a small dog owned by Theodore Roosevelt. This dog was forever getting into fights and forever being beaten. Someone once said to Mr. Roosevelt, "Your dog is a pretty poor fighter."

Mr. Roosevelt said, "Oh, no. He's a very good fighter. He's just a terrible judge of dogs." *General Matthew B. Ridgway*

The Common Man

Among the delusions offered us by fuzzy-minded people is that imaginary creature, the Common Man. It is dinned into us that this is the Century of the Common Man. The whole idea is another cousin of the Soviet proletariat. The Uncommon Man is to be whittled down to size. It is the negation of individual dignity and a slogan of mediocrity and uniformity.

The Common Man dogma may be of use as a vote-getting apparatus. It supposedly proves the humility of demagogues.

The greatest strides of human progress have come from uncommon men and women. You have perhaps heard of George Washington, Abraham Lincoln, or Thomas Edison. They were humble in origin, but that was not their greatness.

The humor of it is that when we get sick, we want an uncommon doctor. When we go to war, we yearn for an uncommon general or admiral. When we choose the President of a University, we want an uncommon educator.

The imperative need of this nation at all times is the leadership of the Uncommon Men or Women. We need men and women who cannot be intimidated, who are not concerned with applause meters, nor those who sell tomorrow for cheers today.

Such leaders are not to be made like queen bees. They must rise by their own merits. America recognizes no frozen social stratifications which prevent this free rise of every individual. They rise by merit from our shops and farms. They rise from the thirty-five million boys and girls in our schools and colleges. That they have the determination to rise is the glorious promise of leadership among free men.

A nation is strong or weak, it thrives or perishes upon what it believes to be true. If our youth is rightly instructed in the faith of our fathers; in the traditions of our country; in the dignity of each individual man, then our power will be stronger than any weapon of destruction that man can devise. *Herbert Hoover*

Confidence

There are voices in our country who daily sound alarms that our civilization is on the way out. Concentrated on the difficulties of our times, they see an early and dour end for us. But civilization does not decline and fall while the people still possess dynamic creative facilities, devotion to religious faith and to liberty. The American people still possess these qualities. We are not at the bedside of a nation in death agony.

Eighty years is a long time for a man to live. As the shadows lengthen over my years, my confidence, my hopes and dreams for my countrymen are undimmed. This confidence is that with advancing knowledge, toil will grow less exacting; that fear, hatred, pain, and tears may subside; that the regenerating sun of creative ability and religious devotion will refresh each morning the strength and progress of my country. *Herbert Hoover*

Not So Bad

After this rather grim recital of the state of the world, I feel I must relieve the gloom created by it by quoting a good lady who had just spent an hour at an exhibition of modern art. "Thank goodness," she said to her companion, as they left the museum, "things are not as bad as they are painted!"
from an address by Warren Lee Pierson,
Chairman of Trans-World Airlines

Moral Strength

Sometimes, as mature, perhaps pseudosophisticates in America, coldly intellectual, we tend to disregard, to set aside arbitrarily, to think unmanly a discussion of God, country, religion and morals. Gentlemen, I say to you today that no matter what rating Dun & Bradstreet gives any corporation represented in this audience, no matter what income you may be paying to the United States Government by way of taxes as a means of establishing your relative affluence, no matter what your material well-being may be, basically, fundamentally, the future of the United States of America is founded on the moral strength of ourselves and our children and our grandchildren, from one end of this country to the other.

I regret to say that as we have moved from an agricultural civilization—where the canopy above us was composed of the stars in the heavens, and where we scrounged in the forest and upon the farms for our food and shelter and clothing, and had close communion with God and allegiance to certain basic moral values—to the civilization where man, from his own inner resourcefulness, ingenuity and enterprise, has fashioned the skyscraper and the submarine and the flying machine, has sent images across thousands of miles without benefit of wires, man has become persuaded to believe that he is self-contained, and that he no longer needs guidance, counsel and inspiration apart and beyond himself, and therefore he has developed for himself a wholly new set of alleged moral values—more material values in the guise of moral values rather than moral values themselves.

I believe that our adult behavior—what we do today—has much more to do with what the younger generation (and those who follow us and assume responsibility in the future) does than those things about which we criticize our youth. It is surprising to me that the young people of America are so good and not so bad, in view of the example set for them by ourselves in our generation.

from an address by Louis B. Seltzer,
Editor, Cleveland Press

Just Between Friends

It is said that George Bernard Shaw once wrote to Winston Churchill as follows:

"Dear Winston: I have just completed a new play which I think is one of my best. We are having the premiere showing of it in London next Monday night. I think it would be a wonderful thing if you could attend, and therefore I am enclosing a complimentary ticket herewith. As a matter of fact, Winston, I am enclosing two complimentary tickets so you can bring along a friend, if you have one left in London."

Churchill, himself a master of the fine are of repartee, answered the letter in kind and wrote: "Dear George: I have received your very thoughtful invitation asking me to attend the opening show of your performance in London next Monday night, and regret exceedingly that due to a previous commitment, (that's an old Parliamentary gag) it is going to be impossible to attend. However, I am retaining the complimentary tickets and assure you I shall be mighty glad to attend the second performance of your play if there is one."

United States Senator Karl E. Mundt

Our Economic Achievements

What has the American economic system achieved? First, of course, a prodigious volume of production. The United States has but 6 per cent of the world's population and land area, but it produces from 40 to 50 per cent of the world's goods. Production here has increased 30 times between 1850 and 1950, while the labor force grew less than 9 times. Many Europeans and even more Asians profess to find this vast stream of production spiritually barren and, indeed, they say that sometimes it is a source of danger. They would be right insofar as Americans make a deity of material production and of material goods, but how many of them really do so? There is nothing spiritually degrading about a pair of shoes. Production can be one means of proving man's God-given capacity to control and to improve his material environment, rising above it.

But we must make spiritual use of the values achieved in our greater mastery of the material elements. We must realize in the fullest, rational sense that God giveth the increase.

The second point about our economic achievement is that it is based upon the shortest working hours in the world. In 1850 the average in American industry was 70 hours a week. Today it is about 40. Again, interpretations must be added to these simple figures. There is nothing evil or undesirable in hard work, and we have not yet adequately learned how to use the new leisure. I am not talking about your leisure, because I am aware of the problems of the executive who is exempt from these 40-hour-week figures, by definition. But, nevertheless, the change in working hours which has come about has a certain importance. It is important to ease the grinding burden of toil, the 70 hours, the six or seven days a week of the last century. And it is valuable to give man the opportunity to live a richer and a more varied life. But we must not forget to place real value on work, hard work, as we congratulate ourselves on the diminishing number of hours worked per week.

The challenge of which work is a partial symbol is a spiritual imperative, and even adversity—short of the breaking point—is the ladder up which men climb. We must therefore keep our economic society lean and vigorous, competitive, restless, unsatisfied.

The third point in the basis of our economic system is, of course, productivity, the constant increase in output per man-hour. This, of course, is different from and, indeed, more important than mere volume of production. Productivity per man-hour has increased sixfold since 1850, and in the past three or four years it has gone ahead at a greater rate of increase than ever.

Economists and labor leaders used to speak of the "speed-up" and what they called "the degradation of labor," but employers now have found out that labor must be a willing and eager partner if really high production is to be achieved.   *Erwin D. Canham,*
editor, Christian Science Monitor

Good Neighbor Policy in Business

"Be a good neighbor" means being neighborly both within and without the plant gates. Inside it represents those leadership attributes which help all members of the organization recognize their true worth as individuals, make the most of opportunities, and turn potential into achievement. It includes training programs for the newest apprentice fresh from a vocational school, and ranges to the grooming of more experienced employes for further managerial responsibilities.

Neighborliness, within the plant also means the development of better two-way communication between management and employes. Here is a field in which none of us has done enough, but where many are now trying. Certainly, anyone who would pretend to call himself an executive must give consideration to all of the problems involved. Long and bitter experience has taught us that communication does not mean "talking to ourselves." Nor are lectures the answer. Our training people know that one discussion is worth an uncounted number of lectures. Lectures, you may recall, have been defined as the process whereby the words of the lecturer get to the notebooks of the audience without passing through the minds of either.

I could mention dozens of other plant activities, such as safety and recreation, which come under this heading of "Neighborliness inside the plant gates."

Outside the plant gates, it seems to me that the first contribution a businessman can make is to operate a successful business—thus feeding the economic life stream of his neighborhood.

Beyond that, as we all recognize, is a definite responsibility to aid in all of those civic projects aimed at the betterment for the city and its people.

Of course, there is an element of self-interest in all of these community activities, just as there is a definite element of community interest in seeing to the successful operation of our businesses and industries. Every desirable community needs the support of the successful enterprises which have contributed so much to its growth. Successful enterprises must be guided and managed by men of vision and vigorous drive by executives who are aware of their various responsibilities and who are able to place them in their proper perspective.   *Clifford F. Hood,*
President of the United States Steel Corporation

Our Way of Life

Our system is based on the belief in the responsibility of the individual citizen who lives in God's world and who, in a general way, is afforded freedom of choice and the right to the pursuit of happiness. On such simple beliefs we have created a civilization which has shown tremendous material power, and today is becoming the cultural center of the world.   *Andrew Heiskell,*
publisher, Life magazine

American Progress

Some of the reasons for our remarkable American record of economic progress are our rich natural resources, the fact that we are a young country, and our large area of internal peace.

Even more fundamental are the following:

One, the free enterprise economy is a real production-for-use economic system; therefore, producers must remain flexible and responsive to consumer preferences freely expressed in the market place.

Two, there is the will to compete; thus productive resources tend to be used only by the more efficient, thereby going farther.

Three, a free enterprise economy places a premium on new ideas by offering large rewards to the fellow with the good idea. Thus, others must quickly follow or be extinguished by competition.

Paul W. McCracken,
Professor of Business Conditions,
University of Michigan

A Gift of God

Fritz Kreisler said of his playing, "It is a gift of God and not my own possession that I can play as I do. It means an opportunity to serve humanity. Music is too sacred to be sold—should the birds ask pay for singing? I never look upon the money I earn as my own; it belongs to the public and is placed in my trust for proper use. So I never spend money for personal pleasure or in high living. I reduce my needs to a minimum and feel morally guilty in ordering a costly meal while there is so much hunger and misery in the world. If music brings people happiness, then it makes me happy to play for them."

Except With God

Until man has found God, and has been found by God, he begins at no beginning and works to no end. Nothing in the universe or in life falls into place except with God.   *H. G. Wells,*
English novelist

He Was Less Trouble

Note attached by a widow to one of the many forms she had filled out for the insurance company: "You have asked me to fill out so many proofs of claim and I've had so much trouble getting my money that I sometimes wish my husband hadn't died."

The Weekly Underwriter,
February 7, 1953

Overrule the Motion

While he was Chief Justice of the Supreme Court, Charles Evans Hughes took several of his associates on a cruise down Chesapeake

Bay. It was rough, and the late Justice Cardozo was having a rougher time of it than the rocking boat. Mr. Hughes found him leaning over the rail, his face about the same shade as the waves beneath them. "I'm sorry," said the host. "If you can think of anything I can do for you, please let me know."

Justice Cardozo lifted his head to mutter: "There certainly is, your Honor—please overrule this motion!"

Correction, Please

About the middle of yesterday's interminable afternoon, Mr. Tex Rickard, the Ebbetts Field announcer, spoke through the public address system thus: "Will the ladies and gentlemen in centerfield kindly remove their wearing apparel—," which was the best suggestion made all day for livening up a shabby entertainment, but Mr. Rickard added prudishly, "—from the outfield railing."

At the moment the Yankees were threatening to splatter Brooklyn's pitching staff all over the premises and witnesses in the front row might have got some dry-cleaning bills. However, there were no fatalities except from boredom as New York won the second game of the World Series, 7 to 1.   *by Red Smith*
in the New York Herald Tribune

Did Sam Goldwyn Really Say Them?

1. Anybody who goes to a psychoanalyst should have his head examined.

2. Include me out.

3. I will tell you in two words—Impossible.

4. You have the mucous of a great idea.

5. I read part of all the way through.

6. I had a terrific idea this morning, but I didn't like it.

7. *To an employee on Saturday noon:* You look all run down. Go home and don't come back until Monday.

8. *To a writer:* I am counting on you. Remember, you are the most important clog in the wheel.

9. I know the man is a genius. But he is a stupid genius.

10. *To an employee who was leaving to take his usual lunch hour:* You don't look well. Take a nap after lunch. Remember, half an hour lunch and half an hour nap.

Do You Have the Time?

For people who "don't know where the time goes," The Royal Bank of Canada has released some interesting figures on leisure hours:

Hours in year, 365 days		8,760
Sleeping hours, eight daily	2,920	
Working hours, eight daily (excluding two weeks vacation and seven holidays)	1,960	
Travel hours, two daily	490	
Eating hours, three daily	1,095	
Dressing and undressing hours, one daily	360	
Total hours consumed		6,830
Do-as-you-please hours		1,930

Thus leisure time averages out to 80 days of 24 hours each, or nearly 22 per cent of the year. It's almost identical with total working hours.   *The Employment Counselor (National Association of Personnel Consultants, Columbus, Ohio)*

Restored, But Not Fully

In a certain lawsuit recently, one of the witnesses was a woman covered with jewels. She had dyed her hair and had hopelessly overdressed and overdecorated herself in a vain effort to conceal the evidence of her age. Asked on the stand how old she was, she replied calmly, "Twenty-six." The judge raised his eyebrows. "Twenty-six? Well, what year were you born?" "1900," the woman admitted reluctantly. "Oh well," said the judge to the clerk, "put, founded in 1900—restored in 1931." Well, if we would spend as much effort in growing up inside as we do in trying to keep youthful outside, we would be better off. Accept your age—Act your age!

Charles M. Crowe,
Pastor, Wilmette Methodist Church,
Wilmette, Illinois

Confusion

Too many of us these days are like the young husband who had been asked to copy a radio recipe. His wife discovered that he had been tuned to two stations. His recipe read, "Hands on hips, place one cup of flour on the shoulders, raise knees and depress toes, mix thoroughly in ½ cup of milk. Repeat six times. Inhale quickly ½ teaspoon baking powder, lower feet and mash hard boiled eggs in a sieve. Exhale, breathe naturally, and sift into a bowl. Lie flat on the floor and roll the white of an egg backward and forward until it comes to a boil. In 10 minutes remove from the fire and rub smartly with a rough towel. Breathe naturally, dress in warm flannels, and serve with fish soup."

You see, too often our minds are divided and confused because we are listening to two sets of voices: the voice of God and the voice of man, the voice of duty and the voice of pleasure, the voice of idealism and the voice of selfishness, the voice of evil and the voice of good, the voice of dishonesty and the voice of conscience.

Charles M. Crowe,
Pastor, Wilmette Methodist Church,
Wilmette, Illinois

A Welcome to New Citizens

It is a real privilege and pleasure to welcome people into one's home, and is even a greater privilege to welcome people like you, into one's country, as new citizens.

So I say, welcome to your new home in the United States!

I know you have looked forward to this day with much hope and expectation. And now the day has come when your plans are to be realized.

My most sincere wish is that your fondest hopes and prayers for a rich and full life here may be fulfilled.

I don't mean rich in the way we speak of money, but rather in spiritual values. The deep satisfaction that comes when we have lived up to the ideals and principles we were taught at our mothers' knees. The pride we felt when we stood fast and were honorable in our dealings—when we gave full value for the services we were paid for—when we exercised our duty and rights as a citizen, and voted, or served on a jury, or used our talents no matter how humble they seemed to us.

That is the kind of person who helped make this a great country.

Recently a friend from Norway said he was not so much impressed with the fact that the vast majority of our people have automobiles, refrigerators, electric stoves, savings accounts, or investments, but he was impressed with the fact that people had come here from every corner of the globe—people of every religious, political, and national view—and in spite of their different views they helped make this a great country.

So don't think of yourself as being only one out of 160,000,000 people—but rather think of yourself as an individual who has something important to contribute to your new country.

I am sure that while this is a happy day for you, that in a way it is also a sad one. You have foresworn allegiance to the country where you were born, where you have left loved ones and friends and where you have spent many happy days, but you have not foresworn your love for it. I know how you feel because I heard my parents who came here from Norway often speak of again seeing their loved ones and the places they knew in their childhood. But they also found, as you will find, a deep and abiding love for their new country.

Some day I hope you will appear before the Jury Commission to qualify for jury service. You will find it a very satisfying experience because you are helping to administer the law by serving on a jury. Also I hope you will exercise your right to vote on every occasion. Remember the only one who has the right to offer, even constructive criticism of his government, is the person who has voted.

There is much more I would like to tell you of this country which I hope you may come to love as much as I do. But I will end this brief but sincere welcome by wishing you God's richest blessing in your new experience.   *an address by Casper Apeland*
to new citizens in the Circuit Court
of Waukegan, Illinois

Tell Me That

John W. Davis once wrote, when he had been asked to sacrifice a principle to help assure his nomination for the presidency: "What is life worth, after all, if one has no philosophy of his own to live by? If one surrenders this to win an office, what will he live by after the office is won? Tell me that."   *Frank W. Abrams*

The Business Republic

The modern business corporation has become a cooperative way of life for large numbers of people. In effect what has happened is that many individuals with varying amounts of available capital and many others with varying skills and experience and energy have pooled their resources and abilities in a joint enterprise, in the belief that they will all get out of their combined efforts more than anyone could get from his own.

The modern business organization *is* a way of life. It is the source from which three out of four people in this country must draw a livelihood for themselves and their families, and to which they must look for not only the economic but even much of the mental and social satisfactions they need to give their lives fullness and meaning.

Perhaps the most drastic change that the business revolution is causing in our business society is in the form and spirit of its government. In typically American fashion, the old fashioned dictatorship or feudal concept of governing the business part of people's lives has been largely replaced by the new "Business Republic."

If there is any one thing that sets the republics of the free world apart from the dictatorships, it is their belief in the inalienable rights of the individuals. I will not deny that natural resources developed by spiritually hungry people who dared to venture from the security of their homelands to the risky frontiers of a new country had a lot to do with the development of America. That we have had within our country the greatest release of human ingenuity and energy in the world's history, however, was only possible because Americans knew what their rights were, generally agreed on them, felt secure in them, and worked together to uphold them. They were clearly set forth in the Constitution of the United States of America.

Of all the changes that are being wrought in our economic society by the business revolution, the most promising from the standpoint of both future profits and future happiness of the people is the growing awareness that individuals have inalienable rights as citizens of the Business Republic.

Most of these rights are still in the process of formulation. They are still being defined and redefined. Few of them are really understood or agreed to by many managements or many employees, let alone by both. Only a handful have been reduced to writing in any statement of principles, Constitution if you please, to serve as the code of business government. So employees cannot yet feel secure in their rights. But all this is coming, and very fast too.

Let me list some of the principles that seem to be gradually emerging and clarifying themselves into a Bill of Rights for the citizens of the Business Republic.

1. *The right of freedom of choice.* This presupposes that the citizen of the business republic is not putting in a term of involuntary servitude—that not only can he be separated from his job for just cause, but that he has the inalienable right to leave it if he so desires. It also means freedom to work out his own destiny in business with the help of, not in spite of, the business.

2. *The right to safe and healthful working conditions.* No one, I am sure, will question the obligation of management to protect people against occupational hazards.

3. *The right to earn a decent living.* This it seems to me, as almost too obvious to mention. Although rare is the man who thinks he is being paid enough, every study of the motivations of workers shows that the pay problem ranks well down the list. By and large American business is paying good wages by any standard.

4. *The right to equitable compensation for the work he performs.* This is not a question of amount of pay, but fairness of pay. The employee has a right to expect that his salary or wage is reasonably close to what others are getting in the business for jobs of equal difficulty and complexity. He also has the right to expect that his pay will not be out of line with what other businesses are paying for the same kind of work.

5. *The right to share in the prosperity of the business.* This is not the time to discuss the advantages and disadvantages of so-called profit sharing. But if we accept the premise that the business republic is a way of life for people, who hope to do better cooperatively than alone, then we must also accept the principle that the better the team does, the more the individual benefits.

6. *The right to earn security.* Since employees usually raise families—with all the hopes, aspirations and problems which that entails—they are entitled to have the opportunity to earn reasonable protection against the financial hazards of illness, accident, death or old age. Minimizing freedom from worry about uncontrollable misfortunes is like removing a millstone from the necks of all of us, even managers.

7. *The right to equal opportunity to progress.* This does not mean that everyone in the organization has an equal chance to be president. But to the full limit of his aptitudes, knowledge and effort he will be given fair and thorough consideration for advancement. It means that working up through the ranks is not just giving lip

service to a time-honored tradition, but that men are encouraged and trained and helped to do so. And it also means that management makes every effort to use people to the limits of their capacity, but not above it or very far behind it.

8. *The right to be productive.* This presupposes confident, intelligent, friendly, aggressive leadership, furnishing a creative climate in the business which stimulates people to want to contribute to it, encourages them to use their heads and not just their backs and nimble fingers, supplies the best of tools to make increased productivity possible, and is generous in giving credit where due.

9. *The right to understand.* Every citizen of the business republic is entitled to know the broad goals of the organization and the reasons for them. He is entitled to know the score of the game and how the business is progressing, and to hope for something better for himself if he helps in that progress. He is entitled to know not only what part he is expected to play in the whole scheme, but how that part fits in with the whole, and why he is asked to do his specific assignments. He is entitled to learn all those things about the business which will help him contribute more to it.

10. *The right to freedom of speech.* In business, as in all other phases of American life, the employee has a right to a voice in matters affecting him and his work. He is entitled to criticize and to advance ideas, and have both his grievances and his ideas considered fairly and decided on their merit by people who are competent to judge. This means, of course, that he must have free access to his superiors.

11. *The right to belong.* Man is by nature gregarious. His largest area of personal satisfaction comes from his relationships with other people. The citizen of the Business Republic has a right to good close group relationships with his fellow workers, both on and off the job. He has the right to join others, either casually or in organizations of his choice for social purposes, for mutual protection or assistance, or for collective bargaining with management. And above everything else, he has the right to be considered on a par with every other employee of the business when it comes to his importance in the whole scheme. To be sure one job may require much less talent or experience or knowledge or skill than another. But it is not one iota less important. The fact that he is on the job presupposes that he is

a *required* member of the cooperative community we call the Business Republic.

Those then are some of the basic rights of employees that are becoming clearer as the Business Republic matures. Others have rights, too, which must be respected if the enterprise is to prosper. Owners are entitled to a reasonable return on a growing value of their investment. Management is entitled to manage without undue interference or harrassment. Consumers are entitled to share in the fruits of improved performance through better values on the products they buy. The strength of this country lies in freedom of choice in the market place, and millions of consumers daily cast their ballots automatically for or against this or that business.

When the basic rights of the citizens of the Business Republics of this country are more clearly defined and understood, and embodied in their written policies, and carried out consistently in management's daily decisions and acts so that all may have confidence in them, then the business revolution will be complete. When this will be, I would not hazard a guess. But it will not take many years at our present rate of progress, and our increasing understanding of the economics of happiness.

If I have any proposition to make to you tonight, it is that business is a way of life for three out of four people in this country; that these people are striving for a good life, liberty, and a chance to attain some degree of happiness in business; that as they approach their goals through the Business Republic they will be more productive; and when they are more productive, your business and mine will be more profitable.   *from an address by Jervis J. Babb,*
President, Lever Brothers Company, New York, N. Y.,
before the Economic Club of New York, New York City

Progress

The past is gone and static. Nothing we can do can change it. The future is before us and dynamic. Everything we do will affect it. Each day brings with it new frontiers, in our homes and in our businesses, if we will only recognize them. We are just at the beginning of progress in every field of human endeavor.

Charles F. Kettering

Self-Evident Truths

The Constitution is your business. It is in a state of neglect. Its ramparts are shot through with apathy and complacency. It is high time for a repair job; it may even be too late.

Let's see the case of the Constitution in perspective, and in order to get that perspective, let's make some stipulations.

First of all, we must stipulate certain facts laid down by the Founding Fathers of this Republic. They called them self-evident truths; I call them facts.

Let's stipulate what the Declaration of Independence says. You can read it as well as I; you haven't done it lately. I advise you to do that. The Declaration of Independence, first of all, stipulates the fact that all men are created by God. God exists not as a matter of faith but as a matter of fact. That we stipulate for the record, and that is basic and fundamental.

Secondly, they stipulate the fact that all men are equal in God's sight, and for that reason, and for that reason alone, they are equal before the law of the land. Beyond that they are unequal in every way in the world, and no one in creation can equalize that. It is just as important for you to advertise the material and physical inequality of human nature as it is to remember that before God, and before the law of the land, everybody is entitled to the same treatment.

Then we stipulate the third great fact of American life, the fact that rights are not the gifts of the state or the government, or the Bill of Rights or the Constitution; rights are the gifts of God, inalienably breathed out into every human soul when the human soul is manifested by the breath of life.

And then life and liberty are linked together as co-equally important. Liberty is just as important as life, according to these stipulations. You can't sell liberty for security. You can't sell liberty for money. You can't sell liberty for tranquility or apathy, any more than you can commit suicide. Liberty is a part of the nature of man, and man is denatured when his liberty is taken from him, just as he is completely murdered when his life is taken. That is stipulation Number 3.

And here is Stipulation Number 4, the fourth and most important fact of life, because up to this time the Founding Fathers were merely looking at the stars and reading the messages they saw in the heavens. Now they went to work. They had to invent something. What to do about this liberty which sparks the inequality, which blossoms civilization? How to preserve liberty? That was the $64 question, and they sat down and invented an entirely new type and kind of government.

Governments are instituted, they said, to secure and protect the God-given rights of man. Government is man's agent for the protection of God's gifts.

Nowhere in the great books, or lesser books, nowhere outside of Holy Writ is there a more profound statement than that—to secure these rights, to protect these gifts of God, and for no other purpose, governments are instituted amongst men, deriving their existence as well as their powers from the consent of the governed.

Government is a device, a tool. Tools are not always perfect. They have special purposes. Government was fabricated as a tool for a special purpose, a protective purpose.

The fact of God, you see, debased government to a point of servitude rather than mastery. There it has stayed throughout this American history of ours, and nowhere else on earth has that concept been maintained.   *Clarence E. Manion*

If You Can Keep It

The American system of government provides investors, producers and consumers with freedom of choice and freedom of opportunity.

In the American system of government the productive facilities of the nation are owned by the people instead of the government.

The American system of government recognizes the dignity of the individual, encourages high moral and ethical standards, and gives its citizens an incentive to do their best and rewards them according to their productive ability.

As long as we keep the spirit and letter of our Constitution alive, we will continue to enjoy our cherished liberties and be a great nation.

Following the signing of the Constitution, a lady asked the venerable Benjamin Franklin, "Mr. Franklin, what have you given us?" The wise old man responded, "we have given you a republic," then the sage hesitated and concluded, "if you can keep it." Franklin knew that one of the saddest facts of history is that republics vanish. For

example, the shift from the Roman Republic to the Roman Empire, with the resultant *concentration* of *power* in the *executive* was so gradual that the people lost their liberty before they realized what had happened.   *George E. Stringfellow,*
Senior Vice-President, Thomas A. Edison,
Incorporated, West Orange, New Jersey

No Guarantee

No guarantee has ever been given to America that it shall continue to enjoy the dominance it now has as a nation. America came to its might and majestic greatness and achieved her present high destiny through a conscious dedication of our fathers to religious truths and principles for they knew that unless the Lord build the city, they labor in vain who build it. We must intensify our religious life as a people. We must restore to our homelife some measure of that inspiration which our fathers and mothers bequeathed to us. We must give our children that sense of responsibility which will give strength to their characters and direction to their lives.

Francis Cardinal Spellman,
Archbishop of New York

"Only So Long"

About sixty years ago someone asked James Russell Lowell, then the American Ambassador to Great Britain, "How long will the American republic endure?" The great statesman and diplomat responded, "Only so long as the ideals of the men who made it great continue dominant."   *George E. Stringfellow,*
Senior Vice-President, Thomas A. Edison,
Incorporated, West Orange, New Jersey

"To Sin By Silence"

"To sin by silence," said Abraham Lincoln, "when they should protest, makes cowards of men." Our liberties were not won by cowards and I assure you they will not be preserved by such characters.

If we would save our republic and avoid tyranny, we must emulate St. Paul who, crying that the days were evil, labored to improve them. We must not follow Hamlet who cried that the days were evil and cursed them. Our forefathers gave us a system of government which has produced greater liberties and higher living standards than ever before experienced in the history of the world. As citizens it is our duty and our responsibility to do our utmost to protect that system and to provide moral leadership for the rest of the world. That is our duty and we cannot escape it if we would.

George E. Stringfellow,
Senior Vice-President, Thomas A. Edison,
Incorporated, West Orange, New Jersey

The Value of Knowledge

All of us are quick to recognize in principle the value of knowledge. Yet we may hesitate to do what is necessary in order to open wider access to knowledge for others or to deepen our own knowledge. Too often we even share in reactions that can be explained only by a fear of knowledge.

This contradiction—so prevalent in our generation, so dangerous to the peace and progress of future generations—is not a new one. Its cause is to be found in attitudes common to all men and all times.

If we fear knowledge, and act under the ban of such fear, is it not often because we fear change? In order fully and freely to accept knowledge, and what flows from knowledge, we have both to muster the courage and possess the humility that enables us to accept change. In the development of human society, knowledge and the fruits of knowledge are revolutionary elements. They have proved to be forces which time and again have driven man from his Eden of accepted forms and privileges. They have led to the creation of new forms of social order that succeed one another in responses to the forces set in motion by new conquests for knowledge...

from an address by Dag Hammarskjold,
Secretary-General, United Nations,
at the Charter Day Dinner of the
Columbia University Bicentennial Year

Educational Opportunity

About two weeks ago I stood on the steps of this building with two distinguished British educators—Sir Philip Morris, vice-chancellor of the University of Bristol, and Dr. Douglas Logan, principal of the great University of London. We looked down the Mall at the substantial buildings, with the towering Mayo Memorial rising into the sky above the older ones. We watched groups of new students on their orientation tours—the advance guard of the thousands here now.

These men, I think, were a bit aghast to see with their own eyes the vast contrast between the American commitment to educational opportunity and that of other lands, including their own. For in all Great Britain, with less than 84,000 fulltime students, only 4 per cent of the young people of college age are enrolled in the universities.

How different the story in our country where 30 per cent of all Americans between the ages of 18 and 21 were attending college or university, as shown by the 1950 census! ...

Despite the smaller percentage of young people attending universities in Great Britain, the fact is that nearly 74 per cent are aided by scholarships, mostly provided by Parliament or local governments. In Canada the figure is 14 per cent. In the United States it is nowhere near even that figure.   *Dr. J. L. Morrell,*
President, University of Minnesota

Dig the Bait

Speaking last spring at Emory University in Georgia, the distinguished historian and former president of this University, Dr. Guy Stanton Ford, recited to the students a little poem by John Masefield, the British poet and dramatist:

"Sitting still and wishing," the verses went,
"Makes no person great.
"The good Lord sends the fishing,
"But you must dig the bait."

"The good Lord certainly sends good fishing when he opens to anyone the opportunities of a college education," President Ford remarked, adding that "the student who deserves them has only to dig the bait."   *Dr. J. L. Morrell,*
President, University of Minnesota

World Trade

It is an elementary fact of economic life that if we expect to receive dollars in payment for our exports, we have to make those dollars available abroad.

What does this mean? It means simply that if we restrict our imports under the theory that we are protecting America, and the

American standard of living, we are in fact doing exactly the opposite. Restriction of our imports means restriction of our exports. And that can mean reduced employment and living standards not only for the many Americans—farmers, manufacturers, workers—depending on exports, but of the American consuming public as a whole which has to pay higher prices for its goods.

Winthrop W. Aldrich,
United States Ambassador to Great Britain

The 19th Hole

I see many of my old 19th hole golfing companions from Glenview here today. I was a member out there when I lived here. I still am a non-resident member. I never was much good on the 18 holes, but on the 19th I got along fairly well.

A crowd of us used to meet in the locker room, and we finally composed a little rhyme that expressed our philosophy which went something like this:

> Our main base is the locker room
>   Where highest winds prevail;
> Where many a squawk and alibi
>   Surmount the foaming ale.
> Where many a wife calls up of eve,
>   Each wife a burning soul;
> But no wife ever reaches us—
>   We're safe at the 19th hole.

from an address by William T. Faricy,
President, Association of American Railroads

Can I Take His Place?

A persistent office seeker rushed to former United States Senator, the late Pat McCarran, on learning of the death of an official. "Can I take Flanagan's place?" he pleaded. The Senator, wearied by previous entreaties, snapped, "It's alright with me if you can square it with the undertaker."   *told by James A. Farley*

Mass Information or Mass Entertainment

The newspaper has had to make great concessions to the ever growing demand on the part of the public to be entertained. Within the last two decades the number of comic strips printed daily and

Sunday has increased by many times. And don't for one minute assume that only children read them. Actually, more adults read the most popular comic strip on a typical day than read the most important news story on the front page.

In a recent study of metropolitan newspapers, it was found that the average amount of time which a reader spends daily on the important news of his country and of the world is less than four minutes. He spends ten times as much time on sports, local gossip, and the service and entertainment features.   *George Gallup,*
Director, American Institute of Public Opinion

Our Lack of Intellectual Interests

Despite the fact that we have the highest level of formal education in the world, fewer people buy and read books in this nation than in any other modern democracy. The typical Englishman, with far less formal education, reads nearly three times as many books as our typical citizen. In fact, an Englishman who leaves school at the age of fourteen reads about as many books as our college graduate.

The lack of interest in books is reflected by the number of book stores in the United States. In this country, about 1450 stores sell a fairly complete line of books. In Denmark, a nation whose population is just about half that of New York City, there are some 650 full-fledged book stores. If we had the same proportion in this country as Denmark, we would have not 1450 book stores—but 23,000!

But some will say that whereas we have few book stores we have a great many free libraries. We do, but certainly not to the extent of the Scandinavian countries. In the United States there are about 7,500 free public libraries. In Sweden a nation only one twenty-fifth the size of the United States in population, there are 6,500 free public libraries. Or to put this comparison in another way, the United States would have to have not 7,500 libraries—but 150,000 to equal Sweden!
George Gallup,
Director, American Institute of Public Opinion

Freedom

Freedom is not an economic or political discovery.
It is not freedom for this or from that.
It is not freedom for the National Association of Manufacturers or the American Federation of Labor.

Freedom is related to people and in the last analysis it is a religious discovery. The religious through the ages have struggled to relate the individual to their Deity. The Judo-Christian philosophy of our Bible is replete with the philosophy of individualism. People are important. The sanctity of persons and their individual relationship with God are all important.

It was 2,000 years ago that Christ came to earth with the revolutionary doctrine that people are significantly important. He said that neither Caesar nor the Temple had the right to come between man and his Maker.

And it was our forefathers that brought that revolutionary conviction to America and for the first time in the history of the world, wove their deep, religious convictions into the political fabric of government. They gave their convictions life in our Declaration of Independence and in our Constitution.

Our forefathers said, "No majority, not even the government itself can interfere with the unalienable, God-given rights of individual people."   *from an address by William J. Grede,*
President, Grede Foundries, Inc., and past President,
National Association of Manufacturers, before the
summer School of Banking at the University of Wisconsin

An Old Saying

There's an old saying in Cheyenne that "if you want a short winter just sign a note that comes due in the spring."   *Harry Henderson,*
former Rotary District Governor, Cheyenne, Wyoming

7

EPIGRAMS

AND

QUIPS

The best way to check the "life of the party" is to let him pick up the check.

Don't make your garden too big if your wife tires easily.
Allegan Gazette, Shelbyville, Michigan

Why is it that some folks, even after they're admitted to a friend's home, keep right on knocking?   *Lexington (Ky.) Herald*

As the Chinese doctor said to his patient, "Long time no fee."

Henry Morgan says a careful driver is something more than a guy who honks his horn as he goes through a red light.

Traffic is so bad that even back seat drivers can't help much.

A man had better buy his wife a new washing machine than to put silver handles on her casket.   *Billy Sunday*

Fisherman's Motto—Bait and See.

The hope of the future lies in people who go to bed weary, instead of getting up all tired out.

If you're wondering what happened to the old-fashioned girl, you'll probably find her at home with her husband.

News-Journal, Campbellsville, Ky.

A radio announcer is a man who tries to get the commercial in before the listener can change stations.

Subtlety is the art of saying what you think, and getting out of range before it is understood.   *American, Oxford, N. Y.*

A small boy is willing to believe almost anything—except that his teacher is just as glad as he is to see vacation coming.

Farmer, Idaho Falls, Idaho

Learn from the mistakes of others—you can't live long enough to make them all yourself.   *Intelligencer, Doylestown, Pa.*

A small town is the place where a fellow with a black eye doesn't have to explain to people; they know.

Herald and Democrat, Siloam Springs, Ark.

Our town is a delightful place to live in if you are a delightful person to live beside.   *Courier, Coffeeville, Miss.*

Tourist—A man in sport clothes with a head cold.

If you think old soldiers just fade away, try getting into your old Army uniform.   *Herald, Bradenton, Fla.*

The hand that lifts the cup that "cheers," should not be used to shift the gears.

A wedding ring may not be as tight as a tourniquet, but it certainly stops the wearer's circulation.   *Journal, Sarasota, Fla.*

Summer—the time of year when the highway authorities close the regular roads and open up the detours.

A far sighted office employee is one who asks for a desk away from the door so he won't get killed at five o'clock.

A chrysanthemum by any other name would be easier to spell.

To put is to place a thing where you want it . . . to putt is a vain attempt to do the same thing.   *Rotary Cog, Mesa, Arizona*

The average girl would rather have beauty than brains, because she knows that the average man can see better than he can think.

Ralph Bellamy of Man Against Crime refers to drama critics as "leading members of the first knife audience."

After a month on a new diet, Mrs. Jones was asked what she weighed. "One hundred and plenty," she replied.

Marriage entitles women to the protection of strong men to hold stepladders for them while they paint the kitchen ceiling.
                                                The Postage Stamp

College professors are the persons who get what's left after the athletic director and football coach are paid off.

The big game hunter was missing in Africa. Apparently something he disagreed with ate him.

It's not hard to spot a fool, unless he's hiding inside you.

Bob Hawk describes his butcher as a clumsy fellow whose hands are always in the weigh.

Can you spell expediency in five letters? Yes, XPDNC.

The office drinking fountain—"Old Faceful."

Algonquin J. Calhoun on Amos 'n' Andy radio show: "I been busier than a flea workin' his way through a dog show."

Dr. Earl Butz: "It is not the High Cost of Living that is bothering the American people, but rather, the Cost of High Living."

New York City sign shop advertisement: "Signs—All Kigns."

Buck passing is not new, but they never passed faster than they do now.

The mechanical lie detector will never be as successful as the one made from Adam's rib.   *Westby Times*

Hardening of the heart ages people more quickly than hardening of the arteries.

Dignity is the capacity to hold back on the tongue what never should have been on the mind in the first place.

Progress involves risk—you can't steal second and keep your foot on first.   *Speed Queen News*

Gossip runs down as many persons as automobiles.

Bob Hope: "The ten most beautiful words in the English language are: 'Dear Sir: Inclosed find your income tax refund for 1952.' "

Weather forecast: "Snow—followed by little boys on sleds."
                    Henry Morgan

You're getting old when the gleam in your eye is from the sun hitting your bifocals.   *American Eagle*

It's nice to be important, but it's more important to be nice.

A Communist is a Socialist in a hurry.   *C. E. Wilson*

Tipping generally calls for at least 10 per cent; 12½ per cent gives better service, which is why people so often tip 15 per cent.

If your wife doesn't treat you as she should, be thankful.

Critic: "A string quartet played Brahms last evening. Brahms lost."

Actor William Drew: Drama pages are "a sort of paper coffin where dead plays are buried."

Mayor—An amiable person who lays corner stones for a living.
Herbert V. Prochnow

Executive ability—The faculty of earning your bread by the work of other people.

Neurotic—A person who thinks you mean it when you ask how he is.

"Smile and the whole world smiles with you," says Bob Crosby, "cry and you sell two million records."

Said the man of tall tales, "My wife is the safest driver in the world—she drives in the safety zone."

The first screw that gets loose in a person's head is the one that controls the tongue.

Some people think they have dynamic personalities because they're always exploding.

There is one advantage of poor handwriting. It covers up a lot of mistakes in spelling.

You can't measure a person's happiness by the amount of money he has. A man with ten million dollars may be no happier than one who has only nine million.

Asked to define "memory," one youngster replied sagely, "The thing I forget with."

Let no one tell you that a fool and his money are soon parted. A fool rarely has any money.

A psychiatrist is a man who doesn't have to worry so long as others do.

No young person will write if he can telegraph, and none will telegraph if he can telephone—collect.

When things turn green, you don't know whether it's spring, envy, or chlorophyll.

The driver is safer when the roads are dry, the roads are safer when the driver is dry.

Don't get discouraged and sell your car. Any day now you may find a place to park it.

Will party who picked up black cocker spaniel Saturday either return him or come get the three-year-old boy he belongs to?
Tribune, Mobridge, S.D.

What fun can a sewing club possibly have when every member shows up? *News, Rolla, Mo.*

Time was when men lost their shirts in the stock markets. Now its in the supermarkets.

There may be a destiny that shapes our ends, but our middles are of our own chewsing.

"Laugh and grow fat" seems like fine advice—until you try it and find that it works.

It is never wise to argue with a fool—the listeners don't know which is which.

You never get ahead of anyone as long as you are trying to get even with him.

Just think how happy you would be if you lost everything you now have, and then suddenly got it back.

The toughest form of mountain climbing is getting out of a rut.

Dictatorship is like a great beech tree—nice to look at, but nothing grows under it.   *Stanley Baldwin*

The hardest tumble any man can take is to fall over his own bluff.

When you help someone up hill, you find yourself closer to the top.

It is always easy to covet another man's success without envying his labors.

Women are not strong physically, but one of them can put the cap on a fruit jar so it takes 20 minutes for her husband to get it off.

Some cause happiness wherever they go; others when they go.

There are those who make speeches and those who are rendered speechless by them.

Love is like eating a mushroom. By the time you know whether it's the real thing, it's too late.

Barber: The village gosnip.

Sam Levenson described George Kaufman as a man the same offstage as on: "He always looks angry; inside he's happy, but his face hasn't heard the news."

Women will never be men's equal until they can sport a bald spot on top of their heads, and still think they're handsome.

In school the best minds are not necessarily those that mind best.

The man with the hoe doesn't get nearly as far as the man with the hokum.

Old gardeners never die; they just spade away.

Caterpillar News and Views

The lazy way to enjoy a beautiful, productive garden is to live next door to one, and cultivate your neighbor.

Caterpillar News and Views

Correspondence in a business efficiency magazine has been discussing how to stop a typist talking. Our own method is to ask her to read back from her shorthand.

The most common impediment of speech today in children is often bubble gum.

An old-timer is one who remembers when a baby-sitter was called mother.

A system of identifying dogs by nose-prints is being tried in America. Our plan is to whistle, and if the animal takes no notice it is ours.   *Times of Brazil*

College football makes hardy young people. You can't sit three hours on cold concrete, eating a cold hot dog and peanuts and be a weakling.

An optimist is a person who saves the pictures in the seed catalog to compare them with the flowers and vegetables he grows.

It is most dangerous nowadays for a husband to pay any attention to his wife in public. It always makes people think that he beats her in private.   *Oscar Wilde*

A man will sometimes devote all his life to the development of one part of his body—the wishbone.   *Robert Frost*

The probable reason some people get lost in thought is because it is unfamiliar territory to them.

A bargain is something you cannot use at a price you cannot resist.

The problem in this country has been whether to participate actively in the United Nations Organization or just butt into the world's arguments from time to time.

Stenographer (back from her vacation): And the sunsets over the lake! There wasn't an evening the clouds wasn't as pink as a petty cash voucher!   *New York World*

The trouble with these "How to Succeed" books is that you find out from them that you have to work for it.

The sun never sets on some part of the world where the American dollar isn't being handed out.

No one is ever too old to learn, and that may be why all of us keep putting it off.   *Herbert V. Prochnow*

Why worry about who's boss at your house. You will be happier if you never find out.

The beauty about the vacation season is that if you don't pay your bills your creditors think you are away.

In life, as in a mirror, you never get more out than you put in.

Perhaps it was because Nero played the fiddle that they burned Rome.   *Oliver Herford*

Soaking a wedding ring in dishwater three times a day makes it last longer.   *Speed Queen News*

When some persons trade in their cars, they should go to the abused car lot.

Laws that favor part of us at the expense of others are wrong, unless they are tariff laws.

William James said algebra was "a form of low cunning."

Making cars longer is a good idea. It forces the driver to take exercise walking to the trunk.   *W. L. Hudson*

To the tariff enthusiasts a thing of duty is a joy forever.

When it comes to tax reductions, never do so many wait so anxiously for so little for so long.

Environment is a wonderful thing. It gives the parents a chance to learn something from the children.   *Herbert V. Prochnow*

We don't suppose all the people of Russia are red. Some of them must be pretty blue.

A braggart produces either satellites or absentees.
                                                    W. L. Hudson

When our country enacts it, it's a protective tariff; when a foreign country adopts it, it's a tariff war.

A great many drivers seem to think the speed limit on a highway is what their cars can do.

It would be wonderful to be so well to do that the Joneses would try to keep up with you.

For demanding money with threats a man was imprisoned. Will the income tax collector please note.

It's a good thing that Moses didn't have to submit the Ten Commandments to a council of foreign ministers for approval.

The pace that kills is that of the pedestrian who strolls casually across a busy street in the middle of the block.   *W. L. Hudson*

It's easy to die with your boots on, if they're on the accelerator.

College football and basketball get the headlines, but they can't hold a scandal to college tennis and golf.

The turn-over is highly important whether it is in business or right after the alarm clock goes off in the morning.

Despite what the cartoonists make him look like, Uncle Sam is a gentleman with a very large waste.

When better business predictions are made, economists won't make them.   *Herbert V. Prochnow*

Well-washed and well-combed domestic pets grow dull; they miss the stimulus of fleas.   *Francis Galton*

Summer is the time when the weather gets too hot to cook and the relatives come to visit you.

There are two kinds of finishes you can put on an automobile— lacquer and liquor.

When you pay $10 for a small bottle of perfume, you are paying through the nose.

In most cities traffic is so jammed motorists sit in their cars and watch the pedestrians whiz by.

A man who owns a summer cottage on a lake may not have a good time during the summer season, but the chances are dozens of his friends who visit him do.

Advice to young men in love: Never tell the girl you are unworthy of her. Let that come later as a complete surprise.

Most moving pictures are more to be pitied than censored.
                                              Herbert V. Prochnow

The only records we would like to break are some the neighbor plays every night.

As we understand it, the world will be wrecked if any nation fails to get from us what she wants.

In September most of the folks return from the summer resorts for a greatly-needed rest.

A pessimist is a person who thought every cloud had a silver lining.

Weatherman's description of his infant son: Dry and sunny, but subject to change.

Millions of American commuters live in a clock-eyed world.

A living wage is a little more than you are making now.

A modest person is one who doesn't blow his knows.

There are children in Europe nine years old who have never seen a war.

John L. Lewis seems to be interested in becoming a banker, and that's not a miner matter.

Dale Evans: He's not exactly polished, but he's awfully slippery.

The best way to get a good, lasting finish on your car is to try and beat the train to the crossing.   *Texaco Safety Digest*

"Reading maketh a full man," but it depends on what he is full of.
                                        Herbert V. Prochnow

In international affairs, a conference is a meeting lasting several weeks to prepare for another meeting lasting several weeks.

Some politicians of the Western nations who criticize the United States should remember it's impolite to talk with your mouth full.

If all the trap drums in the world were placed end to end, and left there, the lull would be extremely soothing.

Sectionalism is an uncontrollable urge to reform a part of the United States you know nothing about.

A scientist predicts that in ten years' time there will be no servant girls. He appears to be just ten years behind the times.

We've found you can always tell the host from the butler because the butler knows how to act.

Conceit is a queer disease; it makes everybody sick but the one who has it.   *Sunshine Magazine*

Nearly everybody nowadays appears to be in favor of Government ownership of something if it belongs to somebody else.
                                                    New York World

It is a socialist idea that making profits is a vice. I consider that the real vice is making losses.   *Winston Churchill*

They say you can't live on bread alone, but some fellows are trying on just the crust.   *Sunshine Magazine*

A servant girl and $10,000 disappeared from the same house the same day; the report does not state, but it probably was her pay-day.

We don't know whether gentlemen prefer blondes, but we think it may be the light-headed ones who marry first.

The professors who complain that football interferes with academic work don't realize how seriously academic work interferes with football.

You may be a fine upstanding citizen, but that never makes any difference to a freshly waxed floor.   *Sunshine Magazine*

The main thing we have learned from our short-wave set is that nearly every country in the world is full of sopranos.

It may be debatable whether a nation would raise its standard of living more by a five-day week or a forty-day month.

If the bravest are the tenderest, the steer that provided our dinner was a coward.

The fellow who rocks the boat is never the fellow at the oars.

Canada won't give relief to any one owning a car. It is diametrically at odds with the American attitude that an automobile is a dependent.   *Detroit News*

To be a gentleman is a worthy trait, but it is a great handicap in an argument.

A good executive not only knows how to take advice, but also how to reject it.   *Herbert V. Prochnow*

This is another year when it won't be necessary to fool all the people all the time—only in the fall election campaigns.

We suppose these are the so-called piping times of peace, and we're paying the piper.

If you want to know how much a man can't remember, call him as a witness to an automobile accident.

"What do the ruins of Ancient Egypt really prove?" wonders a writer. Probably, among other things, that Ancient Egyptian wives insisted on having a shot at backing the chariot into the garage.

Being in a ship is being in a jail, with the chance of being drowned.   *Johnson*

In spite of continued predictions that business will get better, it will.

The best thing a citizen of the Russian satellites can hope to get is out.

It's a little difficult to reconcile the creed of some Christians with their greed.

Judging from our defense budget, the dogs of war are not going to die, only to diet.

A man who trims himself to suit everybody will soon whittle himself away.   *Charles Schwab*

It was absolutely unintelligible, for the reason that it was couched in diplomatic language.   *Anatole France*

I believe that it is better to tell the truth than a lie. I believe it is better to be free than to be a slave. And I believe it is better to know than be ignorant.   *H. L. Mencken*

An instrument has been invented in Russia that is said to be similar to a saxophone but much easier to play. That country seems to get nothing but tough luck.

My wife is using a very efficient weed killer in the garden this year. Me!   *The Mo-Hawker*

Sweet are the uses of your neighbor's adversity.

One should always play fairly when one has the winning cards.
                                                        Oscar Wilde

A false alarm may cost a city fire department $100. In business, one costs even more.

Fog, it is announced, can now be made to order. This will be no news to politicians.

A poet is a person who tells the truth about something that never happened.

A liar is a person who becomes an authority under oath on a witness stand.

An Eskimo is the only person who sits on top of the world, and he lives in an igloo and eats blubber.

Few politicians die because of ideals, but a great many ideals die because of politicians.

If they ever do away with comic books, many American youngsters will quit reading.

In her hope for recognition by the Western world, Red China does not wish to be recognized for what she is.

The Swiss object to our tariff on watches, which proves again that time is money.

Diplomats believe many powwows keep the world from going to the bowwows.

A gentleman is a man who holds the door open for the wife while she carries in a load of groceries.

To be the man of the hour, first learn to make every minute count.

A timely slogan: Work and save, young man, and some day you'll have enough to divide with those who don't.

A woman, provided she knows that her hat is on straight, is prepared to look the whole world in the face at any moment.

There are said to be prunes six inches in diameter. Well, we've seen some even larger.

Always do right. This will gratify some people, and astonish the rest.

There's nothing like scratching to satisfy the itch for money.
Herbert V. Prochnow

A pair of owls came down the chimney into the sitting-room of a Kent schoolmaster. We understand that they exasperated him by repeatedly saying, "To Who" instead of "To Whom."

London Opinion

Experience is the one perpetual best seller—everybody is continually buying it.   ***Boston Transcript***

A pessimist is a person who knows he isn't as smart as those who want to borrow money from him tell him he is.

Wife to husband: "All right, I admit I like to spend money . . . but name one other extravagance."

What we'd like to know is where the people who live beyond their incomes get the money with which to live beyond their incomes.

It is easy enough to restrain our wrath when the other fellow is bigger.

A schoolboy was making a speech on the national debt. He said: "It's too bad that future generations can't be here at this time to see the wonderful things we're doing with their money."

Jack Paar: "If you insist on smoking in bed, the ashes you drop on the floor may be your own."

A coed is a girl who didn't get her man in high school.

More important than the time you get up in the morning is the time you get down to work.

Before marriage he spoons around, and later he forks over.

Herbert V. Prochnow

When a traffic officer stops you, he either gives you a ticket or sells you one.

Business is always improving for the beauty parlor operator.

Business never comes back unless you go after it.

He cut quite a figure among his friends, but his bank account looked like zero.

Progress—In the old days a girl got her good looks from her mother. Now she gets it from the beauty parlor.

When you walk in the park in the spring, you realize love is a great game. In fact, it's the only game where the players want to stay on the bench.   *Bob Hope*

An optimist thinks he is as smart as the fellow who wants to borrow $10 from him tells him he is.

Many a young man who asks for a girl's hand later finds himself under her thumb.

A Parisian was knocked down twice in one day by the same car. Next time, I presume, he becomes the property of the motorist.
                                              Passing Show

He was dull in a new way, and that made many think him great.
                                              Samuel Johnson

Boss: "O.K. now, gang, let's take a ten-minute break for work!"

Heard in the radio studios: "She's smarter than she looks—but then she'd have to be."

Henry Morgan tells of the radio broadcasting executive who retired after 25 years' service . . . so they gave him a silver ulcer.

Modern idea of roughing it: driving a car with a standard shift.
                                              American Eagle

Don McNeill: a first grade teacher knows how to make little things count.

Think how surprised a mink must be who goes to sleep in a Wisconsin marsh and wakes up in the Metropolitan opera house.

The person who says something is "as easy as taking candy from a baby" never had a baby.   *Herbert V. Prochnow*

Now-a-days children are called bright when they make remarks that used to call for a licking.

An Idaho man wants a divorce because his wife would cook nothing but eggs. She just egged him on, as it were.   *Troy Times*

Nothing gets you all up in the air quicker than an inflated ego.
Columbia Record

An aggressive employee is not only on his toes but often on those of his superiors as well.

By working faithfully eight hours a day, you may eventually get to be a boss and work twelve hours a day.   *Robert Frost*

Ernie Simon: "Nowadays it takes a heap of payments to make a house a home."

An economist is a man who tells you what to do with your money after you've done something else with it.
Edmund S. Muskie, Governor of Maine

The hardest job an independent man has today is trying to keep the government from taking care of him.

The motor car will eventually drive people underground, says a traffic expert. It often does now, if it hits a man hard enough.
Punch

Some persons think if they wear their best clothes on Sunday they're observing the Sabbath.

A cultured person is one who has a lot of information for which he can't get cash on the barrel-head.

It's pretty difficult to draw the line between leisure and laziness.

An ignoramus knows how the world should be run, but it takes a wise man to run his own business.

Home is the place where the great are small and the small are great.

Don't try to get something for nothing and then complain about the quality.   *Herbert V. Prochnow*

A Detroit engineer of aeronautics says that in twenty years every motorist will be flying. And by that time every pedestrian will be playing a harp.   *Judge*

A motorist has admitted running over the same man twice. The time has evidently come when there aren't enough pedestrians to go round.

Nothing makes you more tolerant of a neighbor's party than being there.

You can always spot a well-informed man. His views are the same as yours.

Married life: First you carry the bride over the threshold ... then she puts her foot down.

Isn't it terrible how close some motorists drive ahead of you?

Thirty days hath September, April, June, and my uncle for taking bets on the horses.

They laughed when I spoke to the waiter in French—they didn't know I told him to give the check to the other guy.

A girl considers college a success if she quits to get married.

God made everything out of nothing but man seems to make nothing out of everything.

The dinner to which you are not invited is the one that gives you stomach trouble.

We could save time by teaching babies how to drive a car instead of how to walk.

If politicians were obliged to stand on the planks of their party platforms, they would be constructed better.

Those who try to do something and fail are infinitely better than those who try to do nothing and succeed.

Some people are like buttons—continually popping off.

One of the hardest secrets for a man to keep is his opinion of himself.

Demagoguery means to humor the crowd that causes the trouble.

Some persons are like a wheelbarrow. They stand still unless they're pushed.   *Herbert V. Prochnow*

You should bear with people because people have to bear with you.

When your first love is yourself, you never find a good successor.

Here's to my friend who knows I'm not much good, and can forget it.

There is a difference between having an aim in life and just shooting at random.

The best thing for newly-weds to feather their nest with is plenty of cash down.

The person who says he has never told a lie has just told one.

Some persons can be at home everywhere and others can be at home and be everywhere.

Let him who doesn't wish to die yet diet.

Sure money talks, but nowadays you can't hold on to it long enough to start a conversation.

Jean says she never saw a vitamin, but she's sure she'd rather C than B_1.

Amateur shows are a means for people with no talent to prove it.

Doctors advise walking for health, but I've yet to see a mailman who looked as if he could whip a truckdriver.

A conservative is a man who acts impulsively after thinking for a long time. *Herbert V. Prochnow*

When a person apologizes for his religion, he has the kind of religion for which he ought to apologize.

She used to diet on any kind of food she could lay her hands on. *Arthur (Bugs) Baer*

A book-worm may be a person who would rather read than eat, or it may be a worm that would rather eat than read.

The fellow who puts up the bill boards on country roads must have some sense of beauty because he always picks out the best views to obstruct.

A woman may grow old before her time trying to look young after her time. *Herbert V. Prochnow*

Save your pennies and the sales tax will take care of them.

Two can live as cheaply as one, and they generally have to.

The principle of the crawl stroke used by swimmers has been applied to motor boats. It has been applied to motor busses for a long time.

American chewing gum may gain a foothold in Japan. It has here.

No one can ever doubt the miracles who sees a minister living on a salary fixed ten years ago, and keeping out of debt.

A young fellow recently told us that he knew his girl friend could keep a secret, because they had been engaged for two weeks before he knew anything about it.

While some folks are shouting, "Up and atom," other citizens are murmuring, "Let's go fission."   *The Cab Stand*

Success nowadays is making more money to pay the taxes you wouldn't be paying if you hadn't made so much money already.

Home is a place where a man is free to say anything he pleases, because no one will pay the slightest attention to him.

Next to being shot at and missed, nothing is quite as satisfying as an income tax refund.

A fool and his money are invited places.   *Herbert V. Prochnow*

When you tell your troubles to some one else, you should be willing to listen to his.

No one gives out advice with more enthusiasm than an ignorant person.

The line between self-confidence and conceit is very narrow.

In some countries the coroner announces that a president will not run to succeed himself.

Sign on a highway in Connecticut: "Crossroad ahead, better humor it."

If a demagogue goes crazy, how can you ever find out?

One thing you may say for the garage mechanic; he's not finicky or upstage. He'd just as soon wipe his hands on a cheap seat cover as on a costly one.   *Macon Telegraph*

Why not get "Seven Killed in Grade Crossing Smash" stereotyped for the Monday morning papers?   **Boston Transcript**

Hope is the feeling that you will succeed tomorrow in what you failed at today.   *Herbert V. Prochnow*

A motorist's life was miraculously saved the other day. He stopped his car at a grade crossing and waited for an approaching train to pass.

A world's record is claimed by an unskilled Detroit man who recently took an automobile apart in 30 seconds—at a grade crossing.   *Detroit News*

Warren Hull reports that those Texas oil millionaires live on gush money.

The custom of kissing children goodnight is dying out; parents nowadays can't wait up for them.

Bob Hope says that "you haven't lived if you've never ridden in a French taxicab. And if you have—it's eight to five that you won't."

Ambition still may be the main thing that keeps our people moving, but the "No Parking" sign is doing its part.   *Council Bluffs Nonpareil*

If you think the automobile is here to stay, try parking your car an hour.   *Judge*

Accordionist: A person who plays both ends against the middle.

The improvement in padlocks, burglar alarms and atom bombs just about keeps up with the progress of civilization.

A pessimist is a person who thinks the world is going to the dogs because he isn't running it.

The man who broke the record driving a stock sedan from coast to coast probably was looking for a place to park his car.
Atlanta Constitution

It is pitiful to see someone squander money and know you can't help him.

Talk is one thing of which the supply always exceeds the demand.

Giving some drivers the right of way is not courtesy; its prudence.
Herbert V. Prochnow

A woman keeps a secret she doesn't know.

The proper study of mankind is not man but woman.

Laughter is the sound you hear when you stumble, or lose your hat in the wind.

When a major highway is open, it's probably because they're repairing the detour.

Plastic surgeons nowadays can do anything with the human nose except keep it out of other people's business.

An intelligent person is one who understands the obvious.
Herbert V. Prochnow

Gossip is one form of crime for which the law provides no punishment.

Strange things happen. A woman arrested as a pickpocket claims she has never been married.

We wonder if those biologists who assert there isn't a perfect man on the globe ever heard a campaign speech?

The exchange of Christmas presents ought to be reciprocal rather than retaliatory.

Chamber of Commerce executive: A man who will never admit he's seen better days.

Many a middle-aged woman is thick and tired of it.

One place people seem to think they can get just as much as ever for a quarter is in church.

Disc jockey: One who earns his living by putting on airs.

When they award the Pulitzer book prizes for the best definitive biography, we should like to submit our last income tax report.

Sometimes a woman declines a man's marriage proposal, and they both live happily ever after.

An adult is a person who has stopped growing except in the middle.

Good judgment comes from experience and experience comes from poor judgment.   *Herbert V. Prochnow*

A has-been is a person who thinks he has reached the top.

Grief is a form of happiness that comforts.

One way to save face is to keep the lower part of it shut.

The rainy days for which a man saves usually come during his vacation.

He's writing his alibiography.

Household hint: To keep cake from getting stale, put it in a paper box in the children's room.   *Caterpillar News and Views*

University professor—Any eccentric person in horn rimmed glasses wearing a baggy tweed suit and a gold key.

Herbert V. Prochnow

A young man's attitude toward life helps to determine his altitude.

Nothing lasts forever, not even a bath.

An economist is a person who talks about something he doesn't understand and makes you believe you're ignorant.

Herbert V. Prochnow

Most persons expect to get what they pay for except that they try to hire a $10,000 preacher for $3,000 a year.

Genius is the ability to evade work by doing something right the first time it has been done.

Patience is the ability to stand something as long as it happens to the other fellow.

Very few persons who get something for nothing are not disappointed if they don't get more.

Most people can keep a secret, but the folks they tell it to can't.

When a boy holds a girl's hand at the movies, he may be doing it to keep her from eating his popcorn.

Egotism is the art of seeing things in yourself that others cannot see.

Whenever I close a sentence with a preposition, I think of the comment of a well-known American when he said, "Sentence structure is the most important thing which you should be proud of."

A minor operation is one that was performed on the other fellow.

Russell Pettis Askue

John Cameron Swayze says: "If you want to make a long story short, tell it to a traffic cop."

She is intolerable, but that is her only fault.   *Talleyrand*

An eager beaver is a person who works twice as hard but doesn't know why.   *Herbert V. Prochnow*

To the pessimist, O is the last letter in zero, but to the optimist it's the first letter in opportunity.

Most women are as pretty this year as they were five years ago, but it takes quite a little longer.

An American is a man who has two legs, four wheels and a spare tire.

Henry Morgan notes that a counterfeiter is a guy who gets into trouble by following a good example.

Every little girl is in a hurry to grow up and wear the kind of shoes that just kill mother.   *Herbert V. Prochnow*

Alex Dreier has observed that "Very often the chip on a person's shoulder is just bark."

Ed Wynn: "I'm very happy to be here. In fact, at my age I'm very happy to be anywhere."

There is a natural instinct in women which leads them to sew in flocks.   *Bayard Taylor*

"It won't be lawn now," said the motorist, as he backed over his neighbor's front yard.   *Judge*

Too often we live beyond our means to impress people who live beyond their means to impress us.   *Herbert V. Prochnow*

If you can waste an afternoon profitably, you have learned how to live.

John Cameron Swayze defines memory as "where our youth lives after it goes."

Once upon a time, and not more than that, a son asked for the garage keys, and came out with the lawn mower.

Some of the big guns are silenced when a war ends; others begin work on their memoirs.

The millennium will be here when the pedestrians keep inside the traffic safety zones and the automobiles stay outside of them.

A millionaire spent $1,500 in a night club in one night. Next time he will know better than to order a sandwich.

An army travels on its stomach, but some individuals travel on their gall.

When you have trouble, you learn which friends have been waiting with a paddle to find you bent over.

To be frank is to tell the truth about anything that won't hurt you.

Headwaiter: A tyrant without ears or eyes dressed in a tuxedo.
Herbert V. Prochnow

The greatest disadvantage in life is to have too many advantages.

An executive is a man who is able to have everything he needs charged.

Gourmand: a man who dies an early death from being overweight.

Tradition: The widespread acceptance of something which was at first of questionable merit—and still is.   *Herbert V. Prochnow*

Amos 'n' Andy: "As the Australian said when the boomerang hit him in the back of the head: 'Things have taken a turn for the worse.' "

Ralph Bellamy, the actor: "College debts are obligations that with diligence, economy, and stern self-denial, father will be able to pay."

Diet: Something to take the starch out of you.

Some of America's recent novelists will miss immortality by at least a "T."

A white collar man is one who carries his lunch in a briefcase instead of a pail.

He was the kind of office manager who took criticism like a man. He blamed it on his associates.

It might add a little to the next Olympic Games if they were to add a contest to see which nation could run longest with an unbalanced budget.   *Norfolk Virginian-Pilot*

Executive: A person who considers an idea good because he thought of it.   *Herbert V. Prochnow*

Reputation is a large bubble which bursts when you try to blow it up yourself.

A socialist is an unsuccessful person who figures his last chance to get something is to get a part of yours.

Some persons believe you don't need principle to live if you have principal.

A scholar is a person with too much brains to be able to earn a large salary.

Man is an ambitious biped who struggles to eat, dress and live as well as every other biped—and if possible better.

A library is a place where the dead live.

Whenever a foreign ruler plans a visit to this country, it generally means we are going to come across if he does.

Truthful want-ad: Wanted housekeeper, age 30 or over, to take care of family of four. All modern imps.

Television quiz: For $50 and a set of encyclopedias—Is the watermelon a fruit, a vegetable or a bath?

"After the Bawl Was Over," she got her new fur coat.

There are 112 taxes in a pair of shoes. No wonder we feel pinched.

Leo G. Carroll of Topper reports there are two types of people in Hollywood: "Those who own swimming pools and those who can't keep their heads above water."

No man is a hero to the fellow who collects the installment payments.

The modern woman doesn't want a man who can satisfy her smallest wish; what she wants is one who can attend to the larger ones.

The average man has 66 pounds of muscle and 3.3 pounds of brain, according to a physician. Maybe that explains a lot of things.
Rotary Realist, La Salle, Illinois

The thing that keeps a lot of men broke is not the wolf at the door, but the silver fox in the window.
The Rhododendron, White Sulphur Springs, West Virginia

With television, radio, phonograph and musical instruments, the American home is sounder than ever.

Do you remember way back in the old days when you went to silent movies and saw women opening their mouths and not saying anything you could hear?

It is not only a man's sins, but his creditors who find him out.

If you ate two apples a day, would you keep two doctors away?

When you get discouraged at your job and feel like the smallest pebble on the beach, remember that the "big potatoes are on top of the heap because a lot of little potatoes are in there holding them up."   *Rotary News, Hope, Arkansas*

A secret is what you tell someone else not to tell because you can't keep it.   *Herbert V. Prochnow*

The aim of education is to enable a man to continue his learning.

All the average man asks of life is a little peach and quiet.

Only he who can see the invisible can do the impossible.
                                                       Frank L. Gaines

Kindness is one thing you can't give away. It always comes back.

If a woman is good-looking, higher education is unnecessary. If she isn't, it is inadequate.

An optimist is a person who falls in the pool in his tuxedo and thinks he is in the social swim.

With so many showers for brides, nearly everyone gets soaked!
                                                       Vesta Kelly

Many people are like a cat. They lick themselves with their tongues.

Prejudice is an unwillingness to be confused with facts.

Everyone who has done the best he can is a hero.   *Josh Billings*

A pessimist is a person who keeps an optimist from knowing how well off he really is.   *Herbert V. Prochnow*

Money may be the root of all evil, but some of it seems to grow into some mighty fine shrubbery.

The grass next door may look greener, but it's just as hard to cut.

No woman ever makes a fool out of a man without his full co-operation.

A loafer is a person who spends his time keeping busy people idle.

For some persons it is simply life, liberty and the pursuit of a golf ball.

"Hear no evil, see no evil, speak no evil," and you'll certainly be a dull companion.

An onion a day, keeps everybody away.

When two diplomats shake hands, we aren't sure whether it's friendship or time for the fight to start.

Of all the labor-saving devices invented for women none has ever been so popular as a husband with money.

An intellectual is a person so smart that he doesn't understand the obvious.

Any company that will manufacture a mechanical taxpayer is going to make a fortune.

A cemetery is where a lot of careless drivers stop.
Blair, Wisconsin, Press

Except in street cars, one should never be unnecessarily rude to a lady.
O. Henry

What the average woman wants is a great big strong man who can be wrapped around her finger.

Early to bed and early to rise, and you'll miss hearing and seeing a great deal that would make you wise.

A fish gains weight slowly, except the one that got away.

It does a man no good to sit up and take notice, if he keeps on sitting. *Sunshine Magazine*

The fact that boys are allowed to exist at all is evidence of a remarkable Christian forbearance among men. *Ambrose Bierce*

Man is an animal that makes bargains; no other animal does this—no dog exchanges bones with another. *Adam Smith*

Early to bed and early to rise, if you want your head to feel its normal size.

It's always fair weather when a Californian meets a native of Florida.

It's funny how we never get too old to learn some new way to be stupid. *Mrs. Eleanor E. Coffee, Sunshine Magazine*

An executive is a man who can take two hours for lunch without hindering production.

Try to imagine a cracker barrel philosopher holding forth in a supermarket.

You may not know all the answers, but you probably won't be asked all the questions, either.

Money talks and in most families it's the mother tongue. *Herbert V. Prochnow*

At a lake resort a girl landed a fish weighing 150 pounds, standing six feet in its socks and wearing a button-down shirt and tailored slacks.

Everyone may love a fat man, but not when he has the other half of a seat on the bus.

When you have that sinking feeling on a scale, it's time to start reducing.

Before a person tries his hand at something he ought to try his head at it.

About the only thing the farmers don't raise enough of is farm hands.

An expensive summer vacation cometh before a hard fall.

Most husbands want a wife they can love, honor and display.

If you can't sleep, try lying on the end of the bed—then you might drop off.   *Mark Twain*

You can tour the world now on the instalment plan, but don't fall down on the payments in the middle of the Atlantic.

Always borrow from a pessimist. He never expects to be repaid.

A business that makes nothing but money is a poor business.
                                                Henry Ford

The modern idea of roughing it is to camp out without a television set.

A patriot is a person who saves enough of his salary each week to pay his income tax.

When Johnnie acts cute, he deserves to get a big hand—in the right place.   *Herbert V. Prochnow*

The best things in life are still free, but the tax experts are working overtime on the problem.

Worry is like a rocking chair—gives you something to do, but doesn't get you anywhere.

A good deal of the room at the top is made by men who have gone to sleep there, and fallen off.

Not only are the sins of the fathers visited upon the children, but now-a-days the sins of the children are visited upon the fathers.

A small town today is where the runways aren't long enough for a four engine plane.

An honest city is one where no one knows a rich policeman.

When we hear some popular songs, we are sure the illiteracy rate is still pretty high.

It's no disgrace to be poor, and, besides, the instalment salesmen leave you alone.

There may be songs that never die, but it isn't the fault of TV or radio.

Baby sitters: girls you hire to watch your television set.

A monologue is a conversation between a traffic cop and an automobile driver.

If the average husband bought a house costing twice his income, he would get either a wigwam or an igloo.

You can have the guy who's always searching for the bright side; I'll take the one who's in there polishing up the dull.   *Don Marshall*

Safety slogan: "Watch out for school children—especially if they are driving cars."

As the little boy says, "Ignorance is when you don't know something, and somebody finds it out."

Judging from the way some fellows drive, if the road turns the same time they do, it's a coincidence.

A close relative can be very distant.   *Herbert V. Prochnow*

At the age of fifty one settles down into certain well-defined convictions, most of which are wrong.

The fellow who argues that all religions should unite probably doesn't speak to his brother-in-law.

Now-a-days you have a choice of din with your dinner or rest in a restaurant.

A go-getter who becomes his own boss is apt to wind up a nervous wreck.

Any day now we expect to see power steering for backseat drivers.

If all the toastmasters in the world were placed end to end, the silence would be very restful.

Children have been well trained if they don't have to be coached on how to act when they go to a party.

A small town is a place where everybody knows what everybody else is doing, but they read the local paper to see if their neighbors have been caught at it.   *Wilton (Wisconsin) Star Herald News*

The worst thing about getting old is listening to the children's advice.

To train children at home it's necessary for both the parents and children to spend some time there.

The man who says he's a 100 per cent American probably made the appraisal himself.

Robinson Crusoe started the five-day week plan. He had all his work done by Friday.   *Sunshine Magazine*

Some men know exactly what they are going to do immediately after dinner—the dishes.   *Inez Ozburn*

Many a husband argues with his wife about which fork to use when a highway divides.

Life is a constant struggle to keep up appearances and keep down expenses.

A restaurant is the place where the public pays the proprietor for the privilege of tipping the waiters for something to eat.
                                             Sunshine Magazine

Don't throw away the empty seed packets. They are often just the right size to store the crop.   **Wall Street Journal**

Some parents believe in strict obedience; others painfully count to ten before obeying the dictates of their children.   *Don Marshall*

It's strange how you can hear a rattle in your car but not in your head.

Most girls want a spendthrift before they're married and a man who has saved his money after they're married.
                                             Herbert V. Prochnow

We never could understand how a moth lives eating nothing but holes.

We have more high school and college graduates than ever before and fewer of them can read traffic signs.

Give most people credit for anything and they will take it.

Warning: If your wife wants to learn to drive, don't stand in her way.

The alert man gets everything, including the dinner check.
                                             William Feather in Bagology

"I shall not die of a cold, my son. I shall die of having lived."
Willa Cather

The man who sings his own praise invariably sings a solo unaccompanied.

Sign on a country road: "Drive carefully; there isn't a hospital within 50 miles."

We never get anything but sad news out of those envelopes with a window in front.   *Herbert V. Prochnow*

Some people are always taking the joy out of life and a good many of them are in the Internal Revenue Department.

You can lead high school graduates to college, but you cannot make them think.

Always forgive your enemies; nothing annoys them so much.
Oscar Wilde

Success has always operated on the serve-yourself plan.

Optimism: a word meaning the same as Americanism.

The answer to "What is the world coming to?" is "America."

Business may be turning the corner, but not on two wheels.

The world's choice: Disarmament or Disbursement.

Economics Simplified: When buyers do not fall for prices, prices must fall for buyers.

Martyr: a person who sacrifices himself to the unavoidable.

Waiter: a person whose chief business is hiding out.

Opera: where women who are bored at home take their husbands to be bored.

Diplomat: a wealthy person assigned to meddle in other people's business.

Gravitation: what happens to a man's socks without garters.

Lawyer: a person for whose ignorance others pay.

The reason why some people have their backs to the wall is that they've been keeping up a front.   *Inez Ozburn*

Compliment: A remark that need not be true to be gratefully received.

Literary critic: a person who will discuss the social objectives of a book that never had any.

Any married man who agrees with his wife can have his own way.

The bumptious guy usually gets bumped.

We never quite understand the words "professional women." Are there any amateurs?

We suppose a hen gets discouraged because she always finds things missing from where she laid them.

Frenchmen have a sense of humor, as every tourist finds when he tries to talk to them in French.

A pedagogue works against ignorance, but a demagogue gets a profit out of it.

In tax revision the emphasis should be on vision.

It is no sillier for the rich to think the poor are happy than for the poor to think the rich are.

When they asked the movie actress how long she had been married, she said, "This time or all together?"

She had only three requirements for a husband—money, wealth and property.

There is an automobile for every $3\frac{1}{2}$ persons. The missing half is the pedestrian who has been run over.

What the world needs is the peace that passes all misunderstanding.

No opportunity is ever lost. The other fellow takes those you miss.

We suggest that some new issue of postage stamps carry a picture of a weeping taxpayer.

The fellow who does nothing is doing somebody.

Herbert V. Prochnow

A politician will consider every way of reducing taxes except cutting expenses.

An elephant lives several hundred years, but then his trunk doesn't have to travel anywhere.

Don't be conceited. Just because you're sitting in the front seat doesn't mean you're driving the car.

Apparently the Communists' chief complaint is that we won't let them wrest peacefully.

You must give the Russians credit—they haven't claimed yet that they invented baseball.

One of these days the Russian rulers will find out their people can't live forever without eating.

We sympathize with the fellow who occupied two seats in the bus because half the time he didn't get any seat.

He who hesitates is definitely not an income-tax collector.

Inez Ozburn

Sometimes we think the television hero is the one who sits through the program.

If a person wishes to die poor today, the Internal Revenue Department is organized to help him.   *Herbert V. Prochnow*

If they would make men's clothes without pockets, a lot of wives could get to bed earlier.

This is a year when we need emphasis on the try in industry.

Before you call yourself peace-loving, tell us how you act when the umpire calls a close one on the home team.

Woman to her husband: "When I want your opinion, I'll give it to you."

To be unhappily married requires a good income and to be incompatible a couple must be rich.

Adam was the first man to know the meaning of rib-roast.

To the Communist, a wage slave is any American who earns $5,000 a year, drives a car, owns a television set and has a bathroom.

Our foreign policy is slowly changing from an endowment policy.

When the young man said he would die for her, the cynical young lady wanted to know how soon.

Modern youngsters are precocious. They don't read, but name any record and they can tell you what's on the other side.

If you think business is a little slow, how would you like to be an automobile salesman in Russia?

Man has conquered the air but so has our neighbor's radio.

Fishing is just a jerk at one end of the line waiting for a jerk at the other end.   *Ernie Ford*

We understand some sections of the country received less rain under the Republicans than under the Democrats.

Sometimes we think the wicked fleece and no man pursueth.
                                          Herbert V. Prochnow

The surest way to get a job done is to give it to a busy man; he'll have his secretary do it.   *The Mo-Hawker*

My little Margie: "There's no use crying over spilt milk. It only makes it salty for the cat."

Generally the bride looks stunning and the groom stunned.

Rod Brasfield notes that one type of attachment that fits all models of cars is the finance company's.

Why not give everyone a government subsidy who wants one and excuse everyone else from taxation?

"One advantage of being married," says Alex Dreier, "is that you don't make a fool of yourself without finding out about it."

There are times when we understand what the weatherman means by the "mean" temperature.   *Herbert V. Prochnow*

Nothing makes time pass more quickly than an income tax install-ment every three months.

Not only the camel, but Johnnie also could do without water for eight days if his mother would let him.

Gabriel Heatter: "Diamonds may be a girl's best friend, but a man's best friend is overtime. His regular pay all goes to taxes."

The Greeks had their idea of tragedy, but they never sat in the grandstand and watched an outfielder drop an easy one.

Some persons not only expect opportunity to knock, but they want to break the door down.

Many businessmen now would like to hurry along the sweet buy and buy.

I once asked my grandpa why a man is not allowed to have more than one wife, and he said: "Son when you're older you'll realize that the law protects those who are incapable of protecting themselves."   *Ernie Ford*

June is the month when the bride who has never had a broom in her hand sweeps up the aisle.

Some persons never appeal to God unless they're getting licked.

The business man who demands facts in his office buys hair restorer from a bald-headed barber.

The biggest trouble with industry is that it is full of human beings.   *John McCaffery in Fortune*

You can buy a Russian ruble for 25 cents, but no one with any cents would do it.

A pessimist is a person who thinks the world is against him—and it is.   *Herbert V. Prochnow*

When you criticize your child for not being smart, remember a wooden head is one thing that can be inherited.

A person never knows defeat is bitter unless he swallows it.

When a pensive little thing gets married, she often becomes an expensive little thing.

8

LITERARY QUOTATIONS FOR THE TOASTMASTER

ACHIEVEMENT

Sound, sound the clarion, fill the fife,
To all the sensual world proclaim
One crowded hour of glorious life
Is worth an age without a name.

T. O. Mordaunt

The nearest way to glory is to strive to be what you wish to be thought to be. *Socrates*

The mountain groaned in pangs of birth:
Great expectation filled the earth;
And lo! a mouse was born!

Phaedrus

ACTION

Heaven ne'er helps the men who will not act. *Sophocles*

Get good counsel before you begin: and when you have decided, act promptly. *Sallust*

ADVERSITY

Sweet are the uses of adversity;
Which, like the toad, ugly and venomous,
Wears yet a precious jewel in his head.

Shakespeare

Adversity introduces a man to himself.

AGE

Grow old along with me!
The best is yet to be,
The last of life for which the first was made.

R. Browning

As a white candle in a holy place,
So is the beauty of an aged face.

Joseph Campbell

Your old men shall dream dreams, your young men shall see
visions.   *Book of Joel, II, 28*

When you are old and gray and full of sleep,
And nodding by the fire, take down this book.

W. B. Yeats

To me, old age is always fifteen years older than I am.

Bernard Baruch

It is magnificent to grow old, if one keeps young.

Harry Emerson Fosdick

If wrinkles must be written upon our brows, let them not be written upon the heart. The spirit should not grow old.

James A. Garfield

I cannot sing the old songs
I sang long years ago,
For heart and voice would fail me
And foolish tears would flow.

Charlotte A. Barnard

ALONE

I feel like one who treads alone
Some banquet-hall deserted,
Whose lights are fled, whose garlands dead,
And all but he departed!
Thomas Moore

AMBITION

All ambitions are lawful except those which climb upward on the miseries or credulities of mankind. *Joseph Conrad*

I had Ambition, by which sin
The angels fell;
I climbed and, step by step, O Lord,
Ascended into Hell.
W. H. Davies

Cromwell, I charge thee, fling away ambition:
By that sin fell the angels;
Shakespeare

Ambition has but one reward for all:
A little power, a little transient fame,
A grave to rest in, and a fading name!
William Winter

A tomb now suffices him for whom the whole world was not sufficient. *Epitaph on Alexander the Great*

AMERICA

Bring me men to match my mountains,
Bring me men to match my plains,
Men with empires in their purpose,
And new eras in their brains.
S. W. Foss

I am willing to love all mankind except an American.
Samuel Johnson

ANCESTORS

Whoever serves his country well has no need of ancestors.

Voltaire

ANGER

He that is slow to anger is better than the mighty; and he that ruleth his spirit than he that taketh a city.   *Proverbs XVI 32*

Beware the fury of a patient man.   *Dryden*

APRIL

April is the cruelest month, breeding
Lilacs out of the dead land, mixing
Memory and desire, stirring
Dull roots with spring rain.
T. S. Eliot

April, April,
Laugh thy girlish laughter;
Then, the moment after,
Weep thy girlish tears!
William Watson

ARGUE

I never make the mistake of arguing with people for whose opinions I have no respect.   *Gibbon*

I am not arguing with you—I am telling you.   *J. McN. Whistler*

Strong and bitter words indicate a weak cause.   *Victor Hugo*

Those who in quarrels interpose,
Must often wipe a bloody nose.
Gay

ARMAMENTS

The Savior came. With trembling lips
He counted Europe's battleships.

"Yet millions lack their daily bread.
So much for Calvary!" he said.

Norman Gale

AUTHOR

A writer is rarely so well inspired as when he talks about himself.

Anatole France

A pen becomes a clarion. *Longfellow*

AUTUMN

The day is cold, and dark, and dreary;
It rains, and the wind is never weary;
The vine still clings to the mouldering wall,
But at every gust the dead leaves fall,
And the day is dark and dreary.

Longfellow

BABY

When the first baby laughed for the first time, his laugh broke into
a million pieces, and they all went skipping about. That was the
beginning of fairies. *J. M. Barrie*

BALANCE

Evermore in the world is this marvelous balance of beauty and
disgust, magnificence and rats. *Emerson*

BASEBALL

There was ease in Casey's manner as he stepped into his place,
There was pride in Casey's bearing and a smile on Casey's face

. . . .

But there is no joy in Mudville—mighty Casey has struck out.

E. L. Thayer

BEAUTY

A thing of beauty is a joy for ever:
Its loveliness increases; it will never
Pass into nothingness.

Keats

She was good as she was fair.
None, none on earth above her!
As pure in thought as angels are:
To know her was to love her.

Samuel Rogers

Remember that the most beautiful things in the world are the most useless; Peacocks and lilies, for example.   *John Ruskin*

Beauty is a short-lived reign.   *Socrates*

BED

In winter I get up at night
And dress by yellow candle-light.
In summer, quite the other way,
I have to go to bed by day.

R. L. Stevenson

BELIEF

Blessed are they that have not seen, and yet have believed.

John, XX, 29

Lord, I believe; help thou mine unbelief.   *Mark, IX, 24*

BETRAY

And while he yet spake, lo, Judas, one of the twelve, came . . . and forthwith he came to Jesus, and said, Hail! Master; and kissed him.

Matthew XXVI 47, 49

BIOGRAPHY

Every great man nowadays has his disciples, and it is always Judas who writes the biography.   *Oscar Wilde*

BLESSING

"God bless us every one!" said Tiny Tim, the last of all.   *Dickens*

BLINDNESS

They be blind leaders of the blind. And if the blind lead the blind, both shall fall into the ditch.   *Matthew, XV, 14*

There's none so blind as they that won't see.   *Swift*

BOAST

The boast of heraldry, the pomp of pow'r,
And all that beauty, all that wealth e'er gave,
Awaits alike th' inevitable hour.
The paths of glory lead but to the grave.

Gray

BOOKS

Some books are to be tasted, others to be swallowed, and some few
to be chewed and digested.   *Bacon*

Blessings upon Cadmus, the Phoenicians, or whoever it was that
invented books.   *Carlyle*

There is no frigate like a book
To take us lands away,
Nor any coursers like a page
Of prancing poetry.

Emily Dickinson

Comerado, this is no book,
Who touches this, touches a man.

Walt Whitman

My desire is...that mine adversary had written a book.

Job XXXI 35

Everywhere I have sought rest and found it not except sitting
apart in a nook with a little book.   *Thomas À. Kempis*

Except a living man there is nothing more wonderful than a book!
A message to us from...human souls we never saw....And yet
these arouse us, terrify us, teach us, comfort us, open their hearts to
us as brothers.   *Kingsley*

The writings of the wise are the only riches our posterity cannot
squander.   *Landor*

The true university of these days is a collection of books. *Carlyle*

BOY

The boy stood on the burning deck,
Whence all but him had fled;
The flame that lit the battle's wreck
Shone round him o'er the dead.
Felicia D. Hemans

Across the fields of yesterday
He sometimes comes to me,
A little lad just back from play—
The lad I used to be.
T. S. Jones, Jr.

When I was a beggarly boy,
And lived in a cellar damp,
I had not a friend nor a toy,
But I had Aladdin's lamp.
J. R. Lowell

The smiles and tears of boyhood's years,
The words of love then spoken.
Thomas Moore

BRAVERY

True bravery is shown by performing without witness what one might be capable of doing before all the world. *La Rochefoucauld*

Physical bravery is an animal instinct; moral bravery is a much higher and truer courage. *Wendell Phillips*

BREAD

O God! that bread should be so dear,
And flesh and blood so cheap!
Thomas Hood

Man shall not live by bread alone. *Matthew, IV, 4*

Cast thy bread upon the waters: for thou shalt find it after many days.   *Ecclesiastes, XI, 1*

BREVITY

What is the use of brevity if it constitute a book?   *Martial*

The more you say, the less people remember. The fewer the words, the greater the profit.   *Fenelon*

BRIBERY

Few men have virtue to withstand the highest bidder.
                                             George Washington

BUSINESS

Business is religion, and religion is business. The man who does not make a business of his religion has a religious life of no force, and the man who does not make a religion of his business has a business life of no character.   *Maltbie Babcock*

We demand that big business give people a square deal; in return we must insist that when anyone engaged in big business honestly endeavors to do right, he shall himself be given a square deal.
                                             Theodore Roosevelt

BUSY

How doth the busy little bee
Improve each shining hour,
And gather honey all the day
From every opening flower!
                            Isaac Watts

CARE

The night shall be filled with music
And the cares that infest the day
Shall fold their tents like the Arabs,
And as silently steal away.
                            Longfellow

To carry care to bed is to sleep with a pack on your back.

Haliburton

Providence has given us hope and sleep as a compensation for the many cares of life.   *Voltaire*

CAUTION

Little boats should keep near shore.   *Franklin*

Caution is the eldest child of wisdom.   *Victor Hugo*

Among mortals second thoughts are wisest.   *Euripides*

It is a good thing to learn caution by the misfortunes of others.

Syrus

CHANGE

There is a certain relief in change, even though it be from bad to worse; as I have found in travelling in a stagecoach, that it is often a comfort to shift one's position and be bruised in a new place.

Irving

Earth changes, but thy soul and God stand sure.   *Browning*

CHARACTER

When you are in doubt whether an action is good or bad, abstain from it.   *Zoroaster*

Talent is nurtured in solitude; character is formed in the stormy billows of the world.   *Goethe*

Every man has three characters—that which he exhibits, that which he has, and that which he thinks he has.   *Alphonse Karr*

Oh, East is East, and West is West, and never the twain shall meet
Till earth and sky stand presently at God's great judgment seat;
But there is neither East nor West, border nor breed nor birth
When two strong men stand face to face, tho' they come from the
   ends of the earth!   *Kipling*

CHARITY

And now abideth faith, hope, charity, these three; but the greatest of these is charity.   *I Corinthians XIII 13*

As the purse is emptied the heart is filled.   *Victor Hugo*

My poor are my best patients. God pays for them.   *Boerhaave*

Though I have all faith, so that I could remove mountains, and have not charity, I am nothing.   *I Corinthians XIII 2*

The charity which longs to publish itself, ceases to be charity.
Hutton

He who waits to do a great deal of good at once, will never do anything.   *Samuel Johnson*

Our charity begins at home, and mostly ends where it begins.
Horace Smith

Though I speak with the tongues of men and of angels, and have not charity, I am become as sounding brass or a tinkling cymbal.
I Corinthians XIII 1

Verily I say unto you, Inasmuch as ye have done it unto one of the least of these my brethren, ye have done it unto me.
Matthew XXV 40

If a body's ever took charity, it makes a burn that don't come out.
John Steinbeck

Behold, I do not give lectures or a little charity,
When I give I give myself.
Walt Whitman

Not what we give, but what we share,
For the gift without the giver is bare.
J. R. Lowell

That is no true alms which the hand can hold;
He gives only the worthless gold
Who gives from a sense of duty.

J. R. Lowell

God loveth a cheerful giver.   *II Corinthians IX* 7

With malice toward none, with charity for all, with firmness in the right, as God gives us to see the right.   *Lincoln*

He who bestows his goods upon the poor,
Shall have as much again, and ten times more.

Bunyan

Blessed is he that considereth the poor.   *Psalms XLI* 1

CHILDREN

Children have more need of models than of critics.   *Joubert*

Train up a child in the way he should go; and when he is old, he will not depart from it.   *Proverbs XXII 6*

How sharper than a serpent's tooth it is
To have a thankless child!

Shakespeare

A child should always say what's true
And speak when he is spoken to,
And behave mannerly at table;
At least as far as he is able.

R. L. Stevenson

I do not love him because he is good, but because he is my little child.   *Rabindranath Tagore*

He that spareth the rod hateth his son.   *Proverbs XIII 24*

There is no prince or prelate
I envy—no, not one,
No evil can befall me—
By God, I have a son!
Christopher Morley

What is the price of a thousand horses against a son where there is one son only.   *J. M. Synge*

A wise son maketh a glad father.   *Proverbs X 1*

When I was a child, I spake as a child, I understood as a child, I thought as a child; but when I became a man, I put away childish things.   *I Corinthians XIII, 11*

My son is my son till he have got him a wife,
But my daughter's my daughter all the days of her life.
Thomas Fuller

CHRISTIANITY

A Christian is God Almighty's gentleman.   *J. C. and A. W. Hare*

Christianity ruined emperors, but saved peoples.
Alfred de Musset

Christianity is a battle, not a dream.   *Wendell Phillips*

Alexander, Caesar, Charlemagne and I myself have founded empires; but upon what do these creations of our genius depend? Upon force. Jesus alone founded His empire upon love; and to this very day millions would die for Him.   *Napoleon*

CHRISTMAS

Let's dance and sing and make good cheer,
For Christmas comes but once a year.
G. MacFarren

O little town of Bethlehem,
How still we see thee lie!
Above thy deep and dreamless sleep
The silent stars go by.

Phillips Brooks

I heard the bells on Christmas Day
Their old, familiar carols play,
And wild and sweet
The words repeat
of peace on earth, good-will to men!

Longfellow

God rest you merry, gentlemen,
Let nothing you dismay,
For Jesus Christ, our Savior,
Was born upon this day.

Old Carol

'Most all the time, the whole year round, there ain't no flies on me,
But jest 'fore Christmas I'm as good as I kin be!

Eugene Field

CHURCH

I never weary of great churches. It is my favorite kind of mountain scenery. Mankind was never so happily inspired as when it made a cathedral.　　*Stevenson*

CITY

God made the country, and man made the town.　　*Cowper*

Cities force growth, and make men talkative and entertaining, but they make them artificial.　　*Emerson*

Far from gay cities, and the ways of men.　　*Homer*

To one who has been long in city pent,
'Tis very sweet to look into the fair
And open face of heaven.

Keats

Fields and trees teach me nothing, but the people in a city do.

Socrates

The country is lyric—the town dramatic. When mingled they make the most perfect musical drama.   *Longfellow*

> I am tired of four walls and a ceiling;
> I have need of the grass.
>
> *Richard Hovey*

CLERGYMAN

If you would lift me you must be on a higher ground.   *Emerson*

The life of a conscientious clergyman is not easy. I have always considered a clergyman as the father of a larger family than he is able to maintain. I would rather have chancery suits upon my hands than the cure of souls.   *Samuel Johnson*

> A man he was to all the country dear,
> And passing rich with forty pounds a year.
>
> *Goldsmith*

He preaches well who lives well.   *Cervantes*

CLOTHES

The soul of this man is his clothes.   *Shakespeare*

She wears her clothes as if they were thrown on her with a pitch-fork.   *Swift*

> When as in silks my Julia goes,
> Then, then, methinks how sweetly flows
> The liquefaction of her clothes!
>
> *Herrick*

> The tulip and the butterfly
> Appear in gayer coats than I:
> Let me be dressed fine as I will,
> Flies, worms, and flowers exceed me still.
>
> *Isaac Watts*

COLD

There was a small boy of Quebec
Who was buried in snow to the neck;
When they said, "Are you friz?"
He replied, "Yes, I is—
But we don't call this cold in Quebec."

Kipling

COMMUNISM

What is a Communist? One who hath yearnings
For equal division of unequal earnings.
Idler or bungler, or both, he is willing
To fork out his copper and pocket your shilling.

Ebenezer Elliott

The theory of Communism may be summed up in one sentence: Abolish all private property.   *Karl Marx and Friedrich Engels*

Communism is the exploitation of the strong by the weak. In communism, inequality springs from placing mediocrity on a level with excellence.   *Proudhon*

COMPASSION

If we could read the secret history of our enemies we should find in each man's life sorrow and suffering enough to disarm all hostility.

Henry Wadsworth Longfellow

CONCEIT

Conceit causes more conversation than wit.   *La Rochefoucauld*

He was like the cock who thought the sun had risen to hear him crow.   *George Eliot*

I wish I was as sure of anything as Macaulay is of everything.

William Windham

A fly sat on the chariot wheel
And said "What a dust I raise."
La Fontaine

CONQUER

See the conquering hero comes!
Sound the trumpets, beat the drums!
Thomas Morel

CONSCIENCE

Conscience is God's presence in man.   *Swedenborg*

The conscience of the dying belies their lives.   *Vauvenargues*

CONSISTENCY

Inconsistency is the only thing in which men are consistent.
Horace Smith

CONTENT

But if I'm content with a little,
Enough is as good as a feast.
Isaac Bickerstaffe

COOKS

We may live without poetry, music and art;
We may live without conscience and live without heart;
We may live without friends, we may live without books,
But civilized man cannot live without cooks.
Owen Meredith

COW

The friendly cow all red and white,
I love with all my heart:
She gives me cream with all her might
To eat with apple-tart.
R. L. Stevenson

COWARD

Coward: One who in a perilous emergency thinks with his legs.

Bierce

A cowardly cur barks more fiercely than it bites.

Quintus Curtius Rufus

CRITICISM

Critics are the men who have failed in literature and art.   *Disraeli*

Even the lion has to defend himself against flies. *German Proverb*

Who, for the poor renown of being smart,
Would leave a sting within a brother's heart?

Edward Young

DEATH

How well he fell asleep!
Like some proud river, widening toward the sea;
Calmly and grandly, silently and deep,
Life joined eternity.

Samuel T. Coleridge

Man that is born of a woman hath but a short time to live, and is full of misery. He cometh up, and is cut down, like a flower; he fleeth as it were a shadow, and never continueth in one stay.

Book of Common Prayer

O death, where is thy sting?
O grave, where is thy victory?
I Corinthians XV 55

The Lord gave, and the Lord hath taken away; blessed be the name of the Lord.   *Job I 21*

Yet a little sleep, a little slumber, a little folding of the hands to sleep.   *Proverbs VI 10*

No more; and, by a sleep to say we end
The heart-ache and the thousand natural shocks
That flesh is heir to, 'tis a consummation
Devoutly to be wished.

Shakespeare

Nothing in his life became him like the leaving it.   *Shakespeare*

God's finger touched him, and he slept.   *Tennyson*

Pale death, with impartial step, knocks at the poor man's cottage
and the palaces of kings.   *Horace*

I have a rendezvous with Death
At some disputed barricade...
And I to my pledged word am true,
I shall not fail that rendezvous.

Alan Seeger

......death,
The undiscovered country, from whose bourn
No traveller returns.

Shakespeare

Man goeth to his long home.   *Ecclesiastes XII 5*

There the wicked cease from troubling, and there the weary be at
rest.   *Job III 17*

...and man's death diminishes me, because I am involved in Man-
kinde; and therefore never send to know for whom the bell tolls; It
tolls for thee.   *John Donne*

Once in Persia reigned a king
Who upon his signet ring
Graved a maxim true and wise,
Solemn words, and these are they:
"Even this shall pass away."

Theodore Tilton

In Flanders fields the poppies blow
Between the crosses, row on row.

John McCrae

DEBT

Wilt thou seal up the avenues of ill?
Pay every debt as if God wrote the bill!

Emerson

If you want the time to pass quickly, just give your note for 90 days.   *R. B. Thomas*

Debt is the worst poverty.   *M. G. Lichtwer*

DECISION

Once to every man and nation comes the moment to decide,
In the strife of Truth and Falsehood, for the good or evil side;

J. R. Lowell

No man, having put his hand to the plow, and looking back, is fit
for the Kingdom of God.   *Luke IX 62*

DEMAGOGUE

Demagogues and agitators are very unpleasant, but they are incidents to a free and constitutional country, and you must put up with these inconveniences or do without many important advantages.

Disraeli

A wise fellow who is also worthless always charms the rabble.

Euripides

DEMOCRACY

Democracy means not "I am as good as you are," but "You are as good as I am."   *Theodore Parker*

All the ills of democracy can be cured by more democracy.

Alfred E. Smith

While democracy must have its organization and controls, its vital breath is individual liberty.   *Charles Evans Hughes*

On the whole, with scandalous exceptions, Democracy has given the ordinary worker more dignity than he ever had.   *Sinclair Lewis*

Not only our future economic soundness but the very soundness of our democratic institutions depends on the determination of our Government to give employment to idle men.
                                        Franklin D. Roosevelt

DESIRE

It is easier to suppress the first desire than to satisfy all that follow it.   *Franklin*

Our desires always increase with our possessions. The knowledge that something remains yet unenjoyed impairs our enjoyment of the good before us.   *Samuel Johnson*

DESPAIR

Despair is the conclusion of fools.   *Disraeli*

Despair doubles our strength.   *English Proverb*

DESPOTISM

It is the old practice of despots to use a part of the people to keep the rest in order.   *Jefferson*

I will believe in the right of one man to govern a nation despotically when I find a man born unto the world with boots and spurs, and a nation with saddles on their backs.   *Algernon Sidney*

DIFFICULTY

The three things most difficult are—to keep a secret, to forget an injury, and to make good use of leisure.   *Chilo*

The greater the obstacle, the more glory in overcoming it.
                                                    Molière

DIGNITY

Too coy to flatter, and too proud to serve,
Thine be the joyless dignity to starve.

Tobias Smollett

No race can prosper till it learns that there is as much dignity in tilling a field as in writing a poem.   *Booker T. Washington*

DISCRETION

A sound discretion is not so much indicated by never making a mistake as by never repeating it.   *Bovee*

Great ability without discretion comes almost invariably to a tragic end.   *Gambetta*

The better part of valor is discretion.   *Shakespeare*

DOCTRINE

Doctrine is nothing but the skin of truth set up and stuffed.

Henry Ward Beecher

"Orthodoxy, my Lord," said Bishop Warburton, in a whisper, "orthodoxy is my doxy—heterodoxy is another man's doxy."

Joseph Priestley

DOG

Every dog is entitled to one bite.

Oh, the saddest of sights in a world of sin
Is a little lost pup with his tail tucked in!

Arthur Guiterman

Gentlemen of the Jury: The one, absolute, unselfish friend that man can have in this selfish world, the one that never deserts him, the one that never proves ungrateful or treacherous, is his dog.

Senator George Graham

DOUBT

Our doubts are traitors
And make us lose the good we oft might win
By fearing to attempt.

Shakespeare

O Lord—if there is a Lord; save my soul—if I have a soul. Amen.

Ernest Renan

I am cabin'd, cribb'd, confined, bound in
To saucy doubts and fears.

Shakespeare

DREAM

I dreamt that I dwelt in marble halls,
With vassals and serfs at my side.

Alfred Bunn

A pleasing land of drowsy head it was,
Of dreams that wave before the half-shut eye;
And of gay castles in the clouds that pass,
For ever flushing round a summer sky.

Thomson

But I, being poor, have only my dreams;
I have spread my dreams under your feet;
Tread softly, for you tread on my dreams.

W. B. Yeats

DUTY

I slept and dreamed that life was beauty;
I woke, and found that life was duty.

Ellen S. Hooper

Not snow nor rain nor heat nor gloom of night stays these couriers
from the swift completion of their appointed rounds.

Motto of the U.S. Postal Service

ECONOMY

Buy not what you want, but what you have need of; what you do not want is dear at a farthing.   *Cato*

He who will not economize will have to agonize.   *Confucius*

After order and liberty, economy is one of the highest essentials of a free government.... Economy is always a guarantee of peace.
Calvin Coolidge

ELOQUENCE

Eloquence is the poetry of prose.   *Bryant*

Noise proves nothing. Often a hen who has merely laid an egg cackles as if she laid an asteroid.   *Mark Twain*

True eloquence consists in saying all that is necessary, and nothing but what is necessary.   *La Rochefoucauld*

ENEMY

He who has a thousand friends has not a friend to spare,
And he who has one enemy will meet him everywhere.
Emerson

If thine enemy hunger, feed him; if he thirst, give him drink: for in so doing thou shalt heap coals of fire on his head.   *Romans XII 20*

We have met the enemy and they are ours.   *Oliver Hazard Perry*

I choose my friends for their good looks, my acquaintances for their good characters, and my enemies for their good intellects. A man cannot be too careful in the choice of his enemies.
Oscar Wilde

ENGLAND

If I should die, think only this of me:
That there's some corner of a foreign field
That is forever England.
Rupert Brooke

Oh, to be in England
Now that April's there, ...
            R. Browning

God of our fathers, known of old,
Lord of our far-flung battle-line,
Beneath whose awful Hand we hold
Dominion over palm and pine—
Lord God of Hosts, be with us yet,
Lest we forget—lest we forget!
                Kipling

Old England still throbs with the muffled fire
Of a Past she can never forget:
And again shall she banner the world up higher;
For there's life in the Old Land yet.
            Gerald Massey

EQUALITY

Your levellers wish to level down as far as themselves, but they cannot bear levelling up to themselves.   *Samuel Johnson*

We hold these truths to be self-evident: that all men are created equal; that they are endowed by their Creator with certain unalienable rights; that among these are life, liberty and the pursuit of happiness.   *Declaration of Independence*

ERROR

An error gracefully acknowledged is a victory won.
            Caroline L. Gascoigne

When every one is in the wrong, every one is in the right.
            La Chaussee

The man who makes no mistakes does not usually make anything.
            Edward J. Phelps

Errors, like straws, upon the surface flow;
He who would search for pearls must dive below.
                Dryden

Good nature and good sense must ever join;
To err is human, to forgive divine.

Pope

EVIL

Evil events from evil causes spring.   *Aristophanes*

Woe unto them that call evil good, and good evil.   *Isaiah V 20*

As sure as God is good, so surely there is no such thing as necessary evil.   *Southey*

EXPERIENCE

Experience is the best of schoolmasters, only the school-fees are heavy.   *Carlyle*

Experience is the extract of suffering.   *Arthur Helps*

I have but one lamp by which my feet are guided, and that is the lamp of experience.   *Patrick Henry*

Experience is the name men give to their follies or their sorrows.
Alfred de Musset

Men are wise in proportion, not to their experience, but to their capacity for experience.   *George Bernard Shaw*

Is there anyone so wise as to learn by the experience of others?
Voltaire

A sadder and a wiser man
He rose the morrow morn.
S. T. Coleridge

Experience keeps a dear school, yet fools will learn in no other.
Franklin

FACE

He had a face like a benediction.   *Cervantes*

Lift thou up the light of thy countenance upon us.   *Psalms IV 6*

FAILURE

In the lexicon of youth, which
Fate reserves for a bright manhood, there is no such word
As—fail!

Bulwer-Lytton

How are the mighty fallen!   *II Samuel I 25*

And nothing to look backward to with pride,
And nothing to look forward to with hope.

Robert Frost

I sing the hymn of the conquered, who fall in the battle of life,
The hymn of the wounded, the beaten who died overwhelmed in the
strife.

W. W. Story

FAITH

If the stars should appear one night in a thousand years, how men
would believe and adore, and preserve for many generations the
remembrance of the City of God which had been shown! But every
night come out these envoys of beauty, and light the universe with
their admonishing smile. . . .

In the woods we return to reason and faith. Standing on the bare
ground—my head bathed by the blithe air, and uplifted into infinite
space—all mean egotism vanishes. . . . The currents of the Universal
Being circulate through me.   *Ralph Waldo Emerson*

Faith is the continuation of reason.   *William Adams*

We walk by faith, not by sight.   *II Corinthians V 7*

All I have seen teaches me to trust the Creator for all I have not
seen.   *Emerson*

Faith is the substance of things hoped for, the evidence of things
not seen.   *Hebrews XI 1*

Let us have faith that right makes might; and in that faith, let us, to the end, dare to do our duty as we understand it.   *Lincoln*

Here I stand. I can do no otherwise. God help me. Amen.   *Luther*

I have fought a good fight, I have finished my course, I have kept the faith.   *II Timothy IV* 7

I can believe anything, provided it is incredible.   *Wilde*

Faith without works is dead.   *James II* 20

FALL

O' It sets my heart a clickin'
Like the tickin' of a clock,
When the frost is on the punkin
And the fodder's in the shock.
  James Whitcomb Riley

We fall to rise, are baffled to fight better,
Sleep to wake.
  R. Browning

He that is down needs fear no fall,
He that is low, no pride.
  Bunyan

How are the mighty fallen!   *II Samuel I* 19

FAME

If you would not be forgotten as soon as you are dead, either write things worth reading or do things worth writing.   *Franklin*

Men think highly of those who rise rapidly in the world; whereas nothing rises quicker than dust, straw, and feathers.   *Hare*

Fame is but the breath of the people, and that often unwholesome.
  Rousseau

In fame's temple there is always a niche to be found for rich dunces, importunate scoundrels, or successful butchers of the human race.   *Zimmerman*

Fame is the spur that the clear spirit doth raise
(That last infirmity of noble mind)
To scorn delights, and live laborious days.
                                                            Milton

We toil for fame,
We live on crusts,
We make a name,
Then we are busts.
                    L. H. Robbins

Fame is the perfume of heroic deeds.   *Socrates*

Fame has also this great drawback, that if we pursue it we must direct our lives in such a way as to please the fancy of men, avoiding what they dislike and seeking what is pleasing to them.   *Spinoza*

So passes away the glory of the world.   *Thomas à Kempis*

FAMILY

There is little less trouble in governing a private family than a whole kingdom.   *Montaigne*

The family is more sacred than the state.   *Pope Pius XI*

All happy families resemble one another; every unhappy family is unhappy in its own way.   *Tolstoy*

FAREWELL

When we two parted
In silence and tears,
Half broken-hearted
To sever for years,
Pale grew thy cheek and cold
Colder thy kiss. . . .
                    Byron

To meet, to know, to love—and then to part,
Is the sad tale of many a human heart.

S. T. Coleridge

Good night, good night! Parting is such sweet sorrow,
That I shall say good night till it be morrow.

Shakespeare

FARMING

A farmer is always going to be rich next year.   *Philemon*

Farming is a most senseless pursuit, a mere laboring in a circle. You sow that you may reap, and then you reap that you may sow. Nothing ever comes of it.   *Stobaeus*

Those who labor in the earth are the chosen people of God, if He ever had a chosen people, whose breasts He has made his peculiar deposit for substantial and genuine virtue.   *Jefferson*

Slave of the wheel of labor, what to him
Are Plato and the swing of Pleiades.

Edwin Markham

... whoever could make two ears of corn, or two blades of grass, to grow upon a spot of ground where only one grew before, would deserve better of mankind, and do more essential service to his country, than the whole race of politicians put together.   *Swift*

Give fools their gold, and knaves their power;
Let fortune's bubbles rise and fall;
Who sows a field, or trains a flower,
Or plants a tree, is more than all.

Whittier

FASHION

A fashionable woman is always in love—with herself.

La Rochefoucauld

Fashion is a form of ugliness so intolerable that we have to alter it every six months.   *Wilde*

I see that the fashion wears out more apparel than the man.

Shakespeare

FATE

All are architects of Fate,
Working in these walls of Time;
Some with massive deeds and great,
Some with ornaments of rhyme.

Longfellow

Let us, then, be up and doing,
With a heart for any fate.

Longfellow

Oh busy weaver! Unseen weaver! pause! one word! whither flows
the fabric? What palace may it deck? Wherefore all these ceaseless
toilings? Speak, weaver! Stay thy hand!   *Melville*

The Moving Finger writes; and, having writ,
Moves on: nor all your Piety nor Wit
Shall lure it back to cancel half a Line,
Nor all your Tears wash out a Word of it.

Omar Khayyam

FATHER

Call no man your father upon the earth: for one is your Father,
which is in heaven.   *Matthew XXIII 9*

A father is a banker provided by nature.   *French Proverb*

The child is father of the man.   *Wordsworth*

FAULT

The greatest of faults, I should say, is to be conscious of none.

Carlyle

Be to her virtues very kind,
Be to her faults a little blind.

Prior

The fault, dear Brutus, is not in our stars,
But in ourselves, that we are underlings.
Shakespeare

Faultily faultlessly, icily regular, splendidly null,
Dead perfection, no more.

Tennyson

FEET

My feet, they haul me Round the House,
They Hoist me up the Stairs;
I only have to steer them, and
They Ride me Everywheres.

Gelett Burgess

FESTIVITIES

Why should we break up
Our snug and pleasant party?
Time was made for slaves,
But never for us so hearty.
John B. Buckstone

The feast of reason, and the flow of soul.   *Pope*

FIGHT

I have not yet begun to fight.   *John Paul Jones*

Servant of God, well done! Well has thou fought
The better fight.

Milton

FISH

She is neither fish, nor flesh, nor good red herring.   *Heywood*

Why, as men do a-land: the great ones eat up the little ones.
Pericles

You must lose a fly to catch a trout.   *Herbert*

We may say of angling as Dr. Boteler said of strawberries: "Doubtless God could have made a better berry, but doubtless God never did"; and so, (if I might be judge,) God never did make a more calm, quiet, innocent recreation than angling.   *Izaak Walton*

> Oh, the gallant fisher's life!
> It is the best of any;
> 'Tis full of pleasure, void of strife,
> And 'tis beloved by many.
> > *Izaak Walton*

FLATTERY

> 'Tis an old maxim in the schools,
> That flattery's the food of fools;
> Yet now and then your men of wit
> Will condescend to take a bit.
> > *Swift*

Imitation is the sincerest form of flattery.   *Colton*

A man that flattereth his neighbor spreadeth a net for his feet.
> *Proverbs XXIX 5*

FOOD

> He may live without books,—what is knowledge but grieving?
> He may live without hope,—what is hope but deceiving?
> He may live without love,—what is passion but pining?
> But where is the man that can live without dining?
> > *Owen Meredith*

As the Texas darky said: "Dinner-time fur some folks; but just twelve o'clock fur me!"   *Irvin S. Cobb*

Other men live to eat, while I eat to live.   *Socrates*

FOOL

Young men think old men are fools; but old men know young men are the fools.   *George Chapman*

Hain't we got all the fools in town on our side? And ain't that a big enough majority in any town? *Mark Twain*

The fool hath said in his heart, there is no God. *Psalms XIV 1*

Even a fool, when he holdeth his peace, is counted wise. *Proverbs XVII 28*

It is in the half fools and the half wise that the greatest danger lies. *Goethe*

Lord, what fools these mortals be! *Shakespeare*

> But when we play the fool, how wide
> The theatre expands! beside,
> How long the audience sits before us!
> How many prompters! what a chorus!
> *Landor*

Answer a fool according to his folly, lest he be wise in his own conceit. *Proverbs XXVI 5*

FORGIVENESS

He who has not forgiven an enemy has not yet tasted one of the most sublime enjoyments of life. *Johann K. Lavater*

God pardons like a mother, who kisses the offense into everlasting forgetfulness. *Henry Ward Beecher*

His heart was as great as the world, but there was no room in it to hold the memory of a wrong. *Emerson*

Forgive us our trespasses, as we forgive those that trespass against us. *The Lord's Prayer*

Nobuddy ever fergits where he buried a hatchet. *Kin Hubbard*

Father, forgive them; **for** they know not what they do. *Luke XXIII 34*

Forgive us our debts, as we forgive our debtors.   *Matthew VI 12*

FORGOTTEN

The tumult and the shouting dies,
The captains and the kings depart;
Still stands thine ancient sacrifice,
A humble and a contrite heart.
Lord God of Hosts, be with us yet,
Lest we forget—lest we forget.

Kipling

Who is the Forgotten Man? He is the clean, quiet, virtuous, domestic citizen, who pays his debts and his taxes and is never heard of out of his little circle.   *William Graham Sumner*

FORTUNE

Fortune never seems so blind as to those upon whom she has bestowed no favors.   *La Rochefoucauld*

Fortune favors the bold.   *Virgil*

FREEDOM

Personal liberty is the paramount essential to human dignity and human happiness.   *Bulwer-Lytton*

In a free country there is much clamor, with little suffering; in a despotic state there is little complaint, with much grievance. *Carnot*

Many politicians are in the habit of laying it down as a self-evident proposition that no people ought to be free till they are fit to use their freedom. The maxim is worthy of the fool in the old story who resolved not to go into the water till he had learned to swim.

Macaulay

Since the general civilization of mankind I believe there are more instances of the abridgment of the freedom of the people by gradual and silent encroachments of those in power than by violent and sudden usurpations.   *Madison*

No amount of political freedom will satisfy the hungry masses.

Lenin

I would rather sit on a pumpkin, and have it all to myself, than to be crowded on a velvet cushion.   *Thoreau*

Aye, call it holy ground.
The soil where first they trod!
They left unstained what there they found—
Freedom to worship God.
Felicia D. Hemans

They can only set free men free . . .
And there is no need of that:
Free men set themselves free.
James Oppenheim

FRIEND

Prosperity makes friends and adversity tries them.   *Anon.*

A friend is one who dislikes the same people that you dislike.

Anon.

Animals are such agreeable friends—they ask no questions, they pass no criticisms.   *George Eliot*

A friend must not be injured, even in jest.   *Syrus*

Madam, I have been looking for a person who disliked gravy all my life; let us swear eternal friendship.   *Sydney Smith*

I have had playmates, I have had companions,
In my days of childhood, in my joyful schooldays—
All, all are gone, the old familiar faces.
Charles Lamb

He who has a thousand friends has not a friend to spare,
And he who has one enemy shall meet him everywhere.
Emerson

When I remember all
The friends, so link'd together,
I've seen around me fall,
Like leaves in wintry weather,
I feel like one
Who treads alone
Some banquet-hall deserted . . .

Moore

Thou wert my guide, philosopher, and friend.   *Pope*

Against a foe I can myself defend,—
But Heaven protect me from a blundering friend!
D'Arcy W. Thompson

FUTURE

I never think of the future. It comes soon enough.

Albert Einstein

Take therefore no thought for the morrow; for the morrow shall take thought for the things of itself. Sufficient unto the day is the evil thereof.   *Matthew VI 34*

Till the sun grows cold,
And the stars are old,
And the leaves of the Judgment Book unfold.
Bayard Taylor

GAMBLING

There is but one good throw upon the dice, which is to throw them away.   *Chatfield*

It (gaming) is the child of avarice, the brother of iniquity, and the father of mischief.   *Washington*

There are two times in a man's life when he should not speculate: when he can't afford it, and when he can.   *Mark Twain*

GENIUS

There is no great genius without a mixture of madness. *Aristotle*

A gift, like genius, I often think only means an infinite capacity for taking pains.   *Ellice Hopkins*

The lamp of genius burns quicker than the lamp of life.   *Schiller*

Doing easily what others find difficult is talent; doing what is impossible for talent is genius.   *Amiel*

The eagle never lost so much time as when he submitted to learn of the crow.   *Blake*

> Great wits are sure to madness near allied,
> And thin partitions do their bounds divide.
>   *Dryden*

When a true genius appears in the world, you may know him by this sign, that the dunces are all in a confederacy against him. *Swift*

I have nothing to declare except my genius.   *Oscar Wilde*

GENTLEMEN

A gentleman is a man who can disagree without being disagreeable.   *Anon.*

Propriety of manners and consideration for others are the two main characteristics of a gentleman.   *Disraeli*

To make a fine gentleman, several trades are required, but chiefly a barber.   *Goldsmith*

GIFT

You give but little when you give of your possessions. It is when you give of yourself that you truly give.   *Kahlil Gibran*

Or what man is there of you, whom if his son ask bread, will he give him a stone?   *Matthew VII 9*

GOD

That the universe was formed by a fortuitous concourse of atoms, I will no more believe than that the accidental jumbling of the alphabet would fall into a most ingenious treatise of philosophy.   *Swift*

Man proposes, and God disposes.   *Thomas à Kempis*

> God's in His Heaven—
> All's right with the world!
> *Browning*

> God moves in a mysterious way
> His wonders to perform;
> He plants his footsteps in the sea
> And rides upon the storm.
> *Cowper*

God is our refuge and strength, a very present help in trouble.
                                                  Psalms XLVI 1

If God be for us, who can be against us?   *Romans VIII 31*

God is not a cosmic bell-boy for whom we can press a button to
get things.   *Harry Emerson Fosdick*

> A mighty fortress is our God,
> A bulwark never failing.
> *Martin Luther*

> God doth not need
> Either man's work or his own gifts; who best
> Bear his mild yoke, they serve him best; his state
> Is kingly. Thousands at his bidding speed
> And post o'er land and ocean without rest;
> They also serve who only stand and wait.
> *Milton*

God is no respecter of persons.   *Acts X 34*

Though he slay me, yet will I trust him.   *Job XIII 5*

Suppose I had found a watch upon the ground. . . . The mechanism
being observed, . . . the watch must have a maker; . . . *William Paley*

O God, our help in ages past,
Our hope for years to come,
Our shelter from the stormy blast,
And our eternal home.

Isaac Watts

One God, one law, one element,
And one far-off divine event,
To which the whole creation moves.

Tennyson

GOLDEN RULE

Therefore all things whatsoever ye would that men should do unto you, do ye even so unto them.   *Matthew VII 12*

Do unto the other feller the way he'd like to do unto you, an' do it fust.   *E. N. Westcott*

GOOD

Prove all things; hold fast that which is good.

I Thessalonians V 21

Be good and you will be lonesome.   *Mark Twain*

Here's to you, as good as you are,
And here's to me, as bad as I am;
But as good as you are, and as bad as I am,
I am as good as you are, as bad as I am.

Old Scotch toast

Abhor that which is evil; cleave to that which is good.

Romans XII 9

There is some soul of goodness in things evil,
Would men observingly distil it out.

Shakespeare

O, yet we trust that somehow good
Will be the final goal of ill,
To pangs of nature, sins of will,
Defects of doubt, and taints of blood.

Tennyson

Roaming in thought over the Universe, I saw the little that is Good
steadily hastening towards immortality,
And the vast all that is call'd Evil I saw hastening to merge itself and
become lost and dead.

Walt Whitman

Do all the good you can,
By all the means you can,
In all the ways you can,
In all the places you can,
At all the times you can,
To all the people you can,
As long as ever you can.
John Wesley

GOSSIP

There is only one thing in the world worse than being talked
about, and that is not being talked about. *Wilde*

GOVERNMENT

Experience teaches us to be most on our guard to protect liberty
when the government's purposes are beneficent. *Brandeis*

Though the people support the government the government
should not support the people. *Grover Cleveland*

I think we have more machinery of government than is necessary,
too many parasites living on the labor of the industrious. *Jefferson*

Govern a great nation as you would cook a small fish. (Don't
overdo it.) *Lao-Tsze*

No man is good enough to govern another man without that
other's consent. *Lincoln*

The basis of our political systems is the right of the people to make
and to alter their constitutions of government. *Washington*

I desire so to conduct the affairs of this administration that if at the end, when I come to lay down the reins of power, I have lost every other friend on earth, I shall at least have one friend left, and that friend shall be down inside of me.   *Lincoln*

The whole of government consists in the art of being honest.
                                                        Thomas Jefferson

Government, even in its best state, is but a necessary evil; in its worst state, an intolerable one.   *Thomas Paine*

If elected, I shall see to it that every man has a square deal, no less and no more.   *Theodore Roosevelt*

The throne is but a piece of wood covered with velvet.
                                                              Napoleon

In that fierce light which beats upon a throne.   *Tennyson*

Once there were two brothers. One ran away to sea, the other was elected Vice President, and nothing was ever heard of either of them again.   *Thomas R. Marshall*

GRATITUDE

The gratitude of most men is but a secret desire of receiving greater benefits.   *La Rochefoucauld*

He who receives a good turn should never forget it; he who does one should never remember it.   *Charron*

Two kinds of gratitude: the sudden kind
We feel for what we take, the larger kind
We feel for what we give.
                            E. A. Robinson

GREATNESS

All great men come out of the middle classes.   *Emerson*

No man ever yet became great by imitation.   *Samuel Johnson*

It is the prerogative of great men only to have great defects.
La Rochefoucauld

There were giants in the earth in those days.   *Genesis VI 4*

> That man is great, and he alone,
> Who serves a greatness not his own,
> For neither praise nor pelf:
> Content to know and be unknown:
> Whole in himself.
> *Owen Meredith*

> Why, man, he doth bestride the narrow world
> Like a Colossus, and we petty men
> Walk under his huge legs and peep about
> To find ourselves dishonorable graves.
> *Shakespeare*

> Ah vanity of vanities!
> How wayward the decrees of fate are,
> How very weak the very wise,
> How very small the very great are!
> *Thackeray*

> O may I join the choir invisible
> Of those immortal dead who live again
> In minds made better by their presence.
> *George Eliot*

GUEST

No one can be so welcome a guest that he will not annoy his host after three days.   *Plautus*

> Unbidden guests
> Are often welcomest when they are gone.
> *Shakespeare*

HABIT

Habit with him was all the test of truth;
"It must be right: I've done it from my youth."
George Crabbe

HANDS

The voice is Jacob's voice, but the hands are the hands of Esau.
Genesis XXVII 22

All the perfumes of Arabia will not sweeten this little hand.
Shakespeare

HAPPINESS

Most folks are about as happy as they make up their minds to be.
Abraham Lincoln

What happiness is there which is not purchased with more or less of pain?
Margaret Oliphant

I have learned to seek my happiness by limiting my desires, rather than in attempting to satisfy them.
John Stuart Mill

O, how bitter a thing it is to look into happiness through another man's eyes!
Shakespeare

You have no more right to consume happiness without producing it than to consume wealth without producing it.
George Bernard Shaw

On with the dance! let joy be unconfin'd:
No sleep till morn, when Youth and Pleasure meet
To chase the glowing Hours with flying feet.
Byron

HEAD

And still they gaz'd, and still the wonder grew
That one small head could carry all he knew.
Goldsmith

The head is always the dupe of the heart.   *La Rochefoucauld*

HEART

Where your treasure is there will your heart be also. *Luke XII 34*

The heart has its reasons which reason does not know.   *Pascal*

HEAVEN

Lay up for yourselves treasures in heaven.   *Matthew VI 20*

Earth has no sorrow that heaven cannot heal.   *Moore*

A day in thy courts is better than a thousand. I had rather be a doorkeeper in the house of my God than to dwell in the tents of wickedness.   *Psalms LXXXIV 10*

> Heaven is not reached by a single bound
> But we build the ladder by which we rise.
> *J. G. Holland*

> It was a childish ignorance,
> But now 'tis little joy,
> To know I'm farther off from heaven
> Than when I was a boy.
> *Thomas Hood*

... strait is the gate and narrow is the way which leadeth unto life, and few there be that find it.   *Matthew VII 14*

Joy shall be in heaven over one sinner that repenteth, more than over ninety and nine just persons, which need no repentance.
Luke XV 7

HELP

I'm going your way, so let us go hand in hand. You help me and I'll help you. We shall not be here very long, for soon death, the kind old nurse, will come back and rock us all to sleep. Let us help one another while we may.   *William Morris*

HERO

No man is a hero to his valet. *Madame de Cornuel*

See the conquering hero comes!
Sound the trumpets, beat the drums!
Dr. T. Morel

Hero-worship is strongest where there is least regard for human freedom. *Herbert Spencer*

HOME

Home is the place where, when you have to go there,
They have to take you in.
Robert Frost

The foxes have their holes, and the birds of the air have their nests; but the Son of man hath not where to lay his head.
Matthew VIII 20

Happy the man, whose wish and care
A few paternal acres bound,
Content to breathe his native air
In his own ground.
Pope

The house of every one is to him his castle and fortress, as well for his defence against injury and violence, as for his repose.
Sir Edward Coke

HONOR

To me the highest thing, after God, is my honor.
Ludwig van Beethoven

For Brutus is an honorable man;
So are they all, all honorable men.
Shakespeare

HOPE

A woman's hopes are woven of sunbeams; a shadow annihilates them.
George Eliot

Youth fades; love droops, the leaves of friendship fall;
A mother's secret hope outlives them all.
Holmes

Hope says to us constantly, "Go on, go on," and leads us thus to the grave.
Mme. de Maintenon

Hope is the poor man's bread.
Thales

The heart bowed down by weight of woe
To weakest hope will cling.
A. Bunn

Hope springs eternal in the human breast:
Man never is, but always to be blest.
Pope

HUMANITY

Oh, God! that bread should be so dear,
And flesh and blood so cheap!
Hood

Humanity is the Son of God.
Theodore Parker

I am not an Athenian, nor a Greek, but a citizen of the world.
Socrates

We would not listen to those who were wont to say the voice of the people is the voice of God, for the voice of the mob is near akin to madness.
Alcuin

HUMILITY

After crosses and losses, men grow humbler and wiser.   *Franklin*

Whosoever shall smite thee on thy right cheek, turn to him the other also.   *Matthew V 39*

An outward and visible sign of an inward and spiritual grace.
                                             Book of Common Prayer

Blessed are the meek: for they shall inherit the earth.
                                             Matthew V 5

HYPOCRITE

He blam'd and protested, but join'd in the plan;
He shared in the plunder, but pitied the man.
                                             Cowper

Hypocrisy is the homage which vice pays to virtue.
                                             La Rochefoucauld

Thou hypocrite, first cast out the beam out of thine own eye; and then shalt thou see clearly to cast out the mote out of thy brother's eye.   *Matthew VII 5*

Woe unto you, scribes and Pharisees, hypocrites! for ye make clean the outside of the cup and of the platter, but within they are full of extortion and excess.   *Matthew XXIII 25*

With one hand he put
A penny in the urn of poverty,
And with the other took a shilling out.
                                             Robert Pollok

IDEAS

Ideas must work through the brains and the arms of good and brave men, or they are no better than dreams.   *Emerson*

No army can withstand the strength of an idea whose time has come.   *Victor Hugo*

IDLENESS

As idle as a painted ship
Upon a painted ocean.
                                             S. T. Coleridge

He slept beneath the moon,
He basked beneath the sun;
He lived a life of going-to-do,
And died with nothing done.
J. Albert

God loves an idle rainbow,
No less than laboring seas.
Ralph Hodgson

Go to the ant, thou sluggard; consider her ways, and be wise.
Proverbs VI 6

I wish to preach not the doctrine of ignoble ease, but the doctrine
of the strenuous life.   *Theodore Roosevelt*

IGNORANCE

Ignorance never settles a question.   *Disraeli*

To be ignorant of one's ignorance is the malady of the ignorant.
A. B. Alcott

Where ignorance is bliss,
'Tis folly to be wise.
Gray

Ignorance is degrading only when found in company with riches.
Schopenhauer

IMAGINATION

Imagination is more important than knowledge.   *Albert Einstein*

He who has imagination without learning has wings but no feet.
Joubert

The human race is governed by its imagination.   *Napoleon*

IMMORTALITY

A good man never dies.   *Callimachus*

The nearer I approach the end, the plainer I hear around me the immortal symphonies of the worlds which invite me. It is marvelous, yet simple.   *Victor Hugo*

It must be so,—Plato, thou reason'st well!—
Else whence this pleasing hope, this fond desire,
This longing after immortality?
                                                    Addison

Dust thou art, to dust returnest,
Was not spoken of the soul.
                                                    Longfellow

IMPOSSIBLE

You cannot make a crab walk straight.   *Aristophanes*

Never let me hear that foolish word again.   *Mirabeau*

Impossible is a word only to be found in the dictionary of fools.
                                                    Napoleon

To the timid and hesitating everything is impossible because it seems so.   *Scott*

IMPROVEMENT

It is necessary to try to surpass one's self always; this occupation ought to last as long as life.   *Queen Christina*

Slumber not in the tents of your fathers. The world is advancing. Advance with it!   *Mazzini*

INFERIORITY

The feeling of inferiority rules the mental life and can be clearly recognized in the sense of incompleteness and unfulfillment, and in the uninterrupted struggle both of individuals and of humanity.
                                                    Alfred Adler

INSPIRATION

I saw a delicate flower had grown up two feet high, between the horses' path and the wheeltrack. An inch more to right or left had sealed its fate, or an inch higher; and yet it lived to flourish as much as if it had a thousand acres of untrodden space around it, and never knew the danger it incurred. It did not borrow trouble, nor invite an evil fate by apprehending it.   *Henry David Thoreau*

The sky is the daily bread of the eyes.   *Emerson*

THOMAS JEFFERSON

A gentleman of thirty-two who could calculate an eclipse, survey an estate, tie an artery, plan an edifice, try a cause, break a horse, dance a minuet and play the violin.   *James Parton, Life of Jefferson*

Here was buried Thomas Jefferson, author of the Declaration of American Independence, of the statute of Virginia for religious freedom, and father of the University of Virginia.
    Jefferson, Epitaph written by himself

JOURNALISM

Journalism has already come to be the first power in the land.
    Samuel Bowles

Get your facts first, and then you can distort 'em as much as you please.   *Mark Twain*

Writing good editorials is chiefly telling the people what they think, not what you think.   *Arthur Brisbane*

I fear three newspapers more than a hundred thousand bayonets.
    Napoleon

JUDGE

It is better that a judge should lean on the side of compassion than severity.   *Cervantes*

Judges are apt to be naive, simple-minded men.
    Oliver Wendell Holmes

Four things belong to a judge: to hear courteously, to answer wisely, to consider soberly, and to decide impartially.   *Socrates*

Judges ought to be more learned than witty, more reverend than plausible, and more advised than confident. Above all things, integrity is their portion and proper virtue.   *Bacon*

An upright judge, a learned judge!   *Shakespeare*

The administration of justice is the firmest pillar of government.
George Washington

JUDGMENT

One man's word is no man's word; we should quietly hear both sides.   *Goethe*

Give your decisions, never your reasons; your decisions may be right, your reasons are sure to be wrong.   *Lord Mansfield*

Judge not, that ye be not judged.   *Matthew VII 1*

> There is so much good in the worst of us,
> And so much bad in the best of us,
> That it hardly becomes any of us
> To talk about the rest of us.
> *Anon.*

Why beholdest thou the mote that is in thy brother's eye, but considerest not the beam that is in thy own eye?   *Matthew VII 3*

Thou art weighed in the balance, and art found wanting.
Daniel V 27

God will not look you over for medals, degrees or diplomas, but for scars.   *Elbert Hubbard*

And before him shall be gathered all nations: and he shall separate them one from another, as a shepherd divideth his sheep from his goats.   *Matthew XXV 32*

KNOWLEDGE

Strange how much you've got to know
Before you know how little you know.

To be conscious that you are ignorant is a great step to knowledge.

Disraeli

He that increaseth knowledge increaseth sorrow.

Ecclesiastes I 18

He who knows others is learned;
He who knows himself is wise.

Lao-Tsze

It ain't the things you don't know what gets you into trouble; it's the things you know for sure what ain't so.

My name is Benjamin Jowett,
I'm Master of Balliol College;
Whatever is knowledge I know it,
And what I don't know isn't knowledge.

Anon.

There are four sorts of men:
He who knows not and knows not he knows not: he is a fool—
   shun him;
He who knows not and knows he knows not: he is simple—
   teach him.
He who knows and knows not he knows: he is asleep—wake
   him;
He who knows and knows he knows: he is wise—follow him.

Lady Burton

Knowledge is the only instrument of production that is not subject to diminishing returns.   *J. M. Clark*

I know nothing except the fact of my ignorance.   *Socrates*

Knowledge comes, but wisdom lingers.   *Tennyson*

A little learning is a dangerous thing;
Drink deep, or taste not the Pierian spring.

Pope

LABOR

A truly American sentiment recognises the dignity of labor and the fact that honor lies in honest toil.   *Cleveland*

Bowed by the weight of centuries he leans
Upon his hoe and gazes on the ground,
The emptiness of ages in his face,
And on his back the burden of the world.

Edwin Markham

Labor was the first price, the original purchase money that was paid for all things.   *Adam Smith*

The laborer is worthy of his hire.   *Luke X 7*

LAUGH

And the loud laugh that spoke the vacant mind.   *Goldsmith*

Laugh and the world laughs with you,
Weep and you weep alone,
For the sad old earth must borrow its mirth,
But has trouble enough of its own.

Ella Wheeler Wilcox

LAWS

When the state is most corrupt, then laws are most multiplied.

Tacitus

There is no man so good, who, were he to submit all his thoughts and actions to the laws would not deserve hanging ten times in his life.   *Montaigne*

Where law ends, there tyranny begins.   *William Pitt*

The law, in its majestic equality, forbids the rich as well as the poor to sleep under bridges, to beg in the streets, and to steal bread.

Anatole France

The law is the true embodiment
Of everything that's excellent.
It has no kind of fault or flaw,
And I, my Lords, embody the law.
W. S. Gilbert

I know no method to secure the repeal of bad or obnoxious laws so effective as their stringent execution.   *U. S. Grant*

LAWYERS

It is a secret worth knowing that lawyers rarely go to law.
Moses Crowell

A lawyer must first get on, then get honor, and then get honest.

A lawyer's opinion is worth nothing unless paid for.
English Proverb

Most good lawyers live well, work hard, and die poor.
Daniel Webster

And whether you're an honest man or whether you're a thief
Depends on whose solicitor has given me my brief.
W. S. Gilbert

Woe unto you also, ye lawyers, for ye lade men with burdens grievous to be borne, and ye yourselves touch not the burdens with one of your fingers.   *Luke XI 46*

A lawyer art thou?—draw not nigh!
Go carry to some fitter place
The keenness of that practised eye,
The hardness of that sallow face.
Wordsworth

LEARNING

All wish to be learned, but no one is willing to pay the price.
Juvenal

The three foundations of learning: Seeing much, suffering much, and studying much.   *Catherall*

And still they gazed, and still the wonder grew,
That one small head should carry all he knew.
                                             Goldsmith

They have learned nothing, and forgotten nothing.
                                       Chevalier de Panat

LEISURE

Increased means and increased leisure are the two civilizers of man.
                                             Disraeli

Leisure is the mother of philosophy.   *Thomas Hobbes*

LETTER

I have made this letter longer than usual because I lack the time to make it shorter.   *Pascal*

I have received no more than one or two letters in my life that were worth the postage.   *Thoreau*

LIAR

An experienced, industrious, ambitious, and often quite picturesque liar.   *Mark Twain*

The liar's punishment is not in the least that he is not believed, but that he cannot believe anyone else.   *George Bernard Shaw*

A liar needs a good memory.   *Quintilian*

This is the punishment of a liar: He is not believed even when he speaks the truth.   *Babylonian Talmud*

LIBERTY

The people never give up their liberties but under some delusion.
                                             Burke

Give me the liberty to know, to think, to believe, and to utter freely according to conscience, above all other liberties.   *Milton*

The God who gave us life, gave us liberty at the same time.

Jefferson

Is life so dear or peace so sweet as to be purchased at the price of chains and slavery? Forbid it, Almighty God! I know not what course others may take; but as for me, give me liberty, or give me death!   *Patrick Henry*

Eternal vigilance is the price of liberty.   *Wendell Phillips*

LIFE

Take life too seriously, and what is it worth?
If the morning wake us to no new joys, if the evening bring us not
  the hopes of new pleasures, is it worth while to dress and undress?
Does the sun shine on me today that I may reflect on yesterday?
That I may endeavor to foresee and to control what can neither be
  foreseen nor controlled—the destiny of tomorrow?

Goethe

We come and we cry, and that is life; we yawn and we depart, and that is death!   *Ausone de Chancel*

One life—a little gleam of time between two eternities.   *Carlyle*

A useless life is an early death.   *Goethe*

Life is a tragedy for those who feel, and a comedy for those who think.   *La Bruyère*

May you live all the days of your life.   *Swift*

Teach me to live that I may dread
The grave as little as my bed.
Bishop Ken

He who waits to do a great deal of good at once will never do it.
Charles Sumner

The best things are nearest: breath in your nostrils, light in your eyes, flowers at your feet, duties at your hand, the path of Right just before you. Then do not grasp at the stars, but do life's plain, common work as it comes, certain that daily duties and daily bread are the sweetest things of life.   *Robert Louis Stevenson*

> Our hearts, though stout and brave,
> Still like muffled drums are beating
> Funeral marches to the grave.
> *Longfellow*

Is life worth living? That depends on the liver.   *Anon.*

> Why should there be such turmoil and such strife,
> To spin in length this feeble line of life?
> *Bacon*

> When I consider Life, 'tis all a cheat.
> Yet fool'd with hope, men favor the deceit;
> Trust on, and think tomorrow will repay.
> Tomorrow's falser than the former day;
> *Dryden*

> Life is a jest, and all things show it;
> I thought so once, but now I know it.
> *John Gay*

> A crust of bread and a corner to sleep in,
> A minute to smile and an hour to weep in,
> A pint of joy to a peck of trouble,
> And never a laugh but the moans come double;
> And that is life!
> *Paul Laurence Dunbar*

Life is made up of sobs, sniffles, and smiles, with sniffles predominating.   *O. Henry*

> Like leaves on trees the race of man is found,
> Now green in youth, now with'ring on the ground:

Another race the following spring supplies,
They fall successive and successive rise.

Homer

Happy the man, and happy he alone,
He who can call today his own:
He who, secure within, can say:
"Tomorrow do thy worst, for I have liv'd today."

Horace

The weariness, the fever, and the fret
Here, where men sit and hear each other groan.

Keats

Tomorrow will I live, the fool does say;
Today itself's too late; the wise lived yesterday.

Martial

As for man his days are as grass: as a flower of the field, so he
flourisheth. The wind passeth over it, and it is gone; and the place
thereof shall know it no more.   *Psalms CIII 15-16*

Strange interlude! Yes, our lives are merely strange dark interludes
in the electrical display of God the Father!   *Eugene O'Neill*

Life is not a spectacle or a feast; it is a predicament.

George Santayana

Life's but a walking shadow, a poor player
That struts and frets his hour upon the stage
And then is heard no more: it is a tale
Told by an idiot, full of sound and fury,
Signifying nothing.

Shakespeare

And the wild regrets and the bloody sweats
None knew so well as I:
For he who lives more lives than one
More deaths than one must die.

Oscar Wilde

All the world's a stage,
And all the men and women merely players.

Shakespeare

Variety's the very spice of life
That gives it all its flavour.

Cowper

Trust no Future, howe'er pleasant!
Let the dead Past bury its dead!
Act—act in the living Present!
Heart within, and God o'erhead!

Longfellow

ABRAHAM LINCOLN

Lincoln, six feet one in his stocking feet,
The lank man, knotty and tough as a hickory rail,
Whose hands were always too big for white-kid gloves,
Whose wit was a coonskin sack of dry, tall tales,
Whose weathered face was homely as a plowed field.

Stephen Vincent Benét

His heart was as great as the world, but there was no room in it
to hold the memory of a wrong.   *Emerson*

Now he belongs to the ages.   *Edwin M. Stanton*

LISTENING

From listening comes wisdom, and from speaking repentance.

Italian Proverb

A good listener is not only popular everywhere, but after a while
he knows something.   *Wilson Mizner*

LITERATURE

The classics are only primitive literature. They belong to the same
class as primitive machinery and primitive music and primitive medicine.   *Stephen Leacock*

The difference between literature and journalism is that journalism is unreadable, and literature is not read.   *Wilde*

There is first the literature of knowledge, and secondly, the literature of power. The function of the first is—to teach; the function of the second is—to move.   *De Quincey*

Great literature is simply language charged with meaning to the utmost possible degree.   *Ezra Pound*

Literature is the orchestration of platitudes.   *Thornton Wilder*

LOVE

Love in France is a comedy; in England a tragedy; in Italy an opera seria; and in Germany a melodrama.   *Marguerite Blessington*

Love is an ocean of emotions, entirely surrounded by expenses.
                    Lord Dewar

We are all born for love. . . . It is the principle of existence and its only end.   *Disraeli*

> Man's love is of man's life a thing apart,
> 'Tis woman's whole existence.
>   *Byron*

With all thy faults, I love thee still.   *Cowper*

> Oh, I'm in love with the janitor's boy,
> And the janitor's boy loves me;
> He's going to hunt for a desert isle
> In our geography.
>   *Nathalia Crane*

> Two souls with but a single thought,
> Two hearts that beat as one.
>   *Von Munch-Bellinghausen*

Men have died from time to time and worms have eaten them, but not for love.   *Shakespeare*

I hold it true, whate'er befall;
I feel it, when I sorrow most;
'Tis better to have loved and lost
Than never to have loved at all.
Tennyson

MADNESS

Whom the gods would destroy, they first make mad.   *Euripides*

Though this be madness, yet there is method in't.   *Shakespeare*

MAJORITY

A minority may be right; a majority is always wrong.   *Ibsen*

It is my principle that the will of the majority should always prevail.   *Jefferson*

MAN

Man that is born of a woman is of few days, and full of trouble.
Job XIV 1

Thou hast made him a little lower than the angels.   *Psalms VIII 5*

His life was gentle, and the elements
So mix'd in him that Nature might stand up,
And say to all the world, This was a man!
Shakespeare

One man finds pleasure in improving his land, another his horses. My pleasure lies in seeing that I myself grow better day by day.
Socrates

When little men cast long shadows, it is a sign that the sun is setting.   *Walter Savage Landor*

But hearing oftentimes
The still, sad music of humanity.
Wordsworth

I am a man, and nothing human can be of indifference to me.

Terence

Man's inhumanity to man
Makes countless thousands mourn.

Burns

I am seeking a man. *Diogenes (carrying a lantern in the daylight)*

Thou every prospect pleases,
And only man is vile.

Reginald Heber

Man, biologically considered, ... is the most formidable of all the beasts of prey, and, indeed, the only one that preys systematically on its own species. *William James*

So God created man in his own image, in the image of God created he him. *Genesis I 27*

Man is a reed, the weakest in nature, but he is a thinking reed.

Pascal

Man is the only animal that blushes. Or needs to. *Mark Twain*

And much it grieved my heart to think
What Man has made of Man.

Wordsworth

There is
One great society alone on earth:
The noble Living and the noble Dead.

Wordsworth

Know then thyself, presume not God to scan;
The proper study of mankind is Man.

Pope

Great God, I ask thee for no meaner pelf
Than that I may not disappoint myself.

Thoreau

MARRIAGE

The highest happiness on earth is in marriage. Every man who is happily married is a successful man even if he has failed in every-thing else.   *William Lyon Phelps*

To have and to hold from this day forward, for better, for worse, for richer, for poorer, in sickness, and in health, to love and to cherish, till death us do part.   *Book of Common Prayer*

The woman cries before the wedding; the man afterward.
Polish Proverb

What therefore God hath joined together, let not man put asunder.   *Matthew XIX 6*

With this ring I thee wed, with my body I thee worship, and with all my worldly goods I thee endow.   *Book of Common Prayer*

It is not good that man should be alone.   *Genesis II 18*

MEDICINE

The physician heals, Nature makes well.   *Aristotle*

Nature, time, and patience are the three great physicians.
H. G. Bohn

The best doctor is the one you run for and can't find.   *Diderot*

God heals and the doctor takes the fee.   *Franklin*

Doctors are men who prescribe medicines of which they know little, to cure diseases of which they know less, in human beings of whom they know nothing.   *Voltaire*

MEMORY

The true art of memory is the art of attention.   *Samuel Johnson*

The Right Honorable gentleman is indebted to his memory for his jests and to his imagination for his facts.   *R. B. Sheridan*

Oft, in the stilly night,
Ere Slumber's chain has bound me,
Fond memory brings the light
Of other days around me.

Thomas Moore

MERCY

Blessed are the merciful: for they shall obtain mercy.

Matthew V 7

Teach me to feel another's woe,
To hide the fault I see;
That mercy I to others show,
That mercy show to me.

Pope

The quality of mercy is not strain'd;
It droppeth as the gentle rain from heaven
Upon the place beneath: it is twice blest;
It blesseth him that gives and him that takes:
'Tis mightiest in the mightiest: it becomes
The throned monarch better than his crown;

. . . .

And earthly power doth then show likest God's
When mercy seasons justice.

Shakespeare

MISERY

Preach to the storm, and reason with despair,
But tell not Misery's son that life is fair.

H. K. White

MISTAKE

To be positive: to be mistaken at the top of one's voice.

Ambrose Bierce

MODESTY

Modesty is the conscience of the body.   *Balzac*

With people of only moderate ability modesty is mere honesty; but with those who possess great talent it is hypocrisy.

Schopenhauer

MONEY

When I had money everyone called me brother. *Polish Proverb*

Make all you can, sell all you can, give all you can. *John Wesley*

Money is not required to buy one necessity of the soul. *Thoreau*

I cannot afford to waste my time making money. *Agassiz*

If you want to know what God thinks of money, look at the people he gives it to. *Anon.*

Money is honey, my little sonny,
And a rich man's joke is always funny.
T. E. Brown

For the love of money is the root of all evil. *I Timothy VI 10*

The Almighty Dollar, that great object of universal devotion.
Washington Irving

If you lend you either lose the money or gain an enemy.

MONUMENT

I would much rather have men ask why I have no statue than why I have one. *Marcus Cato*

If you would see his monument, look around. *Christopher Wren, Epitaph for his father, Sir C. Wren*

MOTHER

God could not be everywhere and therefore he made mothers.
Jewish Proverb

Her children arise and call her blessed. *Proverbs XXXI 28*

Who ran to help me when I fell,
And would some pretty story tell,
Or kiss the place to make it well?
My Mother.

Ann Taylor

MUSIC

Music hath charms to soothe a savage breast,
To soften rocks, or bend a knotted oak.

Congreve

When the morning stars sang together, and all the sons of God shouted for joy. *Job XXXVIII 7*

The man that hath no music in himself,
Nor is not moved with concord of sweet sounds,
Is fit for treasons, stratagems and spoils.

Shakespeare

NATION

I do not know a method of drawing up an indictment against a whole nation. *Edmund Burke*

The first panacea for a mismanaged nation is inflation of the currency; the second is war. Both bring a temporary prosperity; both bring a permanent ruin. But both are the refuge of political and economic opportunists. *Ernest Hemingway*

Republics are brought to their ends by luxury; monarchies by poverty. *Montesquieu*

NATURE

To him who in the love of Nature holds
Communion with her visible forms, she speaks
A various language.

Bryant

The woods were made for the hunter of dreams,
The brooks for the fishers of song.

Sam Walter Foss

Grass is the forgiveness of nature—her constant benediction...
Forests decay, harvests perish, flowers vanish, but grass is immortal.

Ingalls

Nature, to be commanded, must be obeyed.   *Francis Bacon*

The meanest floweret of the vale,
The simplest note that swells the gale,
The common sun, the air, the skies,
To him are opening Paradise.

Gray

The heavens declare the glory of God, and the firmament sheweth
his handywork.   *Psalms XIX 1*

Nature never did betray the heart that loved her.   *Wordsworth*

NEWNESS

There is nothing new except what is forgotten.   *Mlle. Rose Bertin*

What is valuable is not new, and what is new is not valuable.

Daniel Webster

NEWSPAPER

Were it left to me to decide whether we should have a government
without newspapers or newspapers without government, I should
not hesitate a moment to prefer the latter.   *Jefferson*

Four hostile newspapers are more to be feared than a thousand
bayonets.   *Napoleon*

Our liberty depends on the freedom of the press, and that cannot
be limited without being lost.   *Jefferson*

NIGHT

Night, when deep sleep falleth on men.   *Job IV 13*

And the night shall be filled with music
And the cares, that infest the day,
Shall fold their tents, like the Arabs,
And as silently steal away.

Longfellow

To all, to each, a fair good night,
And pleasing dreams; and slumbers light.

Scott

NONSENSE

No one is exempt from talking nonsense; the misfortune is to do it
solemnly.   *Montaigne*

They dined on mince with slices of quince,
Which they ate with a runcible spoon,
And hand in hand, on the edge of the sand,
They danced by the light of the moon.

Edward Lear

The Pobble who has no toes
Had once as many as we;
When they said, "Some day you may lose them all,"
He replied, "Fish fiddle-de-dee!"
And his Aunt Jobiska made him drink
Lavender water tinged with pink,
For she said, "The World in general knows
There's nothing so good for a Pobble's toes!"

Edward Lear

NOTHING

Blessed be he who expects nothing, for he shall never be disappointed.   *Pope*

They laboriously do nothing.   *Seneca*

OCEAN

Love the sea? I dote upon it—from the beach.   *Douglas Jerrold*

Praise the sea, but keep on land.   *George Herbert*

OPINION

He that complies against his will,
Is of his own opinion still,
Which he may adhere to, yet disown,
For reasons to himself best known.

Butler

Public opinion, a vulgar, impertinent, anonymous tyrant who deliberately makes life unpleasant for anyone who is not content to be the average man.   *Dean W. R. Inge*

The pressure of public opinion is like the pressure of the atmosphere; you can't see it—but, all the same, it is sixteen pounds to the square inch.   *J. R. Lowell*

OPPORTUNITY

It is better to light one small candle than to curse the darkness.

Confucius

With doubt and dismay you are smitten,
You think there's no chance for you son?
Why the best books haven't been written,
The best race hasn't been run.

Berton Braley

There is a tide in the affairs of men, which, taken at the flood, leads on to fortune.   *Shakespeare*

OPTIMISM

Two men look out through the same bars:
One sees the mud, and one the stars.

Frederick Langbridge

God's in his Heaven—
All's right with the world!

R. Browning

A health unto the happy,
A fig for him who frets!
It is not raining rain to me,
It's raining violets.

R. Loveman

Who brought me hither
Will bring me hence; no other guide I seek.

Milton

ORATORY

Oratory is the power to talk people out of their sober and natural opinions.   *Chatfield*

I am not fond of uttering platitudes
In stained-glass attitudes.

W. S. Gilbert

What the orators want in depth, they give you in length.

Montesquieu

PAINTING

Paint me as I am. If you leave out the scars and wrinkles, I will not pay you a shilling.   *Oliver Cromwell*

I mix them with my brains, sir.   *John Opie,*
answering the question
"With what do you mix your paints?"

PARASITE

Great fleas have little fleas upon their backs to bite 'em,
And little fleas have lesser fleas, and so ad infinitum.
And the great fleas themselves, in turn, have greater fleas to go on;
While these again have greater still, and greater still, and so on.

Augustus de Morgan

PAST

O God! Put back Thy universe and give me yesterday.

Henry Arthur Jones

Nor deem the irrevocable Past
As wholly wasted, wholly vain,
If, rising on its wrecks, at last
To something nobler we attain.
Longfellow

Those who cannot remember the past are condemned to repeat it.
Santayana

The penguin flies backwards because he doesn't care to see where he's going, but wants to see where he's been.   *Fred Allen*

PATIENCE

Adopt the pace of nature: her secret is patience.   *Emerson*

Patience is the art of hoping.   *Vauvenargues*

Beware the fury of a patient man.   *Dryden*

Ye have heard of the patience of Job.   *James V 2*

She sat like patience on a monument,
Smiling at grief.
Shakespeare

PATRIOTISM

No man can be a patriot on an empty stomach.   *W. C. Brann*

To make us love our country, our country ought to be lovely.
Edmund Burke

Indeed I tremble for my country when I reflect that God is just.
Thomas Jefferson

Patriotism is the last refuge of a scoundrel.   *Johnson*

God gave all men all earth to love,
But since our hearts are small,
Ordained for each one spot should prove
Beloved over all.
Kipling

PEACE

I prefer the most unfair peace to the most righteous war.   *Cicero*

They shall beat their swords into ploughshares, and their spears into pruninghooks; nation shall not lift up sword against nation neither shall they learn war any more.   *Isaiah II 4*

The wolf also shall dwell with the lamb, and the leopard shall lie down with the kid.   *Isaiah XI 6*

Peace hath her victories, no less renowned than war.   *Milton*

It must be a peace without victory. Only a peace between equals can last: only a peace, the very principle of which is equality, and a common participation in a common benefit.   *Woodrow Wilson*

Blessed are the peace-makers.   *Matthew V 9*

How beautiful upon the mountains are the feet of him that bringeth good tidings, that publisheth peace.   *Isaiah LII 7*

Peace, peace; when there is no peace.   *Jeremiah VI 14*

PEOPLE

The voice of the people is the voice of God.   *Alcuin*

The Lord must love the common people—He made so many of them.   *Lincoln*

You got to have patience. Why Tom, us people will go on livin' when all of them people is gone. . . . Rich fellas come up an' they die, an' their kids ain't no good an' they die out. But we keep a-comin'.   *John Steinbeck from The Grapes of Wrath*

There is not a more mean, stupid, dastardly, pitiless, selfish, spiteful, envious, ungrateful animal than the public.   *Hazlitt*

PERFECTION

Trifles make perfection, but perfection is no trifle.   *Michelangelo*

Be ye therefore perfect even as your Father which is in heaven is perfect.   *Matthew V 48*

PESSIMISM

A pessimist is one who feels bad when he feels good for fear he'll feel worse when he feels better.

A pessimist? A man who thinks everybody as nasty as himself, and hates them for it.   *George Bernard Shaw*

PHILOSOPHY

A little philosophy inclineth man's mind to atheism; but depth in philosophy bringeth men's minds about to religion.   *Bacon*

There are more things in heaven and earth, Horatio,
Than are dreamt of in your philosophy.
                                        Shakespeare

For there was never yet philosopher
That could endure the toothache patiently.
                                        Shakespeare

PLAGIARISM

When 'Omer smote 'is bloomin' lyre,
He'd 'eard men sing by land and sea;
An' what 'e thought 'e might require,
'E went an' took—the same as me!
                                        Kipling

Though old the thought and oft exprest,
'Tis his at last who says it best.
                                        J. R. Lowell

Originality, I fear, is too often only undetected and frequently unconscious plagiarism.   *Dean W. R. Inge*

POET

The bards sublime,
Whose distant footsteps echo
Through the corridors of Time.
Longfellow

Jewels five-words-long,
That on the stretch'd finger of all Time
Sparkle for ever.
Tennyson

Poetry is the spontaneous overflow of powerful feelings: it takes its origin from emotion recollected in tranquillity.   *Wordsworth*

POLITICS

I always voted at my party's call,
And I never thought of thinking for myself at all.
W. S. Gilbert

A majority is always better than the best repartee.   *Disraeli*

I often think it's comical,
How nature always does contrive
That every boy and every gal,
That's born into the world alive,
Is either a little Liberal,
Or else a little Conservative.
W. S. Gilbert

An honest politician is one who, when he is bought, will stay bought.
Simon Cameron

Here lies beneath this mossy stone
A politician who
Touched a live issue without gloves
And never did come to.
Keith Preston

I'm not a politician and my other habits are good.

Artemus Ward

You cannot adopt politics as a profession and remain honest.

Louis McHenry Howe

I tell you Folks, all Politics is Apple Sauce.   *Will Rogers*

. . . it was not best to swap horses while crossing the river, and . . . I am not so poor a horse that they might not make a botch of it in trying to swap.   *Lincoln (when up for re-election)*

POVERTY

The greatest man in history was the poorest.   *Emerson*

I am as poor as Job, my lord, but not too patient.   *Shakespeare*

> O God! that bread should be so dear,
> And flesh and blood so cheap!
>
> *Hood*

He that hath pity upon the poor lendeth unto the Lord.

Proverbs XIX 17

> It's easy 'nough to titter w'en de stew is smokin' hot,
> But hit's mighty ha'd to giggle w'en dey's nuffin' in de pot.
>
> *Paul Laurence Dunbar*

There are only two families in the world, the Haves and the Have Nots.   *Cervantes*

To be poor and independent is very nearly an impossibility.

William Cobbett

> Let not Ambition mock their useful toil,
> Their homely joys and destiny obscure;
> Nor Grandeur hear with a disdainful smile
> The short and simple annals of the poor.
>
> *Gray*

This mournful truth is ev'rywhere confess'd,
Slow rises worth, by poverty depress'd.

Samuel Johnson

Blessed be ye poor: for yours is the Kingdom of God.

Luke VI 20

What mean ye that ye beat my people to pieces and grind the faces of the poor?   *Isaiah III 15*

The child was diseased at birth, stricken with a hereditary ill that only the most vital men are able to shake off. I mean poverty—the most deadly and prevalent of all diseases.   *Eugene O'Neill*

PRAYER

O Divine Master, grant that I may not so much seek to be consoled as to console; to be understood as to understand; to be loved as to love; for it is in giving that we receive, it is in pardoning that we are pardoned, and it is in dying that we are born to eternal life. Amen.   *St. Francis of Assisi*

At church, with meek and unaffected grace,
His looks adorn'd the venerable place;
Truth from his lips prevailed with double sway,
And fools, who came to scoff, remain'd to pray.

Goldsmith

God warms his hands at man's heart when he prays.   *Masefield*

Pray as if everything depended on God, and work as if everything depended upon man.   *Francis Cardinal Spellman*

I have never made but one prayer to God, a very short one: "Oh Lord, make my enemies ridiculous." And God granted it.   *Voltaire*

Holy Father, in Thy mercy,
Hear our anxious prayer.
Keep our loved ones, now far absent,
'Neath Thy care.

Isabella S. Stephenson

They never sought in vain that sought the Lord aright!   *Burns*

When the last sea is sailed and the last shallow charted,
When the last field is reaped and the last harvest stored,
When the last fire is out and the last guest departed,
Grant the last prayer that I shall pray, Be good to me, O Lord.
Masefield

Every one that asketh receiveth; and he that seeketh findeth.
Matthew VII 8

What things soever ye desire, when ye pray, believe that ye receive them, and ye shall receive them.   *Mark XI 24*

My words fly up, my thoughts remain below:
Words without thoughts never to heaven go.
Shakespeare

PREACHING

Alas for the unhappy man that is called to stand in the pulpit, and not give the bread of life.   *Emerson*

The test of a preacher is that his congregation goes away saying, not, what a lovely sermon, but, I will do something!
St. Francis de Sales

PREJUDICE

Prejudice is the child of ignorance.   *Hazlit*

A prejudice is a vagrant opinion without visible means of support
Ambrose Bierce

PRESS

Then hail to the Press! chosen guardian of freedom!
Strong sword-arm of justice! bright sunbeam of truth!
Horace Greeley

An ambassador is a man of virtue sent to lie abroad for his country; a news-writer is a man without virtue who lies at home for himself.   *Sir Henry Wotton*

PRICE

Still as of old, men by themselves are priced—
For thirty pieces Judas sold himself, not Christ.

Hester H. Cholmondeley

Earth gets its price for what Earth gives us;
The beggar is taxed for a corner to die in,
The priest hath his fee who comes and shrives us,
We bargain for the graves we lie in;
At the devil's booth are all things sold,
Each ounce of dross costs its ounce of gold.

J. R. Lowell

PRIDE

And the Devil did grin, for his darling sin
Is pride that apes humility.

S. T. Coleridge

Oh, why should the spirit of mortal be proud?
Like a swift-fleeting meteor, a fast-flying cloud,
A flash of the lightning, a break of the wave,
He passeth from life to his rest in the grave.

William Knox

Pride goeth before destruction, and a haughty spirit before a fall.

Proverbs XVI 18

PROGRESS

The future fairly startles me with its impending greatness. We are on the verge of undreamed progress.   *Henry Ford*

What we call progress is the exchange of one nuisance for another nuisance.   *Havelock Ellis*

Every step of progress which the world has made has been from scaffold to scaffold, and from stake to stake.   *Wendell Phillips*

Rome was not built in a day.   *Cervantes*

I found Rome brick and left it marble.   *Caesar Augustus*

PROPHECY

My gran'ther's rule was safer 'n 'tis to crow:
Don't never prophesy—onless ye know.

J. R. Lowell

PURE

Blessed are the pure in heart: for they shall see God.

Matthew V 8

PURITAN

A puritan is a person who pours righteous indignation into the wrong things.   *G. K. Chesterton*

The Puritan hated bear-baiting, not because it gave pain to the bear, but because it gave pleasure to the spectators.   *Macaulay*

The great artists of the world are never Puritans, and seldom even ordinarily respectable.   *H. L. Mencken*

QUESTION

I keep six honest serving men
(They taught me all I know):
Their names are What and Why and When
And How and Where and Who.

Kipling

Simon Peter said unto him, Lord whither goest thou?

John XIII 36

READING

The art of reading is to skip judiciously.   *P. G. Hamerton*

I love to lose myself in other men's minds. When I am not walking, I am reading; I cannot sit and think. Books think for me.

Charles Lamb

Verily, when the day of judgment comes, we shall not be asked what we have read, but what we have done.   *Thomas à Kempis*

Give a man a pipe he can smoke,
Give a man a book he can read:
And his home is bright with a calm delight,
Though the room be poor indeed.

James Thomson

REASON

Come now, and let us reason together.   *Isaiah I 18*

The feast of reason and the flow of soul.   *Pope*

REFORM

Reform must come from within, not from without. You cannot legislate for virtue.   *Cardinal Gibbons*

Every reform movement has a lunatic fringe.

Theodore Roosevelt

REGRET

For of all sad words of tongue or pen,
The saddest are these: "It might have been."

Whittier

RELIGION

When a man says he can get on without religion it merely means he has a kind of religion he can get on without.

The Rev. Harry Emerson Fosdick

The world embarrasses me: I cannot believe that so beautiful a clock is without a maker.   *Voltaire*

Men will wrangle for religion; write for it; fight for it; die for it; anything but—live it.   *Colton*

If men are so wicked with religion, what would they be without it?   *Franklin*

REPUTATION

A good name is better than precious ointment. *Ecclesiastes VII 1*

Good name in man and woman, dear my lord,
Is the immediate jewel of their souls:
Who steals my purse steals trash; . . .
But he that filches from me my good name
Robs me of that which not enriches him,
And makes me poor indeed.

Shakespeare

RESOLUTION

I will sit down now, but the time will come when you will hear
me.   *Disraeli—First speech in the House of Commons*

I am in earnest—I will not equivocate—I will not excuse—I will not
retreat a single inch and I will be heard.   *William Lloyd Garrison*

Tell your master that if there were as many devils at Worms as
tiles on its roofs, I would enter.   *Luther*

REST

Absence of occupation is not rest,
A mind quite vacant is a mind distress'd.

Cowper

Come unto me, all ye that labour and are heavy laden, and I will
give you rest.   *Matthew XI 28*

Beyond the last horizon's rim,
Beyond adventure's farthest quest,
Somewhere they rise, serene and dim,
The happy, happy Hills of Rest.

A. B. Paine

Rest, rest, perturbed spirit!   *Shakespeare*

RETRIBUTION

Though the mills of God grind slowly,
Yet they grind exceeding small.

Longfellow

And with what measure ye mete, it shall be measured unto you.

Matthew VII 2

Whatsoever a man soweth, that shall he also reap. *Galatians VI 7*

Ye have heard that it hath been said, An eye for an eye, and a tooth for a tooth: But I say unto you, That ye resist not evil: but whosoever shall smite thee on thy right cheek, turn to him the other also. *Matthew V 38-39*

He that diggeth a pit shall fall into it. *Ecclesiastes X 8*

They have sown the wind, and they shall reap the whirlwind.

Hosea VIII 7

REVENGE

In taking revenge a man is but equal to his enemy, but in passing it over he is his superior. *Bacon*

Vengeance is a dish that should be eaten cold. *English Proverb*

Revenge is sweeter than life itself. So think fools. *Juvenal*

Vengeance is mine; I will repay, saith the Lord. Therefore if thine enemy hunger, feed him; if he thirst, give him drink: for in so doing thou shalt heap coals of fire on his head. *Romans XII 19, 20*

REVOLUTION

Revolutions are not about trifles, but spring from trifles.

Aristotle

A reform is a correction of abuses; a revolution is a transfer of power. *Bulwer-Lytton*

At last I perceive that in revolutions the supreme power finally rests with the most abandoned. *Danton*

Let the ruling classes tremble at a Communist revolution. The proletarians have nothing to lose but their chains. They have a world to win. Working men of all countries, unite!

Karl Marx and Friedrich Engels

Every revolution was first a thought in one man's mind. *Emerson*

RICHES

Lay not up for yourselves treasures upon earth, where moth and rust doth corrupt, and where thieves break through and steal.

Matthew VI 19

Nothing is so hard for those who abound in riches as to conceive how others can be in want. *Swift*

That man is the richest whose pleasures are the cheapest. *Thoreau*

ROAD

Any road leads to the end of the world. *Edward FitzGerald*

All roads lead to Rome. *La Fontaine*

SABBATH

Remember the sabbath day, to keep it holy. Six days shalt thou labor, and do all thy work: but the seventh day is the sabbath of the Lord thy God. *Exodus XX 8-11*

God blessed the seventh day, and sanctified it: because that in it he had rested from all his work which God created and made.

Genesis II 3

SALESMAN

... the Romantic Hero was no longer the knight, the wandering poet, the cowpuncher, the aviator, nor the brave young district attorney, but the great sales-manager, who had an Analysis of Merchandizing Problems on his glass-topped desk, whose title of nobility was "go-getter," ... *Sinclair Lewis, from Babbitt*

SCANDAL

Assail'd by scandal and the tongue of strife,
His only answer was, a blameless life;

Cowper

How awful to reflect that what people say of us is true.

L. P. Smith

SCHOOLS

The nation that has the schools has the future.   *Bismarck*

Still sits the school-house by the road,
A ragged beggar sleeping;
Around it still the sumachs grow
And blackberry-vines are creeping.

Whittier

SELFISHNESS

God bless me and my son John,
Me and my wife, him and his wife,
Us four, and no more.

The same people who can deny others everything are famous for
refusing themselves nothing.   *Leigh Hunt*

That man who lives for self alone
Lives for the meanest mortal known.

Joaquin Miller

The least pain in our little finger gives us more concern and un-
easiness, than the destruction of millions of our fellow-beings.

William Hazlitt

SELF-LOVE

He was like a cock who thought the sun had risen to hear him
crow.   *George Eliot*

He that falls in love with himself will have no rivals.   *Franklin*

To love one's self is the beginning of a life-long romance.   *Wilde*

SELF-PRAISE

If you wish in this world to advance
Your merits you're bound to enhance;
You must stir it and stump it,
And blow your own trumpet,
Or, trust me, you haven't a chance.
W. S. Gilbert

Let another man praise thee, and not thine own mouth.
Proverbs XXVII 2

SERVICE

Well done, thou good and faithful servant: thou hast been faithful over a few things, I will make thee ruler over many things.
Matthew XXV 21

Had I but served my God with half the zeal
I served my king, he would not in mine age
have left me naked to mine enemies.
Shakespeare

SHADOW

We are but dust and shadow.   *Horace*

I have a little shadow that goes in and out with me,
And what can be the use of him is more than I can see.
Stevenson

SILENCE

Silence is more eloquent than words.   *Carlyle*

Silence is the unbearable repartee.   *Chesterton*

Vessels never give so great a sound as when they are empty.
Bishop John Jewell

It is a great misfortune neither to have enough wit to talk well nor enough judgment to be silent.   *La Bruyère*

Keep quiet and people will think you a philosopher.

Latin Proverb

Blessed are they who have nothing to say, and who cannot be persuaded to say it.   *Lowell*

There is a time of speaking and a time of being still.

William Caxton

Let him now speak, or else for ever after hold his peace.

Book of Common Prayer

Even a fool, when he holdeth his peace, is counted wise.

Proverbs XVII 28

He had occasional flashes of silence, that made his conversation perfectly delightful.   *Sydney Smith, about Macaulay*

He knew the precise psychological moment when to say nothing.

Oscar Wilde

SIN

In Adam's fall
We sinn'd all.
New England Primer

It is not alone what we do, but also what we do not do, for which we are accountable.   *Molière*

My son, if sinners entice thee, consent thou not.   *Proverbs I 10*

The way of transgressors is hard.   *Proverbs XIII 15*

I am a man
More sinn'd against than sinning.
Shakespeare

The sins ye do by two and two ye must pay for one by one.

Kipling

He that is without sin among you, let him cast the first stone.

John VIII 7

The wages of sin is death.   *Romans VI 3*

Though your sins be as scarlet, they shall be white as snow.

Isaiah I 18

God be merciful to me a sinner.   *Luke XVIII 13*

SLEEP

Fatigue is the best pillow.   *Franklin*

> To all, to each, a fair goodnight,
> And pleasing dreams, and slumbers light.
>
> *Scott*

She slept the sleep of the just.   *Racine*

> O magic sleep! O comfortable bird,
> That broodest o'er the troubled sea of the mind
> Till it is hush'd and smooth!
>
> *Keats*

> Methought I heard a voice cry, "Sleep no more!
> Macbeth doth murder sleep," the innocent sleep,
> Sleep that knits up the ravell'd sleave of care,
> The death of each day's life, sore labour's bath,
> Balm of hurt minds, great nature's second course,
> Chief nourisher of life's feast.
>
> *Shakespeare*

SMILE

> Her very frowns are fairer far
> Than smiles of other maidens are.
>
> *Hartley Coleridge*

He smiled a kind of sickly smile and curled upon the floor,
And the subsequent proceedings interested him no more.

Bret Harte

One may smile, and smile, and be a villain.   *Shakespeare*

'Tis easy enough to be pleasant,
When life flows along like a song;
But the man worth while is the one who will smile
When everything goes dead wrong.
                    Ella Wheeler Wilcox

SNOW

Where are the snows of yesteryear?

Oh! the snow, the beautiful snow,
Filling the sky and the earth below;
                    J. W. Watson

SOLDIER

Eh-oh, my little brother,
They rigged you up in state,
In khaki coat and gun to tote,
But you never could learn to hate.
                    Martin Feinstein

Far and near and low and louder
On the roads of earth go by
Dear to friends and food for powder,
Soldiers marching, all to die.
                    A. E. Housman

For it's Tommy this, an' Tommy that, an' "Chuck 'im out, the
   brute!"
But it's "Saviour of 'is country" when the guns begin to shoot.
                    Kipling

The brave men, living and dead, who struggled here, have con-
secrated it far above our poor power to add or detract. The world
will little note, nor long remember, what we say here, but it can
never forget what they did here.   *Lincoln, Gettysburg Address*

Ninepunce a day fer killin' folks comes kind o'low fer murder.
                    J. R. Lowell

The muffled drum's sad roll has beat
The soldier's last tattoo;
No more on life's parade shall meet
The brave and fallen few.
On fame's eternal camping-ground
Their silent tents are spread,
And Glory guards, with solemn ground,
The bivouac of the dead.

Theodore O'Hara

SOLITUDE

We enter the world alone, we leave it alone.   *Froude*

The strongest man is the one who stands alone.   *Ibsen*

I never found the companion that was so companionable as solitude.

Thoreau

SONG

That which is not worth saying is sung.   *Beaumarchais*

A wandering minstrel I—
A thing of shreds and patches,
Of ballads, songs, and snatches,
And dreamy lullaby.

W. S. Gilbert

Our sweetest songs are those which tell of saddest thought.

Shelley

Many a heart is aching, if you could read them all,
Many the hopes that have vanished, after the ball.

Charles K. Harris

SORROW

Every noble crown is, and on earth will ever be, a crown of thorns.

Carlyle

There can be no rainbow without a cloud and a storm.

J. H. Vincent

Into each life some rain must fall,
Some days must be dark and dreary.
Longfellow

Earth has no sorrow that Heaven cannot heal. *Thomas Moore*

SOUL

Soul, thou hast much goods laid up for many years; take thine
ease, eat, drink and be merry. *Luke XII 19*

What is a man profited, if he shall gain the whole world, and lose
his own soul? *Matthew XVI 26*

Ah, what a dusty answer gets the soul
When hot for certainties in this our life!
George Meredith

SPEECH

A sophistical rhetorician, inebriated with the exuberance of his
own verbosity. *Disraeli*

The hare-brained chatter of irresponsible frivolity. *Disraeli*

His speech flowed from his tongue sweeter than honey. *Homer*

Speech is the index of the mind. *Seneca*

If you were to make little fishes talk, they would talk like whales.
Oliver Goldsmith

Blessed is the man who, having nothing to say, abstains from giving
us wordy evidence of the fact. *George Eliot*

Speech is civilization itself. The word, even the most contradictory
word, preserves contact—it is silence which isolates. *Thomas Mann*

Out of the abundance of the heart the mouth speaketh.
Matthew XII 34

And 'tis remarkable that they
Talk most who have the least to say.

Prior

SPORT

Detested sport,
That owes its pleasures to another's pain.

Cowper

Wild animals never kill for sport. Man is the only one to whom the torture and death of his fellow creatures is amusing in itself.

J. A. Froude

When a man wants to murder a tiger he calls it sport; when a tiger wants to murder him he calls it ferocity.

George Bernard Shaw

SPRING

For, lo! The winter is past, the rain is over and gone; the flowers appear on the earth; the time of the singing of birds is come, and the voice of the turtle is heard in our land.

The Song of Solomon II 11, 12

In the Spring a livelier iris changes on the burnish'd dove;
In the Spring a young man's fancy lightly turns to thoughts of love.

Tennyson

STAR

Silently, one by one, in the infinite meadows of heaven,
Blossomed the lovely stars, the forget-me-nots of the angels.

Longfellow

The morning stars sang together, and all the sons of God shouted for joy.   *Job XXVIII 7*

These blessed candles of the night.   *Shakespeare*

Two things fill the mind with ever new and increasing wonder and awe—the starry heavens above me and the moral law within me.

Kant

The stars
That Nature hung in Heav'n, and filled their lamps
With everlasting oil, to give due light
To the misled and lonely traveller.

Milton

STATESMAN

A statesman is a successful politician who is dead.

Thomas B. Reed

A ginooine statesman should be on his guard,
Ef he must hev beliefs, not to b'lieve 'em tu hard.

J. R. Lowell

In statesmanship get the formalities right, never mind about the moralities.
Mark Twain

SUCCESS

All you need in this life is ignorance and confidence, and then success is sure.
Mark Twain

If you can dream—and not make dreams your master, . . .
If you can fill the unforgiving minute
With sixty seconds' worth of distance run,
Yours is the Earth and everything that's in it,
And—which is more—you'll be a Man, my son!

Kipling

The race is not to the swift nor the battle to the strong. . . .

Ecclesiastes IX 11

TASTE

There can be no disputing about taste. *Latin Proverb*

Well, for those who like that sort of thing I should think that it
is just about the sort of thing they would like. *Lincoln*

TAXES

The marvel of all history is the patience with which men and women submit to burdens unnecessarily laid upon them by their governments.   *William E. Borah*

... in this world nothing is certain but death and taxes.   *Franklin*

TEACHER

A teacher affects eternity; he can never tell where his influence stops.   *Henry Adams*

> There, in his noisy mansion, skill'd to rule,
> The village master taught his little school; ...
> Full well they laugh'd, with counterfeited glee,
> At all his jokes, for many a joke had he;
> Full well the busy whisper, circling round,
> Convey'd the dismal tidings when he frown'd.
>   *Goldsmith*

Our American professors like their literature clear, cold, pure, and very dead.   *Sinclair Lewis*

Those having torches will pass them on to others.   *Plato*

TEARS

Tears are Summer showers to the soul.   *Alfred Austin*

Jesus wept.   *John XI 35 (Shortest Bible verse)*

There shall be weeping and gnashing of teeth.   *Matthew VIII 12*

If you have tears, prepare to shed them now.   *Shakespeare*

Tears are the silent language of grief.   *Voltaire*

It is the wisdom of crocodiles, that shed tears when they would devour.   *Francis Bacon*

If you would have me weep, you must feel grief yourself. *Horace*

THANKFULNESS

O give thanks unto the Lord, for he is good: for his mercy en-
dureth forever.   *Psalms CVII 1*

Beggar that I am, I am even poor in thanks.   *Shakespeare*

THANKSGIVING

Heap high the board with plenteous cheer, and gather to the feast,
And toast the sturdy Pilgrim band whose courage never ceased.
                                                Alice W. Brotherton

> Over the river and through the wood,
> Now grandmother's cap I spy!
> Hurrah for the fun!
> Is the pudding done?
> Hurrah for the pumpkin pie!
>   *Lydia M. Child*

THIEF

For de little stealin' dey gits you in jail soon or late. For de big
stealin' dey makes you emperor and puts you in de Hall o' Fame
when you croaks. If dey's one thing I learns in ten years on de
Pullman cars listenin' to de white quality talk, it's dat same fact.
                                Eugene O'Neill, from The Emperor Jones

> 'Twas a thief said the last kind word to Christ;
> Christ took the kindness and forgave the theft.
>   *R. Browning*

THOUGHT

Thoughts that breathe and words that burn.   *Gray*

> Yon Cassius has a lean and hungry look;
> He thinks too much: such men are dangerous.
>   *Shakespeare*

Man is but a reed, the weakest in nature, but he is a thinking reed.
                                                        Pascal

To me the meanest flower that blows can give   5
Thoughts that do often lie too deep for tears.
Wordsworth

TIME

Backward, turn backward, O
Time in your flight;
Make me a child again just for tonight.
Elizabeth Akers Allen

Now is the accepted time.   *II Corinthians VI 2*

Gather ye rose-buds while ye may,
Old Time is still aflying,
And this same flower that smiles today,
Tomorrow will be dying.

Herrick

A thousand years in thy sight are but as yesterday when it is past,
and as a watch in the night.   *Psalms XC 4*

Once in Persia reigned a king
Who upon his signet ring
Graved a maxim true and wise,
Which if held before the eyes
Gave him counsel at a glance
Fit for every change and chance,
Solemn words, and these are they:
"Even this shall pass away."
Theodore Tilton

A wonderful stream is the River Time,
As it runs through the realm of Tears,
With a faultless rhythm, and a musical rhyme,
And a broader sweep, and a surge sublime,
As it blends with the Ocean of Years.
B. F. Taylor

The years like great black oxen tread the world
And God, the herdsman, goads them on behind.
W. B. Yeats

Out of Eternity the new Day is born;
Into Eternity at night will return.
Carlyle

I've shut the door on yesterday
And thrown the key away—
Tomorrow holds no fears for me,
Since I have found today.
Vivian Y. Laramore

Tomorrow, and tomorrow, and tomorrow,
Creeps in this petty pace from day to day
To the last syllable of recorded time.
Shakespeare

TODAY

Out of Eternity
The new Day is born;
Into Eternity
At night will return.
Carlyle

Happy the man, and happy he alone,
He, who can call today his own:
He who, secure within, can say
Tomorrow, do thy worst, for I have liv'd today.
Dryden

TRAVELING

The more I see of other countries the more I love my own.
Mme. de Stael

The little Road says, Go;
The little House says, Stay;
And oh, it's bonny here at home,
But I must go away.
Josephine P. Peabody

From going to and fro in the earth, and from walking up and down it.   *Job I* 7

See one promontory, one mountain, one sea, one river, and see all.
Socrates

I pity the man who can travel from Dan to Beersheba, and cry, " 'Tis all barren!"   *Sterne*

It is not worth while to go around the world to count the cats in Zanzibar.   *Thoreau*

Beyond the East the sunrise, beyond the West the sea,
And East and West the wander-thirst that will not let me be.
Gerald Gould

I am fevered with the sunset,
I am fretted with the bay,
For the wander-thirst is on me
And my soul is in Cathay.
Richard Hovey

TREASON

Treason doth never prosper, what's the reason?
For if it prosper none dare call it Treason.
Sir John Harington

Caesar had his Brutus; Charles the First, his Cromwell; and George the Third [*cries of "Treason, treason!"*] may profit by their example. If this be treason, make the most of it.   *Patrick Henry*

TREE

I remember, I remember
The fir-trees dark and high;
I used to think their slender tops
Were close against the sky.
Thomas Hood

I think that I shall never see
A poem lovely as a tree.

.   .   .   .

Poems are made by fools like me,
But only God can make a tree.
Joyce Kilmer

Woodman, spare that tree!
Touch not a single bough!
In youth it sheltered me,
And I'll protect it now.
G. P. Morris

TRIUMPH

Hail to the Chief who in triumph advances!   *Scott*

There are some defeats more triumphant than victories.
Montaigne

TROUBLE

So Nat'ralists observe, a Flea
Hath smaller Fleas that on him prey;
And these have smaller still to bite 'em,
And so proceed ad infinitum.
Swift

But never trouble Trouble
Until Trouble troubles you;
For you only make your trouble
Double-trouble when you do.
David Keppel

Man is born unto trouble, as the sparks fly upward.   *Job V 7*

TRUTH

And ye shall know the truth, and the truth shall make you free.
John VIII 32

There is no truth in him.   *John VIII 44*

To thine own self be true,
And it must follow, as the night the day,
Thou canst not then be false to any man.
Shakespeare

A truth that's told with bad intent
Beats all the lies you can invent.
Blake

God offers to every mind its choice between truth and repose.
Take which you please,—you can never have both.   *Emerson*

Once to every man and nation comes the moment to decide,
In the strife of Truth with Falsehood, for the good or evil side.
J. R. Lowell

I speak truth, not so much as I would, but as much as I dare; and
I dare a little more as I grow older.   *Montaigne*

My way of joking is to tell the truth. It's the funniest joke in the
world.   *George Bernard Shaw*

Truth is the most valuable thing we have. Let us economize it.
Mark Twain

I do not know what I may appear to the world, but to myself I
seem to have been only like a boy playing on the seashore and
diverting myself in now and then finding a smoothe pebble or a
prettier shell than ordinary whilst the great ocean of truth lay all
undiscovered before me.   *Isaac Newton*

UNDERSTAND

Whatever you cannot understand, you cannot possess.   *Goethe*

I shall light a candle of understanding in thine heart, which shall
not be put out.   *Apocrypha, II Esdras, XIV 25*

UNIVERSITY

The true University of these days is a Collection of Books.
Carlyle

A pine bench, with Mark Hopkins at one end of it and me at the other, is a good enough college for me.   *James A. Garfield*

VANITY

And the name of that town is Vanity; and at the town there is a fair kept, called Vanity Fair.   *Bunyan*

Lo, all our pomp of yesterday
Is one with Nineveh and Tyre!
Kipling

Oh, Vanity of Vanities!
How wayward the decrees of Fate are;
How very weak the very wise,
How very small the very great are!
Thackeray

VICE

When our vices leave us, we flatter ourselves with the credit of having left them.   *La Rochefoucauld*

Saint Augustine! Well hast thou said,
That of our vices we can frame
A ladder, if we will but tread
Beneath our feet each deed of shame.
Longfellow

Vice is a monster of so frightful mien,
As to be hated needs but to be seen;
Yet seen too oft, familiar with her face,
We, first endure, then pity, then embrace.
Pope

VICTORY

Who overcomes
By force, hath overcome but half his foe.
Milton

There are some defeats more triumphant than victories.
Montaigne

There is nothing so dreadful as a great victory—except a great
defeat.   *Attributed to Wellington*

VIRTUE

The only reward of virtue is virtue.   *Emerson*

Virtue often trips and falls on the sharp-edged rock of poverty.
                                                       Eugene Sue

Virtue is its own reward.   *Cicero*

Whatsoever things are true, whatsoever things are honest, whatsoever things are just, whatsoever things are pure, whatsoever things
are lovely, whatsoever things are of good report: if there be any
virtue, and if there be any praise, think on these things.
                                               Philippians IV 8

VISION

And it shall come to pass afterward, that I will pour out my Spirit
upon all flesh; and your sons and your daughters shall prophesy,
your old men shall dream dreams, your young men shall see visions.
                                                       Joel II 28

Where there is no vision, the people perish.   *Proverbs XXIX 18*

VOICE

The voice is Jacob's voice, but the hands are the hands of Esau.
                                               Genesis XXVII 22

The voice of him that crieth in the wilderness.   *Isaiah XL 3*

Her voice was ever soft,
Gentle, and low, an excellent thing in woman.
                                                   Shakespeare

But O for the touch of a vanish'd hand,
And the sound of a voice that is still!
                                                      Tennyson

WAR

Every war is a national calamity whether victorious or not.

General Von Moltke

Hail, Caesar, those who are about to die salute thee!

Salutation of Roman Gladiators, according to Suetonius

I believe without a shadow of doubt that science and peace will finally triumph over ignorance and war, and that the nations of the earth will ultimately agree not to destroy but to build up.

Louis Pasteur

War is the science of destruction. *John S. C. Abbott*

War never leaves, where it found a nation. *Burke*

I came, I saw, I conquered. *Julius Caesar*

What millions died—that Caesar might be great! *Campbell*

What distinguishes war is, not that man is slain, but that he is slain, spoiled, crushed by the cruelty, the injustice, the treachery, the murderous hand of man. *William Ellery Channing*

War, he sung, is toil and trouble;
Honor but an empty bubble.
Dryden

The essence of war is violence. Moderation in war is imbecility.

Attributed to Lord Fisher

There never was a good war or a bad peace. *Franklin*

It is not right to exult over slain men. *Homer*

War is as much a punishment to the punisher as to the sufferer.

Jefferson

There is no such thing as an inevitable war. If war comes it will be from failure of human wisdom.

Bonar Law

War is the greatest plague that can afflict humanity; it destroys religion, it destroys states, it destroys families. Any scourge is preferable to it.

Martin Luther

War hath no fury like a non-combatant.

C. E. Montague

> God how the dead men
> Grin by the wall,
> Watching the fun
> Of the Victory Ball.
>
> Alfred Noyes

O war! thou son of Hell!

Shakespeare

... all they that shall take a sword shall perish with the sword.

Matthew XXVI 52

Another such victory over the Romans, and we are undone.

Pyrrhus

> "But what good came of it at last?"
> Quoth little Peterkin.
> "Why that I cannot tell," said he
> "But 't was a famous victory."
>
> Southey

> By the rude bridge that arched the flood,
> Their flag to April's breeze unfurled,
> Here once the embattled farmers stood,
> And fired the shot heard round the world.
>
> Emerson

They wrote in the old days that it is sweet and fitting to die for one's country. But in modern war there is nothing sweet nor fitting in your dying. You will die like a dog for no good reason.

Ernest Hemingway,
from Notes on the Next War

The tumult and the shouting dies,
The captains and the kings depart.
Kipling

Doughboys were paid a whole dollar a day
and received free burial under the clay.
And movie heroes are paid even more
shooting one another in a Hollywood war.
Kreymborg, from What Price Glory?

The American people will not relish the idea of any American
citizen growing rich and fat in an emergency of blood and slaughter
and human suffering.   *Franklin D. Roosevelt*

There's many a boy here today who looks on war as all glory, but,
boys, it is all hell.   *General William T. Sherman*

WEALTH

Surplus wealth is a sacred trust which its possessor is bound to
administer in his lifetime for the good of the community.
Andrew Carnegie

It is easier for a camel to go through the eye of a needle, than for
a rich man to enter into the kingdom of God.   *Matthew XIX 24*

Riches certainly make themselves wings.   *Proverbs XXIII 5*

He heapeth up riches, and knoweth not who shall gather them.
Psalms XXXIX 6

I am the owner of the sphere,
Of the seven stars and the solar year,
Of Caesar's hand, and Plato's brain,
Of Lord Christ's heart, and Shakespeare's strain.
Emerson

Lay not up for yourself treasure upon earth; where the rust and
moth doth corrupt.   *Book of Common Prayer*

The man who dies rich dies disgraced.   *Andrew Carnegie*

WEATHER

As a rule man is a fool,
When it's hot he wants it cool,
When it's cool he wants it hot,
Always wanting what is not.

Change of weather is the discourse of fools.   *Thomas Fuller*

I was born with a chronic anxiety about the weather.

John Burroughs

WEST

Westward the course of empire takes its way.   *George Berkeley,
Bishop of Cloyne*

Out where the handclasp's a little stronger,
Out where the smile dwells a little longer,
That's where the West begins.

Arthur Chapman

Go West, young man, and grow up with the country.

Horace Greeley

WIFE

She looketh well to the ways of her household, and eateth not the
bread of idleness.   *Proverbs XXXI 27*

It is a woman's business to get married as soon as possible, and a
man's to keep unmarried as long as he can.   *George Bernard Shaw*

Here lies my wife: here let her lie!
Now she's at rest, and so am I.

Dryden

Giving honour unto the wife, as unto the weaker vessel.

I Peter II 7

A virtuous woman is a crown to her husband.   *Proverbs XII 4*

WINTER

Winter lingered so long in the lap of Spring, that it occasioned a great deal of talk.   *Bill Nye*

If Winter comes, can Spring be far behind?   *Shelley*

WISDOM

In youth and beauty wisdom is but rare!   *Homer*

The fear of the Lord is the beginning of wisdom.   *Psalms CXI 10*

As for me, all I know is that I know nothing.   *Socrates*

The doorstep to the temple of wisdom is a knowledge of our own ignorance.   *Spurgeon*

> A wise old owl sat on an oak,
> The more he sat the less he spoke;
> The less he spoke the more he heard;
> Why aren't we like that wise old bird?
> *E. H. Richards*

> A sadder and a wiser man,
> He rose the morrow morn.
> *S. T. Coleridge*

The children of this world are in their generation wiser than the children of light.   *Luke XVI 8*

The wisdom of this world is foolishness with God.
I Corinthians III 19

WOMAN

But what is woman? Only one of nature's agreeable blunders.
Cowley

Men say of women what pleases them; women do with men what pleases them.   *De Segur*

An' I learned about women from 'er.   *Kipling*

> Grace was in all her steps, heaven in her eye,
> In every gesture dignity and love.
>   *Milton*

There is no such thing as romance in our day, women have become too brilliant; nothing spoils a romance so much as a sense of humor in the woman.   *Wilde*

I'm not denyin' the women are foolish: God Almighty made 'em to match the men.   *George Eliot*

I am very fond of the company of ladies; I like their beauty, I like their delicacy, I like their vivacity, and I like their silence.
                                   Samuel Johnson

I expect that woman will be the last thing civilized by man.
                                   George Meredith

> For never was it given to mortal man
> To lie so boldly as we women can.
>   *Pope*

> As for the women, though we scorn and flout 'em,
> We may live with, but cannot live without 'em.
>   *Frederic Reynolds*

Women are wiser than men because they know less and understand more.   *James Stephens*

> The time I've lost in wooing,
> In watching and pursuing
> The light that lies
> In woman's eyes,
> Has been my heart's undoing.
>   *Thomas Moore*

WORDS

Words will build no walls.   *Plutarch*

The words of his mouth were smoother than butter, but war was in his heart; his words were softer than oil, yet were they drawn swords.   *Psalms LV 21*

My words fly up, my thoughts remain below:
Words without thoughts never to heaven go.
                                    Shakespeare

He utters empty words, he utters sound without mind.   *Vergil*

But yesterday the word of Caesar might
Have stood against the world; now lies he there,
And none so poor to do him reverence.
                                    Shakespeare

Father is rather vulgar, my dear. The word Papa, besides, gives a very pretty form to the lips. Papa, potatoes, poultry, prunes and prism are all very good words for the lips, especially prunes and prism.   *Dickens*

WORK

It is only well with me when I have a chisel in my hand.
                                    Michelangelo

I never did anything worth doing by accident, nor did any of my inventions come by accident; they came by work.   *Edison*

In the sweat of thy face shalt thou eat bread.   *Genesis III 19*

I like work; it fascinates me. I can sit and look at it for hours. I love to keep it by me: the idea of getting rid of it nearly breaks my heart.   *Jerome K. Jerome*

And only the Master shall praise us, and only the Master shall blame;
And no one shall work for money, and no one shall work for fame;

But each for the joy of the working, and each, in his separate star,
Shall draw the Thing as he sees It, for the God of things as They
  Are!

Kipling

Blessed is he who has found his work; let him ask no other blessed-
ness.   *Carlyle*

If any would not work, neither should he eat.

II Thessalonians III 10

WORLD

Socrates, indeed, when he was asked of what country he called
himself, said, "Of the world"; for he considered himself an inhabitant
and a citizen of the whole world.   *Cicero*

All the world's a stage,
And all the men and women merely players.

Shakespeare

Why, then, the world's mine oyster,
Which I with sword will open.

Shakespeare

The world is so full of a number of things,
I'm sure we should all be as happy as kings.

R. L. Stevenson

The world is too much with us; late and soon,
Getting and spending, we lay waste our powers.

Wordsworth

The optimist proclaims that we live in the best of all possible
worlds; and the pessimist fears this is true.   *Branch Cabell*

WORRY

Consider the lilies of the field, how they grow; they toil not, neither do they spin: And yet I say unto you, That even Solomon in all his glory was not arrayed like one of these.   *Matthew VI 28*

YOUTH

Ah! happy years! once more who would not be a boy!

I remember my youth and the feeling that will never come back any more—the feeling that I could last forever, outlast the sea, the earth, and all men.   *Joseph Conrad*

> How beautiful is youth! how bright it gleams
> With its illusions, aspirations, dreams!
> Book of Beginnings, Story without End,
> Each maid a heroine, and each man a friend!
> *Longfellow*

For God's sake give me the young man who has brains enough to make a fool of himself.   *Stevenson*

ZEAL

My zeal hath consumed me.   *Psalms CXIX 139*

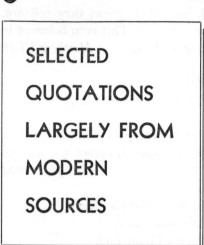

9

SELECTED
QUOTATIONS
LARGELY FROM
MODERN
SOURCES

The welfare of the United States calls for stable prosperity and a rising standard of living in all parts of the free world.

David Rockefeller

It is not enough for us to dwell on our past achievements. The dynamic growth of the American economy must continue if we are to maintain our position as the leading nation of the free world and if we are to keep America's living standards rising.

What can be done to make sure that this growth and the rise in real income will continue? Any large rise in real income can come only from more output per man-hour. Fortunately, the outlook for continuing the rate of growth our economy has enjoyed in the past is good.

Thomas B. McCabe

The businessman owes a tremendous debt to our capitalistic democracy which he can effectively repay only by lifting it to even greater heights and making it a living example for all to see.

Thomas B. McCabe

The cure for crime is not the electric chair but the high chair.

J. Edgar Hoover

The spectacle of a nation praying is more awe-inspiring than the explosion of an atomic bomb. The force of prayer is greater than any possible combination of man-controlled powers because prayer is man's greatest means of tapping the resources of God.

J. Edgar Hoover

Our salvation, and our only salvation, lies in controlling the arm of Western science by the mind of a Western philosophy guided by the eternal truths of God.   *Gen. Chas. A. Lindbergh*

If you don't have philanthropy in your heart, none will come from your pocketbook, however fat it may become.   *B. C. Forbes*

Unquestionably, there is progress. The average American now pays out twice as much in taxes as he formerly got in wages.

Henry L. Mencken

America is a state of the mind—a point of view—a love of moving on—beyond the next hill—the next filling station—the next frontier. Expanding—growing—living beyond the horizon.
That's America! That's the U. S. A.   *Thomas Wolfe*

When an archer misses the mark he turns and looks for the fault within himself. Failure to hit the bull's eye is never the fault of the target. To improve your aim, improve yourself.   *Forbes Magazine*

Trouble is only opportunity in work clothes.   *Henry J. Kaiser*

A man's biggest mistake is to believe that he's working only for someone else.   *Nashua Cavalier*

We cannot all be great but we can always attach ourselves to something that is great.   *Harry Emerson Fosdick*

One thing scientists have discovered is that often-praised children become more intelligent than often-blamed ones. If some of your employees are a bit dumb, perhaps your treatment of them is to blame. There's a creative element in praise.   *Thomas Dreier*

It's good to have money, and the things that money can buy, but it's good, too, to check up once in a while and be sure you haven't lost the things money can't buy.   *George Horace Lorimer*

Man has become a superman . . . because he not only disposes of innate, physical forces, but because he is in command . . . of latent forces in nature and because he can put them to his service . . . But the essential fact we must surely all feel in our hearts . . . is that we are becoming inhuman in proportion as we become supermen.
      Dr. Albert Schweitzer

The successful person is one who is able to take his talents and invest them in the business of living in a manner that leads to the accomplishment of a full life of service. The medium of exchange is not the dollar but services rendered.   *Rabbi Sol Roth*

All growth depends upon activity. There is no development physically or intellectually without effort, and effort means work. Work is not a curse; it is the prerogative of intelligence, the only means to manhood, and the measure of civilization.   *Calvin Coolidge*

Worry kills more people than work—because more people tackle it.   *Elbert Hubbard*

I am certainly not one of those who need to be prodded. In fact, if anything, I am the prod. . . . I am by no means sure I have been right. It is no part of my case that I am always right. . . . I give my opinion. I dare say it will weigh as much as a mocking giggle. . . . Personally I am always ready to learn, although I do not always like being taught. . . . I have been a journalist and half my lifetime I have earned my living by selling words and I hope thoughts.
      Sir Winston Churchill

Russia is a land animal . . . the British are sea animals.
      Sir Winston Churchill

Writing a book was an adventure. To begin with it was a toy, an amusement; then it became a mistress, and then a master, and then a tyrant.   *Sir Winston Churchill*

Any clever person can make plans for winning a war if he has no responsibility for carrying them out.   *Sir Winston Churchill*

Make yourself indispensable, and you will move up. Act as though you are indispensable, and you will move out.   *Jules Ormont*

My country wants to be constructive, not destructive. It wants agreements, not wars, among nations. It wants itself to live in freedom, and in the confidence that the people of every other nation enjoy equally the right of choosing their own way of life.
                                                 Dwight D. Eisenhower

Our defense is not in armaments, nor in science, nor in going underground. Our defense is in LAW and ORDER.
                                                 Albert Einstein

The most influential of all educational factors is the conversation in a child's home.   *William Temple*

The great use of a life is to spend it for something that outlasts it.
                                                 William James

Teach us, GOOD LORD, to serve THEE as THOU deservest;
    To give and not to count the cost;
To fight and not to heed the wounds; to toil and not to seek for rest;
    To labor and not to ask for any reward save that
    of knowing that we do THY will.
                                                 Ignatius Loyola

For the finer spirits of the world there are two dwelling places: Our earthly FATHERLAND, and that other CITY of GOD. Of the one we are the guests, of the other the builders. *Romain Rolland*

Man's capacity for justice makes democracy POSSIBLE; but man's inclination to injustice makes democracy NECESSARY.
                                                 Reinhold Niebuhr

I found HIM very easily among the pots and pans.   *St. Theresa*

Our way of getting things done is the newest, youngest, most dynamic the world has ever known. Our way is the real revolution. It offers more rewards than any other, for a given amount of effort put into it. It has repeatedly demonstrated that it can carry bigger loads and deliver higher performance than any other.
L. L. Colbert, President, Chrysler Corporation

Our economic and political order has survived war, the threat of war and the competition of totalitarian, socialistic economies. Invariably it has performed best when allowed to operate with a minimum of restrictions. Ill-advised and unnecessary tampering can in time dry up its basic productive force, which is the incentive of profits. Profits are not only the incentive to produce, but they provide means for more production.
L. L. Colbert, President, Chrysler Corporation

General John J. Pershing once told me, "I always tell the truth. After a lifetime, I find I can remember it longer."   *John J. McCloy*

The world should tolerate history—or the study of it—only to the extent that its lessons are tutors for tomorrow. A dedication to the past, with its attendant nostalgia, should at the same time be a dedication to the days that will follow.   *Thomas B. McCabe*

The annals of American business carry page after sorry page of concerns who were left by the wayside. . . . of those who doggedly hung on to the old while the new went on all around them. It is an unfailing maxim in the business world that the man who looks to the future will indeed have a past, and the poor unfortunate who looks to the past will indeed have no future.   *Thomas B. McCabe*

The so-called salesman you saw in the play, "Death of a Salesman" —the jovial gent who disinterestedly asks "What do you need this week?"—has no role in our contemporary economy. We mass produce and we must mass sell. Only the well-equipped salesman will survive.   *Thomas B. McCabe*

Search as you will in his long career, and you can never find a mean, petty or dishonest thing which Abraham Lincoln did consciously and deliberately. Honest Abe, they called him! A political tag, perhaps, but one which shines like a gem of indestructible luster. It epitomizes a life and career which shall ever stand as an example for all who would give themselves to public service. He never lied to gain an end. He never compromised a conviction to secure a political advantage. With vision and wisdom, he faced realities, recognized short-comings, understood weaknesses, and accepted human frailties; but through it all he never lost sight of the honest and just determination of every problem he faced.   *Dr. Robert L. Kincaid*

As long as people are ready to die for a great cause, that cause can never die.   *George Meany*

Piety toward God is meaningless unless it encourages compassion toward one's fellow man.   *Rabbi Jacob J. Weinstein*

It is still generally true, as Secretary Stimson used to say—and I think he gave credit to Mr. Root for originating the thought—that there were two types of public servants: those who did all they could for the office and the other that did the office for all they could.   *John J. McCloy*

Wars are great catastrophes. Winston Churchill said to Briand after World War I that victory in many of its aspects is hardly distinguishable from defeat. Defeat is dismal and, as he said, "it has a habit of laying its heavy hand on victors as well as vanquished."   *John J. McCloy*

Through all modern history centralized government has been the chief threat to personal liberty.   *Winthrop W. Aldrich*

A business must be profitable to remain healthy, but a maximum immediate profit is no longer considered to be the sole guide of private enterprise. Management is earnestly dedicated to maintaining a workable and acceptable balance among its shareholders, its employees, its customers and the public at large.   *Frank W. Abrams*

Freedom—human freedom—is an indivisible value. We must all understand and act in the knowledge that you cannot have free management unless you have free labor, and you can't have free labor unless you have free management, and that neither can be free unless they learn to work together to preserve our free society in a free world.   *Walter P. Reuther*

Human freedom is not an absolute value. Human freedom is a value that you can enjoy only in your relationship to other people. Human freedom is possible only within the social context of an organized society.   *Walter P. Reuther*

America is a world symbol of productive power, of military strength, and of great material wealth. Our standard of living is the envy of the world; our technical know-how is unsurpassed, but this is not enough. We must demonstrate the qualities of moral leadership, for power without morality is power without purpose.
                                             Walter P. Reuther

I believe that the American economy is freedom's greatest material asset. I believe also that what we do—and I say "We"; I mean management, labor and the American people—with the American economy, how effectively we mobilize its productive power, and how intelligently we distribute the wealth that we can create by our joint efforts, will, in my opinion, be one of the most decisive factors in whether freedom can win in the struggle against Communist tyranny.   *Walter P. Reuther*

I think that no greater disservice can be performed to America and to the free world than to sell the economic future of America short. Our future is still ahead of us, if we've got the courage to accept the challenge.   *Walter P. Reuther*

I believe strongly in the free enterprise system. I think that it has given us the highest living standard of any people in the world. I think its possibilities are unlimited, if it is geared to the concept of abundance, and if it demonstrates a sense of social responsibility in terms of the welfare of the whole community.

The only thing I'm afraid of is that people may underestimate its great potential. You can never over-estimate in my opinion.

Walter P. Reuther

A nation of free men cannot survive without education. A nation of slaves cannot survive with it—provided we define education in its true sense to include not only technical competence but the ability to evaluate and make sound judgments. Free men pursue truth; the enslaved are forced to fly from it, for the dictator knows that if man's mind is free, he will tear off his chains.   *Robert E. Wilson*

While the socialists and the communists have been *talking* about a classless society without accomplishing much except the cutting off of the peaks of wealth, ability, and leadership, America has largely *achieved* it by broadening the base of education and offering opportunity to all who are willing to work. By emphasis on incentives, production, and freedom, America has attained a standard of living that is the envy of the rest of the world, and with this standard of living has come not only material advancement, but possibilities of cultural and spiritual enrichments that no other nation possesses.

Robert E. Wilson

Through free competition in business we achieve material progress. Through the free competition of ideas we arrive at truth.

Robert E. Wilson

It is a truism that we are living in a world in which we have tremendously increased our information without having appreciably increased our wisdom. We are living in a world in which we have fantastically multiplied our riches without having fully learned to use those riches wisely. We have developed our natural resources without having developed correspondingly greater resources of the spirit.   *Robert E. Wilson*

We have shared our riches with less fortunate nations to a degree never before known. We have worked hard at other aspects of international cooperation, and if there are occasional lapses or reactions from time to time which seem to alter our general course of conduct they are understandable. To have it otherwise would be to exact a degree of perfection from us that has never been achieved by any other nation. *John J. McCloy*

In the American design—as we perceive it—each group in our nation has special problems. None has special rights. Each has peculiar needs. None has peculiar privileges. *Dwight D. Eisenhower*

The good life is not possible without freedom. It is not possible without freedom of inquiry and freedom of thought. It is not possible without freedom of worship and of the individual conscience before God. It is not possible without freedom from fear—fear of oppression that may come from a foreign foe or from a domestic source. And, lastly, the good life is not possible without the assurance of good health and daily bread for everyone. *Harry S. Truman*

The basic requirement of executive capacity is the ability to create a harmonious whole out of what the academic world calls dissimilar disciplines. That's simply a fancy way of saying that an executive is good when he can make a smoothly functioning team out of people with the many different skills required in the operation of a modern business. His most important function is to reconcile, to coordinate, to compromise and to appraise the various viewpoints and talents under his direction to the end that each individual contributes his full measure to the business at hand.

Perhaps the best analogy to an executive's job is that of the symphony conductor under whose hand one hundred or so highly specialized and very different talents become a single effort of great effectiveness. No conductor can play every musical instrument and no more can an executive be skilled in every talent he is called upon to supervise. There was a time when the boss prided himself on personal experience with every job in the shop. If this view ever had merit, it has long since become entirely unrealistic. Today, specific skill in any field becomes less and less important as the executive advances through successive levels of responsibility.

Crawford H. Greenewalt

The nice thing about money is that it has such a wide circle of admirers. *Crawford H. Greenewalt*

For countless centuries, men have thought the horrors of "modern" war would make war impossible. This has been a persistent fallacy. Therefore we all look at the belief skeptically today. But it cannot be denied that today's conditions have changed, and that warfare based on atomic or thermo-nuclear weapons, or upon germs, or upon other devices and concepts of transcendent horror, has become warfare in which no real victor is conceivable and all mankind is manifestly the victim. As has often been pointed out, men and nations rarely have embarked upon war except with the conviction that they could win.

There is a great deal of evidence to show that nobody could win a total, global war. *Erwin D. Canham*

To improve and extend higher education in the United States must be more than a pious hope. It must be recognized as a vital necessity. Increasingly, our whole economic life depends upon the kind and quality of our education. The American people can no longer spread out across the ranges to new and fertile plains, or count upon the discovery of more and richer natural resources. The only frontier that still lies before us is the frontier of knowledge, and we must develop the skills to conquer its vast and difficult reaches. *Robert G. Sproul*

The best answer to a false idea is the truth. *Richard M. Nixon*

Nothing is more important or has contributed more to the American achievement than the spiritual foundation on which our Republic was consciously based.

The founding wise men wrote that men are endowed by their Creator with certain inalienable rights—life, liberty and the pursuit of happiness, and so on. The men who wrote those words were the greatest political scientists of their—and perhaps, of any—time. They had read and understood the political fears of the 18th Century, and they transcended all the rest of them. And their Republic was consciously founded on a recognition of man's debt to God. Thus it was spiritually buttressed. *Erwin D. Canham*

The degree to which Americans have put mechanical power to work for them explains a large part of the increase in production and productivity. Men and animals in 1850 contributed 74 per cent of the total energy used in American production. Men and animals in 1950 contributed only 7 per cent of the total energy; machines did 93 per cent of the work.   *Erwin D. Canham*

The United States cannot long succeed in maintaining an internationalist foreign policy *politically* if we are going to pursue an isolationist policy *economically*.   *Gardner Cowles*

Civilization has risen along trade routes and has been controlled and dominated by the cities and the peoples that control those trade routes.   *Dr. Will Durant*

Look at the arts, literature, any walk of life you want to, and you'll find that Harvard men are in all of them. The thing that is characteristic about them is—as one of them told me (an old gentleman we call "Mr. Harvard,")—that there never was anything that came up in public life where some Harvard man wasn't on the other side. And that's perfectly true, and we consider this to be a good thing.   *Dr. Nathan M. Pusey*

No people can survive and no free nation can endure unless its roots are imbedded in moral principle. Our Christian faith is basic to the spirit which motivates our society. It pointed the road to our way of life long before our forefathers gave it political meaning.
Walter B. Smith

The thing that makes America, and will continue to make it, great and give it leadership in the world is the spiritual strength of our people.   *Arthur B. Langlie*

It is a wonderful thing to be an American; it is a greater thing to be a Christian. But let us be dynamic Christians.   *Arthur B. Langlie*

I do not see how anyone who understands the Constitution of the United States and the history that brought it forth and subsequently refined it can fail to look upon any form of totalitarian dictatorship as utterly abhorrent.   *A. Whitney Griswold*

As we take just and full measure of all authority, let neither time nor the times press us so hard to render unto Caesar the things which are Caesar's that we neglect to render unto God the things that are God's.   *A. Whitney Griswold*

The free world must come to recognize that trade barriers, although intended to protect their country's economy often in fact shackle its prosperity. In the United States there is a growing recognition that free nations cannot expand their productivity and economic strength without a high level of international trade.

Dwight D. Eisenhower

It is to competition more than anything else that we in America owe our unparalleled standard of living and our unmatched proficiency in production and distribution.   *Eric Johnston*

The economic strength and stability of the United States is the greatest safeguard for a free world, and therefore for a free Europe, and a free Germany. This means that nothing that we may think of, desire, or propose in the field of our economic cooperation could be aimed at, or should be interpreted as, seeking either to weaken or undermine the economic strength of the United States. Your strength is the world's greatest bulwark against slavery.

Heinz L. Krekeler

Nobody who deals with foreign affairs must ever expect quick results or think that the barometer is set fair. "Squalls in some quarters" is our daily forecast at the Foreign Office.   *Anthony Eden*

The foundation and prime purpose of the British and American constitutions and indeed of the French constitution is to safeguard themselves against falling under the rule of dictators or oligarchies.

Sir Winston Churchill

I believe myself that the mass of the people in all countries are kind, decent folk who wish to live their lives in neighborly fashion with their fellow men and women. Naught but ruin awaits the world if communities of scores of millions are taught and allow themselves to journey along dominated by feelings of hatred against other vast collections of bewildered mortals.   *Sir Winston Churchill*

Our ever deeper knowledge of nature and of the laws which govern it has made possible an ever-growing technological mastery. We have gained power over forces which may lead us to a new world of plenty but, so far, we have spent most of our energy and skills in putting them to the service of man's fight against man. Is that a sign of wisdom or spiritual maturity? Does this show that we are willing to learn from history?   *Dag Hammarskjold*

The fact we have to face squarely is that the diversity of the nations makes world government still impossible, while the interdependence of nations has already made our world organization necessary. Our knowledge of the past, and the results of our new knowledge in the present, combine to force us to find a middle road: a world organization respecting the sovereignty of nations—a middle road on which we can move, slowly but surely, towards that world community which for our civilization is the only alternative to disaster. Following that middle road, we must establish a cooperation with others which gives true life and direction to the mere existence which we cannot escape from sharing with all mankind, friends and foes alike. In this, as in so many other fields of human activity, anything short of progress will mean regression. Neighbours forced to exist together will end up as enemies unless they act and live animated by a hope one day to become friends.   *Dag Hammarskjold*

Competition is the only effective regulator of economic enterprise and the great protector not only of economic freedom but of all freedom and opportunity. Competition stimulates and channels productive effort, spurs initiative and imagination, attracts customers and determines prices. In simplest terms, it provides people with the goods and services they want at prices they are both able and willing to pay.   *Willard W. Wright*

Our market is so huge that a small upward or downward movement in our imports, unimportant as it may be in relation to our total consumption, may mean the difference between prosperity and depression for many other countries. And if things go seriously wrong with our economy and if we do not behave reasonably, intelligently and fairly in the manner in which we handle our large share of world trade, economic havoc can be created in many places where it is to our national interest to see prosperity, stability and good will.

Winthrop W. Aldrich

In peace America grew great. It was in peace that we grew strong and rich and accumulated the homes, plants, farms, mines and transportation that saw us through two wars. It was wars that brought us debt and taxes and inflation.   *George M. Humphrey*

History demonstrates that whenever currency deterioration has started it tends to continue at an ever increasing rate, the faster and further it goes. Unless courageous, determined, corrective action is taken in time it finally speeds entirely out of control and finishes in utter collapse.   *George M. Humphrey*

Competition is the life of trade. It is what has made our American system. More and better goods at less cost for more people is our national slogan.   *George M. Humphrey*

America is not immortal and there are today signs in American life of an alarming deterioration in the things of the spirit.

Francis Cardinal Spellman

The struggle for Asia is a struggle for the minds and hearts of men.

Sir Percy Spender

Do you not feel what great enterprises, constructive enterprises, this country, France, is capable of, if only all its children are finally animated by a common will?   *Pierre Mendes-France*

One of the things that is wrong with America is that everybody who has done anything at all in his own field is expected to be an authority on every subject under the sun.   *Elmer Davis*

Truly each new book is as a ship that bears us away from the fixity of our limitations into the movement and splendor of life's infinite ocean.   *Helen Keller*

Business is a combination of war and sport.   *André Maurois*

Charm is almost as poor a butter for parsnips as good intentions.
Heywood Broun

If you want to kill any idea in the world today, get a committee
working on it.   *C. F. Kettering*

Conceit is God's gift to little men.   *Bruce Barton*

Sometimes one pays most for the things one gets for nothing.
Albert Einstein

There are some literary critics...who remind me of a gong at
a grade crossing clanging loudly and vainly as the train roars by.
Christopher Morley

The country still has faith in the rule of the people it's going to
elect next.   *Ted Cook*

Democracy is ever eager for rapid progress, and the only progress
which can be rapid is progress down hill.   *Sir James Jeans*

Democracy has not failed; the intelligence of the race has failed
before the problems the race has raised.   *Robert M. Hutchins*

Economists have not yet earned the right to be listened to atten-
tively.   *John Maynard Keynes*

Economy is going without something you do want in case you
should, some day, want something which you probably won't want.
Anthony Hope Hawkins

It is more than probable that the average man could, with no injury to his health, increase his efficiency fifty per cent.
Walter Dill Scott

Executive ability is deciding quickly and getting somebody else to
do the work.   *J. G. Pollard*

Never give a man up until he has failed at something he likes.

Lewis E. Lawes

Freedom is not worth having if it does not connote freedom to err.

Mahatma Gandhi

If we are to have genius we must put up with the inconvenience of genius, a thing the world will never do; it wants geniuses, but would like them just like other people.   *George Moore*

What I like about Hollywood is that one can get along quite well by knowing two words of English—swell and lousy.   *Vicki Baum*

New ideas can be good or bad, just the same as old ones.

Franklin D. Roosevelt

Any frontal attack on ignorance is bound to fail because the masses are always ready to defend their most precious possession— their ignorance.   *Hendrik Van Loon*

Individuality is either the mark of genius or the reverse. Mediocrity finds safety in standardization.   *Frederick E. Crane*

Jazz will endure as long as people hear it through their feet instead of their brains.   *John Philip Sousa*

The trouble with law and government is lawyers.

Clarence Darrow

I don't know a better preparation for life than a love of poetry and a good digestion.   *Zona Gale*

We owe to the Middle Ages the two worst inventions of humanity —romantic love and gunpowder.   *André Maurois*

Of middle age the best that can be said is that a middle-aged person has likely learned to have a little fun in spite of his troubles.

Don Marquis

Monotony is the awful reward of the careful.   *A. G. Buckham*

An open mind is all very well in its way, but it ought not to be so open that there is no keeping anything in or out of it. It should be capable of shutting its doors sometimes, or it may be found a little draughty.   *Samuel Butler*

A pessimist is a man who thinks everybody as nasty as himself, and hates them for it.   *George Bernard Shaw*

Bad officials are elected by good citizens who do not vote.
                                                       Chicago Poster

Politics is like a race horse. A good jockey must know how to fall with the least possible damage.   *Edouard Herriot*

Most statesmen have long noses. But I suppose that is very lucky, because most of them cannot see further than the length of them, so that a statesman with a short nose is handicapped by nature.
                                                         Paul Claudel

How a minority, reaching majority, seizing authority, hates a minority.   *L. H. Robbins*

A wonderful discovery—psychoanalysis. Makes quite simple people feel they're complex.   *S. N. Behrman*

Most reformers, like a pair of trousers on a windy clothesline, go through a vast deal of vehement motion, but stay in the same place.
                                                     Austin O'Malley

Satire is a lonely and introspective occupation, for nobody can describe a fool to the life without much patient self-inspection.
                                                   Frank Moore Colby

The showmanship idea of yesterday was to give the public what it wanted. This is a fallacy. You don't know what they want and they don't know what they want.   *S. L. Rothafel*

Slang is just sport-model language stripped down to get more speed with less horsepower.   *Buffalo Evening News*

If you think of "standardization" as the best that you know today, but which is to be improved tomorrow—you get somewhere.
Henry Ford

Who wants to get on? ... It is only changing what you are for something no better.   *Anthony Hope Hawkins*

Temperance is the control of all the functions of our bodies. The man who refuses liquor, goes in for apple pie and develops a paunch is no ethical leader for me.   *John Erskine*

Truth is beautiful and divine no matter how humble its origin.
Michael Idvorsky Pupin

You are not going to get peace with millions of armed men. The chariot of peace cannot advance over a road littered with cannon.
Lloyd George

There are a few things that never go out of style, and a feminine woman is one of them.   *Jobyna Ralston*

Being a woman is a terribly difficult task, since it consists principally in dealing with men.   *Joseph Conrad*

A capacity for self-pity is one of the last things that any woman surrenders.   *Irvin S. Cobb*

As any psychologist will tell you, the worst thing you can possibly do to a woman is to deprive her of a grievance.   *Beverly Nichols*

It ain't no use putting up your umbrella till it rains.
Alice Hegan Rice

Youth, though it may lack knowledge, is certainly not devoid of intelligence; it sees through shams with sharp and terrible eyes.
H. L. Mencken

Advertising may be described as the science of arresting the human intelligence long enough to get money from it.

Stephen Leacock

Few things are harder to put up with than the annoyance of a good example.   *Mark Twain*

There is no such thing as modern art. There is art—and there is advertising.   *Albert Sterner*

All the blessings of civilization are either curses or superfluous.

August Strindberg

I wonder if we have really grown to the point where the size of a house in which a person lives will have little interest to his neighbors, but what he contributes in mind and character to the community will bring him respect and admiration.   *Eleanor Roosevelt*

Democracy is based upon the conviction that there are extraordinary possibilities in ordinary people.   *Harry Emerson Fosdick*

The greatest destroyer of democracy in the world is war itself.

Harry Emerson Fosdick

It is nonsense to talk of the college years as only a preparation for life. They are part of life, just as much as any other four-year period.

Paul Swain Havens

How can it be that mathematics, being after all a product of human thought independent of experience, is so admirably adapted to the objects of reality?   *Albert Einstein*

Long live also the forward march of the common people in all the lands towards their just and true inheritance, and toward the broader and fuller age.   *Winston Churchill*

The function of language is twofold: to communicate emotion and to give information. ...   *Aldous Huxley*

If you don't say anything, you won't be called on to repeat it.

Calvin Coolidge

Everyone wonders what a man who never says anything sounds like.   *Oscar Levant*

While the right to talk may be the beginning of freedom, the necessity of listening is what makes the right important.

Walter Lippman

Of course sometimes it is not possible to prepare an address fully, but it is much better to do so even if you intend to speak extemporaneously.   *Robert A. Taft*

It is impossible to defeat an ignorant man in argument.

William G. McAdoo

Men like fly-fishing because it is difficult; they will not shoot a bird sitting, because it is easy.... *Bertrand Russell*

Golf was, I should say offhand, the most useless outdoor game ever devised to waste the time and try the spirit of man.

Westbrook Pegler

Like so many people in the theatre, she acted her part continually.

Thomas Wolfe

Fullness of knowledge always and necessarily means some understanding of the depths of our ignorance, and that is always conducive to both humility and reverence.   *Robert A. Millikan*

History repeats itself, that's one of the things that's wrong with history.   *Clarence Darrow*

The men who made the world wiser, better and holier were ever battling with the laws and customs and institutions of the world.

Clarence Darrow

Any event, once it has occurred, can be made to appear inevitable by a competent historian.   *Lee Simonson*

I have written too much history to have faith in it; and if anyone
thinks I'm wrong, I am inclined to agree with him.

Henry B. Adams

History is rather interesting when it repeats itself; historians are
not.   *Philip Guedalla*

When we say that a man has no sense of humor, what we really
mean is that he hasn't the same sense of humor we have. *Frank Case*

As a physician, I have seen men, after all other therapy had failed,
lifted out of disease and melancholy by the serene effort of prayer.

Dr. Alexis Carrel

What I mean is this—all good doctors must be primarily enthusiasts. They must have, like writers and painters, and priests, a sense of
vocation—a deep-rooted, unsentimental desire to do good.

Noel Coward

A liberal is a man who is willing to spend somebody else's money.

Carter Glass

It is not necessary to understand music; it is only necessary that
one enjoy it.   *Leopold Stokowski*

God puts something good and something lovable in every man His
hands create.   *Mark Twain*

The requisites of a singer—a big chest, a big mouth, 90 per cent
memory, ten per cent intelligence, lots of hard work, and something
in the heart.   *Enrico Caruso*

Nature knows nothing of rights. She knows only laws. Man, on
the other hand, has ideals and aspirations.   *James Truslow Adams*

Nothing so needs reforming as other people's habits. *Mark Twain*

The American people never carry an umbrella. They prepare to
walk in eternal sunshine. . . .   *Alfred E. Smith*

In the United States there is more space where nobody is than where anybody is. This is what makes America what she is.

Gertrude Stein

There are two kinds of people in one's life—people whom one keeps waiting—and the people for whom one waits....

S. N. Behrman

A conservative is a man who does not think that anything should be done for the first time. *Frank Vanderlip*

I would rather have my ignorance than another man's knowledge, because I have got so much more of it. *Mark Twain*

Christian charity in fact is not confined to not hating our enemies and loving them as brothers; it desires also that we do good to them.

Pope Benedict XV

A little knowledge often estranges men from religion, a deeper knowledge brings them back to it.... *Dean Inge*

Hollywood is no place for the professional comedian—there's too much amateur competition. *Fred Allen*

When audiences come to see us authors lecture, it is largely in the hope that we'll be funnier to look at than to read. *Sinclair Lewis*

Children love laughter, but not when directed at themselves. To be laughed at seems ridiculous, and to the child that is agony.

Harry Emerson Fosdick

The young man who has not shed tears is a savage, and the old man who will not laugh is a fool. *George Santayana*

Children are a great comfort in your old age—and they help you reach it faster too. *Lionel M. Kauffman*

One of the many things nobody ever tells you about middle age is that it's such a nice change from being young.

Dorothy Canfield Fisher

If a man's curve of efficiency is ascending at 45, and keeps on ascending just after that period, it may well move upward for his whole life; but if there is a turn downward at 45, he will never recover.   *Nicholas Murray Butler*

The fear of ridicule causes our worst cowardice.   *André Gide*

I have learned a great truth which I shall always cherish—that people are pretty much the same the world over when you get down to fundamentals, and that it does not much matter what is their race, creed or color.   *Louis Bromfield*

The most difficult of all virtues is the forgiving spirit. Revenge seems to be natural with man; it is human to want to get even with an enemy.   *William Jennings Bryan*

If you wish to make a man your enemy, tell him simply, "You are wrong." This method works every time.   *Henry C. Link*

We all have weaknesses. But I have figured that others have put up with mine so tolerably that I would be much less than fair not to make a reasonable discount for theirs.   *William Allen White*

Generosity is giving more than you can, and pride is taking less than you need.   *Kahlil Gibran*

Do not put off till tomorrow what can be put off till day-after-tomorrow just as well.   *Mark Twain*

Fear is nature's warning signal to get busy.   *Henry C. Link*

I don't know how the people will feel towards me, but I will take to my grave my love for them which has sustained me through life.
                                    Robert M. LaFollette

Results! Why, man, I have gotten a lot of results. I know several thousand things that won't work.   *Thomas A. Edison*

Slowly and painfully man is learning that he must do to others what he would have them do to him.   *Anthony Eden*

It is well for people who think to change their minds occasionally in order to keep them clean. For those who do not think, it is best at least to rearrange their prejudices once in a while.   *Luther Burbank*

Time was invented by Almighty God in order to give ideas a chance.   *Nicholas Murray Butler*

No grand idea was ever born in a conference, but a lot of foolish ideas have died there.   *F. Scott Fitzgerald*

The obvious is that which is never seen until someone expresses it simply.   *Kahlil Gibran*

There are two kinds of fools. One says, "This is old, therefore it is good." The other says, "This is new, therefore it is better."
Dean Inge

So I should say that civilizations begin with religion and stoicism; they end with skepticism and unbelief, and the undisciplined pursuit of individual pleasure. A civilization is born stoic and dies epicurean.
Will Durant

Vegetarianism is harmless enough, although it is apt to fill a man with wind and self-righteousness.   *Robert Hutchinson*

There is no nation on earth so dangerous as a nation fully armed, and bankrupt at home.   *Henry Cabot Lodge*

He had been rejected from military service. He had weak ribs. He had poor eyes. He was flat-footed. He was a professor.
Will Durant

The most conservative persons I ever met are college undergraduates.   *Woodrow Wilson*

The Constitution is what the judges say it is.
Charles Evans Hughes

We mean to hold our own. I did not become His Majesty's first minister in order to preside over the liquidation of the British Empire.   *Winston Churchill*

A verbal contract isn't worth the paper it's written on.
                                        Samuel Goldwyn

As long as a union remains the servant of the worker and not his master, both are safe.   *Cecil B. De Mille*

A ration of one newspaper a day ought to be enough for anyone who still prefers to retain a little mental balance.   *Clifton Fadiman*

The law and the stage—both are a form of exhibitionism.
                                        Orson Welles

A witness on the stand has some rights, or so the lawbooks say—freedom of speech is not one of them.   *Mitchell Dawson*

It isn't the common man at all who is important; it's the uncommon man.   *Lady Nancy Astor*

Some of man's greatest achievements lie in his successful adaptation to the available raw materials, in his rendering more of them accessible and with his genius in discovering new ones.   *Karl Brandt*

The great secret of successful marriage is to treat all disasters as incidents and none of the incidents as disasters.   *Harold Nicolson*

Success in marriage is much more than finding the right person: it is a matter of being the right person.   *B. R. Brickner*

Woman knows what man has too long forgotten, that the ultimate economic and spiritual unit of any civilization is still the family.
                                        Clare Booth Luce

The city is the place where men are constantly seeking to find their door and where they are doomed to wandering forever.
                                        Thomas Wolfe

The reason American cities are prosperous is that there is no place to sit down.   *A. J. Talley*

... one of the charms of Hollywood is that almost nothing they do is real or true or practical or anything resembling life ...

Frank Case

The very ink with which all history is written is merely fluid prejudice.   *Mark Twain*

Foreigners are people, you know. Some of them are rather nice.

S. N. Behrman

Hollywood is the town where inferior people have a way of making superior people feel inferior.   *Dudley Field Malone*

They say that when the acid test was applied, the prophet turned politician, and the realist was lost in the rhetorician.

Dr. Glenn Frank

You can always get the truth from an American statesman after he has turned seventy, or given up all hope for the presidency.

Ralph Woods

A statesman is a politician who is held upright by equal pressure from all directions.   *Eric A. Johnston*

Adherent—a follower who has not yet obtained all that he expects to get...   *Ambrose Bierce*

A conservative is a man with two perfectly good legs who, however, has never learned to walk.   *Franklin D. Roosevelt*

A radical is a man with both feet firmly planted—in the air.

Franklin D. Roosevelt

You may have noticed that the less I know about a subject the more confidence I have, and the more new light I throw on it.

Mark Twain

All musicians must feel gratitude to the radio. It has done so much for musical taste.   *Lily Pons*

The Church after all is not a club of saints; it is a hospital for sinners.   *George Craig Stewart*

Prayer, our deepest source of power and perfection, has been left miserably undeveloped.   *Dr. Alexis Carrel*

Only through love can we attain to communion with God.
                    Dr. Albert Schweitzer

I am never more tickled than when I laugh at myself.
                    Mark Twain

I often quote myself. It adds spice to my conversation.
                    George Bernard Shaw

I could hear the cadence of his voice and that was all, nothing but the measured rise and fall of syllables. . . .   *J. P. Marquand*

Punning, like poetry, is something every person belittles and everyone attempts.   *Louis Untermeyer*

. . . those who cannot endure vigorous attacks on their opinion should retire from public controversy.   *Dorothy Thompson*

Automobiles continue to be driven at just two speeds—lawful and awful.   *Frederick C. Russell*

The atomic bomb may help to decide a future war; like any other weapon it solves none of the problems which made for war.
                    Hans Kohn

At last war is being made so horrible for the civilian population that perhaps its ultimate stupidity will become clear.
                    Raymond Clapper

War comes as the great failure of man, out of fear, lust for power, injustice, or misery left unrectified.   *Cordell Hull*

Heroic men can die upon the battlefields in vain, because of what occurs after a war, as well as because of what happens during a war.

Harold E. Stassen

War is not a moral picnic.   *Lancelot Hogben*

The Army must get rid of the theory that an officer breathes special air and is a gentleman while the enlisted man is not.

Bill Mauldin

Certainly, we cannot say that our individual freedom is guaranteed if every twenty years we have to stop production of consumer goods and waste all our energies and resources in the manufacture of the tools of war.   *Emery Reeves*

You don't write because you want to say something; you write because you've got something to say.   *F. Scott Fitzgerald*

Age acquires no value save through thought and discipline.

James Truslow Adams

Beauty comes and passes, is lost the moment that we touch it, can no more be stayed or held than one can stay the flowing of a river.

Thomas Wolfe

With me, a change of trouble is as good as a vacation.

David Lloyd George

All change is not growth, as all movement is not forward.

Ellen Glasgow

Half a man's life is devoted to what he calls improvements, yet the original had some quality which he lost in the process.   *E. B. White*

Enthusiasm always exaggerates the importance of important things and overlooks their deficiencies.   *Hugh Stevenson Tigner*

There is no sadder sight than a young pessimist, except an old optimist.   *Mark Twain*

I like him. He is every other inch a gentleman.   *Noel Coward*

He's the kind of a bore who's here today and here tomorrow.

Binnie Barnes

We are likely to believe the worst about another because the capacity for evil is so pronounced in ourselves.   *Louis Nizer*

To be thoroughly religious, one must, I believe, be sorely disappointed. One's faith in God increases as one's faith in the world decreases. The happier the man, the farther he is from God.

George Jean Nathan

This makes me so sore it gets my dandruff up.   *Samuel Goldwyn*

Few of us can stand prosperity. Another man's I mean.

Mark Twain

I'm a self-made man, but I think if I had it to do over again, I'd call in someone else.   *Roland Young*

...the beginning of wise ambition lies in a man's accepting himself as himself and not as someone else, and in trying to make the most and the best of that self and not of another.

Harry Emerson Fosdick

There is always one man to state the case for freedom. That's all we need, one.   *Clarence Darrow*

...Life is like a cash register, in that every account, every thought, every deed, like every sale, is registered and recorded.

Monsignor Fulton J. Sheen

The radical of one century is the conservative of the next. The radical invents the views. When he has worn them out, the conservative adopts them.   *Mark Twain*

The significant questions of human destiny are not to be approached with a smile. God, misery, and salvation are no joke.

Irwin Edman

When you have saved a boy from the possibility of making any mistake, you have also prevented him from developing initiative.
John Erskine

...there is nothing more demoralizing than a small but adequate income.
Edmund Wilson

People who are hard, grasping...and always ready to take advantage of their neighbors, become very rich....
George Bernard Shaw

A heavy guilt rests upon us for what the whites of all nations have done to the colored peoples. When we do good to them, it is not benevolence—it is atonement.
Dr. Albert Schweitzer

People like to imagine that because all our mechanical equipment moves so much faster, that we are thinking faster too.
Christopher Morley

This is the most unselfish of eras because hardly anyone is egotist enough to wish to do his own thinking. There are always so many ready and eager to do it for us.
Christopher Morley

An advertising agency—85 per cent confusion and 15 per cent commission.
Fred Allen

Good breeding consists in concealing how much we think of ourselves and how little we think of the other person.
Mark Twain

Bees are not as busy as we think they are. They just can't buzz any slower.
Kin Hubbard

I never wanted to see anybody die, but there are a few obituary notices I have read with pleasure.
Clarence Darrow

Civilization, is, after all, but a coat of paint that washes away when the rain falls.
Auguste Rodin

Abscond—to "move in a mysterious way," commonly with the property of another....
Ambrose Bierce

We believe in democracy; we believe in freedom; we believe in peace. We offer to every nation of the world the handclasp of the good neighbor. Let those who wish our friendship look us in the eye and take our hand.   *Franklin D. Roosevelt*

In a democracy, the individual enjoys not only the ultimate power but carries the ultimate responsibility.   *Norman Cousins*

The only sound opinions some people have about world affairs are a lot of noise.   *Louis Hirsch*

A man who overindulges lives in a dream. He becomes conceited. He thinks the whole world revolves around him—and it usually does.
                                                                      W. C. Fields

When we teach a child to read, our primary aim is not to enable it to decipher a way-bill or receipt, but to kindle its imagination, enlarge its vision, and open for it the avenues of knowledge.
                                                                  Charles W. Eliot

Education is not salesmanship. No genuine teacher is trying to put something over.   *Alexander Meiklejohn*

It is the utmost folly—it is just short of suicide—to take the position that citizens of any country should hold their tongues for fear of causing distress to the immediate and sometimes torturous policies of their leaders.   *Wendell L. Willkie*

People think too historically. They are always living half in a cemetery.   *Aristide Briand*

The history of the world is the record of a man in quest of his daily bread and butter.   *Hendrik van Loon*

I always avoid prophesying beforehand, because it is much better policy to prophesy after the event already has taken place.
                                                              Winston Churchill

A limitation on the production of the individual is pure waste.
                                                              Louis D. Brandeis

Business men who would blush to be seen in a five-year-old car proudly made medieval pronouncements on economics.

Henry Morton Robinson

The size of a man can be measured by the size of the thing that makes him angry ...   *J. K. Morley*

We have learned from hard experience that stronger, more rigorous world institutions must be created to preserve peace and to forestall the causes of future wars.   *Winston Churchill*

No world settlement that affords nations only a place on relief rolls will provide the basis for a just and durable peace.

William O. Douglas

10

STORIES OF
STATESMEN
AND DIPLOMATS[1]

Companionship

United States Agriculture Secretary Benson has always preached the desirability of increasing efficiency on the farm, and among other things he has urged improvement of dairy herds. He quoted one of his experts as saying that the only thing a farmer gets out of a cow that gives less than 5,000 pounds of milk a year is her companionship.

No Time to Think

Senator Morse was rushing to the senate floor to participate in a filibuster when a reporter cornered him outside the door to the senate chamber.

"Senator, what do you think . . ." the reporter began.

"This is the time for talking," Morse cut in. "I haven't got time to think."

Tact

At a Washington dinner party the subject of tact came up for discussion. "Well," said former Senator Ferguson of Michigan, "I've

---

[1] Many of the stories in this chapter appear through the courtesy and permission of Walter Trohan and the *Chicago Tribune*.

never been able to solve one facet of the problem. When a woman in politics asks me to guess her age, I don't know whether it's wiser to make her 10 years younger on the basis of her looks or 10 years older on the basis of her intelligence."

What's a Million?

Senator Ferguson of Michigan who handled the defense department multi-billion dollar budgets as chairman of the senate defense appropriations subcommittee, always said:

"Thanks a billion." Then he often added apologetically, "I've gotten out of the habit of talking in millions."

Would Do It Again

Former Vice-President Barkley delighted in telling, especially in the presence of Governor Dewey of New York, a mythical story about a mythical retainer on the mythical Barkley acres at Paducah, Kentucky. The story goes:

"How did you vote, Sam?" Barkley asked.

"Same as I did in 1948, for Dewey," was the answer.

"You mean to tell me that with me running for Vice-President as a Democrat you voted Republican?" Barkley asked in amazement.

"Yes, suh, boss," was the reply. "I voted for him then and I voted for him now and I'll vote for him again, because each time I vote for him I never had it so good."

White House Mess

White House staff members have their own dining room in the executive wing, and each has his own wooden napkin ring, carrying the inscription, "White House mess." Presidential aids hasten to head off wiseacres by declaring that this is the only part of the former administration's "mess" that hasn't been cleaned up.

Tried on its Merits

Senator Ferguson of Michigan tells a story of a judge who offered himself as a model of judicial propriety.

"I have here two checks," the judge announced at the opening of a civil suit. "One from the plaintiff for $10,000 and one from the defendant for $15,000. I am now executing my personal check to the defendant for $5,000 so that I can try this case on its merits."

A Lot More Good

When Arthur Larson, United States undersecretary of labor, makes a public address, he likes to tell about the first speech of his career.

"I was addressing a group of farmers in South Dakota," he relates. "I had memorized the speech, and delivered it in my best public-speaking class style. After it was all over, I was talking to one of the farmers and asked him what he thought of the speech.

" 'Well,' he said, 'it wasn't too bad, but a half hour of rain would have done a sight more good.' "

Lose All of Ours, Please

A rather novel method of avoiding the payment of income taxes was offered the United States internal revenue service. A taxpayer wrote:

"Dear sir: I hear about government papers getting lost; please lose my account."

Warm, Isn't It?

When deep summer heat rolls around, David C. Mearns, scholarly chief of the manuscripts division of the library of Congress in Washington, is reminded of his most trying and embarrassing day. During the Coolidge administration, Mearns received a hurry up call from the White House, telling him the President was returning unexpectedly during remodeling of the White House and that it would be necessary to arrange the library in case the President wanted to go to work on a speech.

Mearns found the library in complete disorder and the heat well nigh unbearable. When he began sorting the books into piles according to subject matter, he was hampered by a large and overly friendly white collie. By lunch time Mearns was exhausted more by fighting off the affection of the dog friend than he was by his labors. He repaired to the home of a friend, who fortified him with beakers of courage for the afternoon ordeal. When Mearns returned the dog was overjoyed and raced toward him. The librarian picked up a heavy volume and heaved it at the bounding animal. Unfortunately he misjudged the distance and the tome sailed toward the doorway, and to Mearns' horror, struck Calvin Coolidge who had just entered. Coolidge retrieved the volume and then turned toward Mearns.

"Warm, isn't it?" he said gravely.

Poor Judge of Dogs

General Ridgway, army chief of staff, thinks American foreign policy makers should take some advice from a story about the late Teddy Roosevelt's dog. The mutt was always getting into fights and getting chewed badly. Someone suggested to the late President, "Your dog is a pretty poor fighter." Mr. Roosevelt answered, "Oh, no. He's a very good fighter, but he's just a terrible judge of dogs."

Helpful Notes

Senator Dirksen of Illinois tells the story of the preacher in a little Illinois town who lost his sermon notes. "He had left them on the pulpit," as Dirksen tells it, "and the sexton found them. The sexton got out his specs and began to peer at them, and saw many strange little markings. In the second paragraph, the minister had written, 'throw up your hands in a great and reverent gesture.' A few paragraphs further on, he had written 'throw up your arms with a wide open gesture and glower at the congregation.' When the sexton got to the next paragraph, the notation was, 'argument weak here. Yell like everything.' "

Can't Hold a Job

Livingston T. Merchant, United States Assistant State Secretary for European affairs, has held numerous important posts at home and abroad in his 12 years with the department, but his son, Gerald, isn't impressed, Livingston concedes.

Merchant addressed an American Legion group when the Legion held its national convention in Washington. In introducing him the chairman rattled off the list of assignments Merchant has filled. Responding, Merchant smiled and said:

"When my young son hears that list recited he says, 'Dad, it sure looks like you can't hold a job very long.' "

Correct Title

T. Coleman Andrews, United States commissioner of internal revenue service, recently received a communication from a long-suffering taxpayer which was addressed to "the eternal revenue service."

How to Lose Votes

When former Vice-President Alben W. Barkley was campaigning in Kentucky for the senate seat he held for more than 20 years, he told of encountering a man who was belligerently announcing that he planned to vote against him.

"Did I not put your girl on the FHA?" Barkley asked.

"So you did," the man conceded.

"Did I not get your boy a job with the FCC?"

"So you did."

"And did I not get you a job with the TVA?"

"So you did."

"Then why aren't you for me?"

"Well, you just ain't done nothing for me lately."

Hey You Guys

Army Chief of Staff Matthew B. Ridgway was reminiscing about his days as a second lieutenant fresh out of West Point.

"I can still hear our first sergeant calling for volunteers," he sighed. "And what a musical call it was: 'Hey you guys, I want three volunteers for KP duty and I mean you and you and you.' "

Point of View

Everything depends on the point of view, says Representative Dorn of South Carolina, even in the case of a man being bitten by a dog. "The man screams that the dog is biting him while the dog is growling because the man won't take his foot out of the dog's mouth."

So to Speak

George V. Allen, American Ambassador to India, is the master of the mixed metaphor. Said Allen in his report to the Senate foreign relations committee on India:

"Practically all of Syngman Rhee's (President of South Korea) equipment and supplies have been furnished by the United States and, consequently, even tho Rhee sometimes quarrels with the United States bitterly, Indians believe that when the chips are down, we have got him under our thumb because we can, to use the illustration, jerk the rug out from under him anytime we want to by cutting off his supplies. He is dependent upon us because he is eating out of our hand."

Never Mind the House

Letters about housing windfalls piled up on the desk of Norman P. Mason, federal housing administration commissioner. One of the oddest came from an elderly Louisiana rural route dweller who went on record with his name and address.

"Sir," he wrote, "I've been reading about windfalls in the paper. I would like to build about a $10,000 house and get about a $2,500 windfall. Please send me instructions how to do this."

A few days later he sent another letter.

"Never mind building the house," this one suggested. "Just send me the $2,500 windfall."

A Silly Answer

At the dinner given by President Syngman Rhee of Korea for President Eisenhower, Dr. Howard Rusk, Professor of rehabilitation and physical medicine at New York university, told the story of the two farm boys who were puzzled by fingerbowls at their first dinner in a swank city hotel.

"Can't be for drinking because we got a glass of water right here," said the first farm boy. "Let's ask the waiter."

The second farm boy protested that questioning such a rigid character would lead to no good, but the first farm boy insisted and posed his question.

"That, sir, is a bowl of tepid water for washing one's fingers should they be soiled during the course of the repast," said the waiter haughtily. "After washing, the extremities are dried on the serviette."

"See, what did I tell you," the second farm boy observed. "You ask a silly question and you get a silly answer."

Can't Be

Senator Welker of Idaho was driving Senator Byrd of Virginia through beautiful Rock Creek park. Where the roadway neared the bridle path their car passed one horseman, Senator Morse of Oregon and then another, Senator Malone, of Nevada, who have seldom if ever voted on the same side of any question.

"There go Senators Morse and Malone," observed Byrd.

"Can't be," Welker insisted. "Those fellows are riding in the same direction."

Any Cord Will Do

On the closing night of Congress, Senator Dirksen of Illinois took the floor to spread cheer and harmony among the handful of tired solons sticking it out until the final gavel. Dirksen told stories and praised the work of the party floor leaders—Knowland of California, Johnson of Texas, and even Morse of Oregon, the maverick and self-styled "head of the independent party."

When he came to lauding Morse, Dirksen declared "I pray for him in the hope that somehow he may yet come to his knees to confess the error of his ways." Dirksen said this reminded him of a story about two deacons, one Republican and the other Democratic, kneeling together in church in a small village in Illinois.

"The Republican deacon," said Dirksen, "was praying to the Lord and saying: 'O, Lord make us Republicans unlike the Democrats; make us hang together in accord; make us hang together in concord.' And just then his Democratic brother said, 'Lord, any cord will do.' "

He Knows Better Now

United States Welfare Secretary Hobby tells of a little boy who came home from his first day at school with a black eye. His mother sternly demanded to know whether the shiner was part of his education.

"Yes, mother," was the reply. "I learned why a young gentleman should never hit a young lady."

Take That and That

In his early days in New York City, James A. Farley, former Postmaster General and former Democratic national chairman, recalls a nominating session at Tammany hall which brought forth the most unusual nominating and de-nominating speeches in politics.

The nominator launched into an alphabet of reasons as to why his man should be selected.

"A, he's able; B, he's bountiful; C, he's cautious; D, he's diligent; E, he's efficient; F, he's frank; G, he's general; H, he's honest; I, he's intelligent. . . ."

At this point another man who had a candidate of his own leaped to his feet to break in. He shouted:

"J, he's a jerk; K, he's a krook; L, he's a louse; M, he's a mouse; N, he's a no-good; O, he's onreliable; P, he's a punk; Q, he's quarrelsome; R, he's a rotter; S, he stinks; T, he's treacherous; UVW, U von't want 'im, and XYZ, for good measure he's exactly the kind of man the ticket doesn't need."

Looks Like a Billion

Commenting upon present high prices and inflationary conditions, United States Representative Hunter of California says: "It is only a mild compliment to tell a girl she looks like a million; and to tell a man he appears sound as a dollar is a downright insult."

Outlived Them All

Herbert Hoover celebrated his 80th birthday in his home town of West Branch, Iowa. When the former President mentioned the impending anniversary, a friend was reminded of the preacher who delivered a powerful sermon on "enemies and enmity," warning that the making of enemies warped the soul and blighted the joys of life. Carried away by his own fervor the preacher called upon those in his congregation who were without enmity and without enemies to arise. One old man tottered to his feet. The preacher expressed chagrin that there was only one in the congregation who could profess himself without hate for his fellow men and who could say he did not have an enemy in the world, but he asked the old man to impart his secret to the others so they might benefit from it. The old man cleared his throat and said in a quavering voice, "I outlived all of them."

"Now, Chief, I'm sure that you rejoice in being in the position of the surviving old man," the friend said to Hoover.

"Not exactly," the former President said with a twinkle and a sigh, "in my case they have been mighty slow in dying."

A Chip off the Old Block

In questioning a prisoner, whose father had been sent to Alcatraz by the Federal Bureau of Investigation, J. Edgar Hoover observed: "I see you are following in your father's fingerprints."

A Vacant Chair

On his last concert appearance in Washington, Jascha Heifetz, the celebrated violinist, told of the greatest compliment that had ever been paid him as a virtuoso.

The will of an ancient Japanese, who had heard Heifetz play and treasured the artist's recording, directed his children to purchase a front row seat at the first Heifetz appearance in Tokyo after their aged father's death and to place the urn containing his ashes on that seat at the performance.

That's Telling Them

Public officials are constantly badgered by persons they have met casually in campaigning, who open a second meeting with a challenging: "You don't remember me, do you?"

Representative Judd of Minnesota has devised an effective way of meeting this gambit at the hands of women.

"Madame," Judd says gallantly, "If I remembered a beautiful woman like you, how could I get any work done?"

He Liked Him

During a recent closed committee session, Senator Dirksen of Illinois, who is acknowledged to be one of the greatest orators in Congress, was interrupted in the course of an exposition.

"My dear and distinguished colleague," said Dirksen, "you are interrupting the man I love to hear."

Nothing Unusual

Senator Holland of Florida tells the story of a horse, who wandered into the Senate restaurant and ordered a plate of the famous bean soup and a bottle of catsup.

"Isn't that most odd," an astonished visitor asked the Senator.

"Nope," was the reply, "I like mine the same way."

Internal Beauty

Spruille Braden was alternately coy as a maiden and stubborn as a Missouri mule when the Senate internal security subcommittee tried to get him to tell what he and Harry Truman talked about when Braden presented his resignation as Assistant State Secretary. The subcommittee persisted, certain that it was hot on the trail of something tremendous. Finally Braden waved his hand in token of submission, blushed, and told. "It was largely," he confessed, "a discussion of a gabardine suit I had on."

His Reason

During a lengthy debate on the floor of the United States Senate, Senator Jenner of Indiana looked up and paused as he was delivering a scathing attack on another Senator. The pause was so noticeable that Jenner was asked about it when he finished his speech.

"Well, I looked up toward heaven to ask the Good Lord to spare me until I finished what I had to say," Jenner said. "I knew that if I was suddenly stricken I wouldn't have enough friends on the floor to carry me off."

Who Do You Think You Are?

Joao Carlos Muniz, the ambassador of Brazil, asked Mr. and Mrs. John D. Rockefeller, Jr. whether they had difficulty rearing their children in view of their great wealth. The diplomat wondered how they could deny their children anything, even when they knew that what the children sought might "not be good for them at all." Said Rockefeller: "Whenever such a situation arose we merely asked the children, " 'Who do you think we are, the John Jacob Astors?' "

Couldn't Change Her Mind

United States Under Secretary of Labor Arthur Larson has had difficulty in getting some lawyers to understand that he is opposed to federalization of workmen's compensation and that he favors maintaining such compensation as a state matter. He has frequently spoken against federalization, but still gets mail denouncing him for support of federalization.

Larson says he got into a similar fix in Milwaukee once, when a young friend, a minister, asked him to preach. Larson preached on atheism, denouncing atheism, ridiculing atheism, and disproving atheism. After he trampled all over atheism and satisfied himself he had thoroughly demolished atheism, a sweet old lady approached him.

"Young man," she said, "You're a mighty convincing talker, but I still believe in God."

Is the Senator Certain?

Senator Kerr of Oklahoma circulated a story about President Eisenhower's golf game.

"I've solved the mystery of Ike's golf score," Kerr says. "He shot 108—'in' in '52, 'out' in '56."

Guess That Settles It

The United States internal revenue service is puzzling over a letter it has received in answer to one of its standard "dear sir or madam" letters asking for additional taxes. The reply read:

"Dear sir or madam:

"I do not have the money."

Abated Slightly

Former State Under Secretary Sumner Welles is known for the cold precision of his speech and icy calmness of language. At the state department the story is told that when Welles was two years old the index finger of his right hand was painfully mashed in a door. A lady rushed to him in great concern.

"Did oo hurt oo's itty-bitty finger," she cooed.

"Madame," Welles is reputed to have answered, "the agony has abated slightly."

He Recognized the Voice

During a tour of Venezuela for the purpose of inspecting the strategic resources of that country, Senator Malone of Nevada and his Senatorial party were startled by the unusually loud bray of a donkey.

"If it weren't for the touchy question of censure," Malone observed, "I could tell you the name of the Senator who just answered the roll call."

Long Time No See

At a capital reception a gushing woman rushed up to former Representative Jesse H. Tinkham of Massachusetts, who wears a beard.

"Why, Senator Lewis," she gurgled, "I haven't seen you in ages."

"I'm not at all surprised, madame," Tinkham responded, recalling to mind the late Senator J. Hamilton Lewis of Illinois, "I've been dead 15 years."

Surplus Egg Problem

The speech of a certain governor was long and labored. As he droned on, Senator Knowland of California whispered to Representative Martin of Massachusetts:

"The governor is laying so many eggs, he has Agriculture Secretary Benson worried about the surplus egg program."

The Genuine Article

The favorite story around President Eisenhower's vacation headquarters in Augusta is about the wealthy woman whose husband was dragged out half drowned after a swim. "We'll have to give artificial respiration," said the lifeguard. "Artificial nothing!" screamed the man's wife. "Give him the genuine thing. I can pay for it."

Room for Improvement

Cal Johnson, the former Republican congressman from Illinois, tells the story about the minister who knew he was preaching the worst sermon of his life. When he had finished, a normally testy member of the congregation praised the sermon to the skies.

"But why?" asked the minister.

"Because," answered his new admirer, "I don't like no preachin' at all, and that's as near no preachin' at all as I ever heard."

Texas

Representative Sheehan of Illinois tells a story which has many variations concerning a football game between Southern Methodist University and the University of Notre Dame. A priest came to the game with a pennant which he waved enthusiastically every time S.M.U. scored or made a gain. When a puzzled fellow spectator asked why a priest was rooting against the team representing a Catholic institution, the clergyman drew himself up and answered: "Son, once a Texan, always a Texan."

It Ain't Fair

Senator Malone of Nevada insists there has been too much talking and too little concentration in American diplomacy. The situation soviet propaganda is presenting to the world reminds him of a heated poker game in Reno which exploded into shooting when one of the players announced:

"I protest. Dangerous Dan ain't playing the hand I dealt him."

Was That Nice?

Senator Walter F. George of Georgia, the dean of the Senate, recalls a famous Senatorial insult in his first year in the Senate in 1922.

A former Senator had just been married for the second time, to a very wealthy widow. On his return to the Senate, he stepped aboard an elevator carrying several of his colleagues, including the late Senator Thaddeus H. Caraway of Arkansas. As the former Senator entered, Caraway observed pointedly:

"Isn't it surprising how little money will buy these days?"

For Only $1000 More

At a gathering in New Orleans of leaders of the Democratic party to elect a new national chairman a group of politicians got to discussing a departed friend.

"He had a fine funeral," one man observed. "Understand it cost $3,500."

"For another thousand dollars they could have buried him in a Cadillac," observed David L. Lawrence, mayor of Pittsburgh.

Accusing Others of Your Practices?

Allen Dulles, chief of the American Central Intelligence Agency, the super-secret agency which gathers and evaluates intelligence, was attending a diplomatic function which included Jozef Winiewicz, Ambassador of Red Poland.

The flow of liquor released diplomatic frigidity. There was some singing. Someone suggested the ambassador sing a song.

"Yes, Mr. Ambassador," Dulles urged, "do sing for us. I understand you have an excellent voice."

"You should know, Mr. Dulles," said Winiewicz, who is well aware of the soviet practice of tapping telephones of diplomats behind the iron curtain. "You have enough recordings of it."

Didn't Like the Book

A man attended a movie and was amazed to find himself seated right behind a young lady and a beautiful collie, according to Senator Langer of North Dakota. The dog laughed continually in the right places, all through the comedy. The man could take this no longer. Leaning forward he told the young lady, "Excuse me, miss, but I think it is simply astounding that your dog enjoys the movie so much."

"I'm surprised myself," the girl replied. "He hated the book."

Yes, Suh

An army rookie from the South ran afoul of the loyalty investigation system that requires everyone in the defense department to fill out a loyalty questionnaire. When he came to the question about whether anyone in his family had ever advocated the overthrow of the government he replied, "yes" in bold block letters. He was called up for an interview.

"Yes, suh," he told the interrogator, "it was my grandpappy. He fought for the Confederacy."

You Ain't Seen Nothin'

United States Agriculture Secretary Benson is a man who believes that exciting times are ahead for the farmer. No man knows, he says, what magic atomic developments may bring.

"The atom will teach us more about the effective use of fertilizers than we know today," he said recently. "Rain making may become a normal part of crop production. Deserts may bloom.

"It's like the cab driver who told the tourist who was riding past the government archives building. The tourist looked at the carved words, 'What Is Past Is Prologue,' and wanted to know what it meant.

" 'It means,' said the driver, 'that you ain't seen nothing yet.' "

Despite His Arguments He Won

Young lawyers are taught never to give up their efforts for a client who has lost his suit, but law schools have neglected to teach them to quit when the battle is won.

Chief Justice Harold M. Stephens of the Circuit Court of Appeals once broke in upon a young lawyer who was arguing at great length and with more enthusiasm than law.

"Despite your arguments," the judge said wearily but not unkindly, "the court has already concluded the case in your favor."

This Is One Way to Do It

When John Rankin was in the House of Representatives, he used to offer his colleagues short courses in history. One was on how to remember the Presidents in order. Here it is, in the words of the fiery Mississippi Democrat himself:

> Washington and Jefferson met many a jeer.
> Van Buren had troubles plenty to fear.
> Poor bank-bills let Johnson go home grumbling.
> And Cleveland heard cagy McKinley's rumbling,
> 'Til Wilson held currency Hooverly rare to eat.

"Old Jawn" explained it this way: The first letter of each word is the first letter of the name of a President. So the first line represents Washington, Adams, Jefferson, Madison, Monroe, Adams, and Jackson. The other lines continue Presidential succession. The last two words for Truman and Eisenhower have been added since the congressman departed.

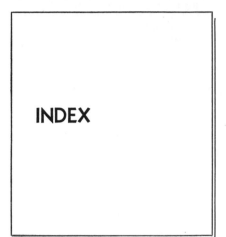

INDEX